EMBRACE

the

JOURNEY

Stories of Life and Finance

by

John T. McCarthy, CFP®

John T. McCarthy

Maggie Publishing Co.
Wauwatosa, WI

Address inquiries to:
     John T. McCarthy
     c/o Maggie Publishing
     8207 Brookside Place
     Wauwatosa, WI 53213

For copies of this self-published and distributed book, contact the author:
     John T. McCarthy
     McCarthy Grittinger Weil Financial Group, LLC
     125 South 84th Street, Suite 130
     Milwaukee, WI 53214-1498

     Phone: 414-475-1369
     Fax: 414-475-0613
     E-mail: JohnM@mgfin.com
     Website: www.mgfin.com

Edited by Chris Roerden
Printed in the USA

ISBN13: 978-0-9660577-1-3   ISBN: 0-9660577-1-6

DEDICATION

To my wife, Cathy.

CONTENTS

PREFACE

I t is the middle of the night. I have awakened from a deep sleep, my mind swimming with material for this book. After an hour of attempting to fall back to sleep, I give in. Bleary-eyed, I trudge down to my basement home office and put pen to yellow pad, trying to capture my thoughts. This preface is the result of the last of many nocturnal awakenings I have experienced over the many months of writing this book.

Writing *Embrace the Journey* has served to remind me of how truly blessed I have been over the course of my own life journey, which began in May 1951. I was welcomed to the world as the first-born of two phenomenally caring and strong parents. My childhood was a sheltering cocoon, where love was a constant. I benefited greatly as a member of a large, close, extended Irish American family. How rich it was to have all four of my grandparents live within a short hop and to spend precious time with them on a regular basis. My wealth can be measured in an abundance of family, from my six brothers and sisters to aunts, uncles, and two dozen cousins whom I count as friends. Their stories are a big part of the fabric of my life.

My good fortune continued when I met and married Cathy. This year marks our silver, twenty-fifth year as husband and wife. I hope and pray we can go on to witness our golden fiftieth. Together, we have three beautiful children in Maggie, Martha, and Jack, each of whom makes life wonderful. Martha and Jack are truly gifted children, and we are proud of them and their accomplishments. Maggie, our firstborn, is a special gift. She has enriched our lives, as well as those of her siblings. Maggie is cognitively disabled, a grown woman of 22, with many attributes of a seven-year-old child. She is a star character, making many appearances in this book. You can go to the website (www.mgfin.com) to see our smiling, gold–medal-winning Special Olympian.

A challenging chapter in my life story is that of a cancer survivor. Millions of people have been touched by cancer. In my case, I was knocked down, but thanks to my faith in God and the wonders of modern medicine, along with early intervention and top-flight care, I became an extremely fortunate survivor. Having been branded with cancer, I feel compelled to embrace fellow members of this vast community, be it tragic victims, fellow survivors, frightened families, or frontline medical personnel.

These pages likely would not have been turned into a published book without the inspiration of two remarkable women and fellow victims of cancer. My friend and former neighbor, Shirley Leszczynski, has waged an intense battle against a dastardly cancer for the past year and a half. I placed a photo of a healthy Shirley at eye level on my writing desk. She is a profile in courage, and her will to live has provided me with a steady source of inspiration to persevere and finally complete this book.

Although this is my third book, I do not consider myself a professional writer but, at best, a journeyman author. What I do possess is a treasure trove of life experiences and stories gleaned from the hundreds of clients I am privileged to know through our financial and investment advisory firm. Yet I am convinced this material would never have come to light in written form without the editing assistance of my friend Jan Lennon. Jan knows me, my voice, and what I am trying to say. Her enthusiastic support has been invaluable.

We mark the milestones of our life journey by anniversaries. In October 2005, we celebrated the tenth anniversary of my founding of our investment advisory firm by hosting a dinner attended by 250 clients, family, and friends. As part of the festivities, I presented an award to Jan to recognize her volunteer involvement in our community, especially with the MACC Fund, whose worthy mission is to defeat childhood cancer. That evening, Jan gave me a lapel boutonniere along with a handwritten note that I cherish and display on my writing desk. It reads, "Here's to 5 years of renewed life, 10 years of business success, 20 years of friendship. Here's to 20 more."

The very next day, Jan came to my office to confide in me her own cancer diagnosis. That day marked my determination to accelerate my efforts to make this book happen. Despite waging a heated battle against a difficult form of breast cancer, Jan persevered through treatment and plugged away with multiple drafts to move my project along. I felt some pressure to finish the manuscript, because Jan now has become a proud grandmother, directing her considerable energy and abundant love to doting on Audrey Kathleen.

Another inspiring individual has been our daughter, Martha, who is heading off to college this fall. She excelled in both academics and athletics in high school and exhibited a talent for writing. Martha has been a valuable asset to me as a publishing assistant. She willingly typed countless pages of drafts, made numerous revisions and edits, and provided necessary research support.

I am fortunate also to have Chris Roerden in my corner as a professional editor. Chris is tops in her field, as evidenced by her landing the prestigious 2007 Agatha Award.

As a practicing financial planner, I have been blessed to pursue a career and a business that allow me to get to know personally and professionally many genuinely nice and interesting people. We are not in the cold business of strictly managing money; rather, we deal up-close and personally in our clients' total lives. I am thankful to our valued clients. A piece of each of them runs through the pages of this financial life-planning book.

I am indebted to all the members of what we refer to as our Anxiety Removal Team. For without the contributions of my partners Scott

Grittinger and Mike Weil, and the dedicated support of our assembled team, it would be difficult to offer our unique services. A special nod goes to Avis Haasch, who with her big heart has been with me since our modest beginning, and instrumental in pulling the pieces of this book together. Finally, I am grateful to all who have contributed in some way to shaping this book. My hope is that these stories of life and finance will encourage readers to live strong and embrace each day of their own life's journey.

John T. McCarthy
July 2007

CHAPTER 1

A TOUR DOWN THE ROAD

Live your life each day as you would climb a mountain.
Climb slowly, steadily, enjoying each passing moment;
and the view from the summit will serve as a
fitting climax for the journey.

Harold V. Melchert

Eulogies offered at funerals and memorial services leave a powerful impression on me. A lot is to be learned about what is really important about living from recalling the lives of those who, as St. Paul said, "have fought the good fight and have finished the race." After more than five decades of life on this earth, I find myself attending an ever-increasing number of farewell ceremonies and reflecting on my own life and the limited time on earth allotted to us all. A reminder I take to heart was penned by Henry David Thoreau: "When it's time to die, let us not discover that we have never lived."

I was privileged to cross paths with Warren P. Knowles in the final years of his life. Affectionately known as "the Governor" because of his position as political leader of Wisconsin from 1965 to 1971, he was a gentleman in every sense of the word. At Knowles' memorial service, his closest friend, Ody Fish, read from a poem the

Governor had said captured the essence of his life philosophy. It spoke of life as a long and unending journey. The reward is not in reaching the destination, but in the journey itself.

Philosophical observer of the financial planning industry and journalist Bob Veres speaks to us in this same vein. "We are learning that the process of improving our lives and achieving greater fulfillment and success doesn't have any end; it is always an endless beginning. This is perhaps the hardest lesson of all, because as humans, we are hard-wired to think in terms of beginnings and destinations."

Champion cyclist and seven-time winner of the *Tour de France,* Lance Armstrong, hits the same note in the subtitle of his bestseller, *It's Not About the Bike: My Journey Back to Life.* The book chronicles his life-and-death struggle with cancer. In spite of his remarkable athletic achievements, Armstrong puts it all in perspective with his words, "Surviving cancer is still the biggest victory of my life."

Esteemed soldier and statesman Colin Powell, in his best-selling personal memoir, *My American Journey,* shares with his fellow Americans his extraordinary life's journey. His rough spots include the loss of his father to cancer and the ugliness of racism. Yet, mostly good times come together for him and add up to a self-described great life. Of all his heady accomplishments and triumphs, this distinguished gentleman is proudest of his marriage partnership with Alma and of the family they raised together.

I heard Powell say that the most interest from readers of his book did not center on his having rubbed shoulders with presidents, queens, and prime ministers or Hollywood and sports celebrities, but rather on his early years growing up in the Bronx as the son of Jamaican-born Luther and Arie.

Powell clearly understands that the attainment of fame and fortune is not what makes for a great life. The richness of family *is.* The dedication in his book reads, "To my family…past, present, and future."

My book, *Embrace the Journey: Stories of Life and Finance,* explores my life and the influence that personal finances have on the course of one's passage. As a financial planning practitioner for 25 years, I have adopted the emerging industry movement emphasizing life planning. Life planning is more holistic in scope than pure "crunching the numbers" financial planning and much more encompassing than a narrow focus on investing. In practical terms, life planning balances the management of one's wealth with the hopes, dreams, and values that go into making a happy and productive life.

I agree with this thought-provoking quote by Frederic G. Donner, "When you come right down to it, almost any problem eventually becomes a financial problem."

Based on the premise that sound financial planning is actually life planning, these pages amount to a course on life planning. I have no doubt that such planning pays off in a richer and more rewarding life in every way.

One of my favorite books and a frequent gift from me to clients is *The Millionaire Next Door*. Academics Thomas Stanley and William Danko wrote a lively text supporting their thesis that high income alone does not result in accumulated real net worth. Their case is buttressed in story form with examples such as: You aren't what you drive—the fortunes of Dr. North and Dr. South heading in opposite directions; and the ostentatious display of wealth is likely to be, as they say in Texas, "all hat and no cattle." My hope is for the reader to perceive that *Embrace the Journey* follows their example and disdains technical finance chatter. To that end, I tell real life stories of people I have known and helped, while guarding the privacy of the individuals involved.

Unlike most personal finance books, including my own two previous publications, this one avoids the traditional practice of grouping chapters by subject, such as estate planning, taxes, and investments. Instead, I follow the back roads, weaving into each chapter snippets from assorted experiences to tell a story.

My own life story took an abrupt turn on May 2, 2000, when a surgeon pronounced ominously, "I'm sorry, but you have cancer." Reality hit home that his message was not a bad dream when I was wheeled to the hospital's oncology floor. Facing the prospect of death does color one's view of life. Now, as a fortunate cancer survivor, the experience frames my personal story and life experience.

That summer I mailed a letter to my clients announcing the condition of my health, and I received the following elegant observation from a retired physician: "Life is such a mystery. It takes us places we would never choose or anticipate. However, it is the unwanted journeys that often are the most enriching and purifying."

The remarkable woman who wrote those lines has since then suffered increasingly from a baffling gastrointestinal condition she believes traces to the time she spent decades earlier as a medical missionary in Africa. Coincidentally, the doctor has herself been diagnosed with cancer, and, like all its victims, faces the uncertainty of the disease's prospects.

Another chapter in my life experience is that our eldest child, easy-to-love Maggie, bears the weight of a cognitive disability and an associated neurological disease. My wife, Cathy, and I are not alone in loving a special child. One in five Americans has a relative living with a disability; and one in ten people, a severe disability, such as Maggie's. Maggie is a gift and a blessing, and in so many ways this Special Olympian enriches our lives. Yet she commands much of our attention, as we navigate the challenges her disabilities present.

The father of a blind and severely disabled son once reminded me gently of the age-old adage that in every life some rain must fall. All in all, our journey with Maggie has brought far more sunshine than rain.

A high school English teacher of mine, Peter Gilmour, is now an associate professor at Chicago's Loyola University and author of the book *The Wisdom of Memoir.* Peter is someone I credit for instilling in me an interest in reading and writing. We have stayed in touch through the years at St. George High School reunions and have kept abreast with our careers, a shared cancer scare, and happenings around my old neighborhood, where he continues to reside.

Aware of my work on this book, Peter passed along a copy of *The Wisdom of Memoir,* believing rightly it would be pertinent. He writes of how impressed he is with the power that life stories of real people possess. According to Peter, "Memoir presumes serious and substantial reflection on life and living. If, as Socrates said, the unexamined life is not worth living, then, as the late Fulton J. Sheen said, through memoir life is worth living."

Retired journalist Dorothy Austin told me the most important aspect of writing a book is to have something worthwhile to say. A priest I know has been living the past few years under the dark cloud of two primary forms of cancer, each of which limits treatment of the other. After discussing my personal cancer ordeal with this seasoned listener, the brave priest opined that the stories I have to tell are, indeed, worthwhile.

To be complete, a life planning book should address the issue of eventual demise. Robert Half reminds us, "Death is the penalty we all pay for the privilege of life." The reality of a cancer diagnosis is that it encompasses both life and death. Roughly half of all the individuals stricken with cancer survive. Sadly, the other half do not.

My first experience with the devastating disease that ended a life too soon happened when I was an impressionable seven-year-old child. My recollection, hazy though it is, is of lining up outside the first grade classroom at St. Ignatius grammar school on the last day of the school year in early June 1958. My first grade teacher was Sister Francis Xavier, a nun who had taken her religious name from a sixteenth-century Spanish Jesuit missionary.

Sister was telling all of us little ones to have a good summer recess and she would see us again when school resumed in the fall. I may have responded to her goodbye by saying aloud that, if she died, she would not see us. To my chagrin, through all these years I don't know if I actually said what I was thinking or not. However, I do recall vividly being in the chapel hand-in-hand with my mother at Sister's wake that summer and viewing my first grade teacher laid out in her casket. This experience is seared in my memory. I often think of Sister Francis Xavier Clark, who died that summer from cancer on August 18, 1958, at the age of 46.

Last summer I participated in a golf outing fundraiser put on by the American Cancer Society. The event coordinator phoned me to say that as a benefit of my corporate sponsorship they were making up cardboard flags in memory of cancer victims. These flags would line the finishing eighteenth hole. She asked me to call her back the next day with four names I would want to remember in this fashion. That night as I thought about possible choices, dozens of names came to mind, enough to fill a small cemetery with memory flags.

I take cancer very personally. It is the culprit that prematurely took the lives of my mother, father, father-in-law, brother-in-law, favorite aunt, and first grade teacher, as well as too many clients, coworkers, neighbors, and friends.

This scourge is at epidemic proportions. A full 40 percent of all Americans now living will face cancer in their lifetimes—one in two men and one in three women. As frequently as every couple of weeks, it seems I learn of a client diagnosed with what the great actor John Wayne, himself a cancer victim, referred to as "the big C."

Statistics aside, cancer touches all our lives in some way. As a survivor, I am not afraid to address this major life event. I believe in the healing power of a positive attitude. Because the cure rate has advanced in the past quarter of a century from 33 percent to over 50 percent, cancer mercifully is no longer an automatic death sentence. Real progress is being made in the battle against this universally feared disease.

The beautifully written columns and books of former Reagan speechwriter Peggy Noonan stir me. In her 2005 book about the late Pope, *John Paul the Great*, she tells us that "the great deserve our loyalty and that those who have added to life, who have inspired the living and pointed to a better way, should be learned from and lauded." She goes on to say that great individuals "lift us up. They tell us by their presence that everything is possible."

As a student of history, I agree with the historians who rate Abraham Lincoln as our greatest president and the greatest man of the nineteenth century. Winston Churchill is regarded as the greatest statesman of the twentieth century, and John Paul II as the greatest worldwide leader over his span as Pope.

Look for brief examinations throughout my book of the lives of this trio of greatness. The hardships each faced, challenges overcome, and successes realized are not only inspiring but also illuminating.

Noonan further observes that Pope John Paul "was an obscure Polish boy with no connections, no standing, without even, by the time he was of college age, a family. He worked in a factory and ate potatoes in water for dinner during a war. He went on to become the most famous man of his age, and famous for that finest of reasons: a life well lived."

What drives my inspiration for *Embrace the Journey* are the many stories I have accumulated since I joined the early wave of advisors in 1984 to earn my Certified Financial Planner (CFP®) designation. As a practicing financial planner in the ensuing years, I peered into the financial closets of over a thousand individuals. From this treasure trove of confidences, I learned valuable lessons on life, finances and successful investing techniques that I'm convinced can benefit many others.

One such wonderful client was Bernice, a gentlewoman if there ever was one, who died surrounded by her two loving daughters at the age of 93.

I was privileged to visit with Bernice three days before the end of her long life and share a cup of tea around the kitchen table at her daughter's house in Madison. We talked about life and reminisced on the 15 years I had been so fortunate to know her.

Driving home from Madison that day, and again at her memorial service, I had a warm feeling come over me as I reflected on what made my relationship with Bernice so special. Somehow she had taken to me right away, and over the years shared confidences with

me in a score of beautifully handwritten letters. Rereading those touching notes, I realized the debt of gratitude I owe to Bernice for helping
me become a better person and planner.

Bernice helped me to more fully understand that money does not
buy happiness. If it did, trust fund babies would not be so frequently
off-course, and Hollywood stars would not play out their lives in
public misery and despair. Count the perceptive genius Benjamin
Franklin among those who understood this eternal truth. "Money
never made a man happy yet, nor will it. There is nothing in its nature to promote happiness."

It should not be surprising that when lottery winners have been
tracked, in a majority of cases their non-material wealth was not appreciably better after they hit pay dirt.

As a cancer survivor, I take to heart the Old English proverb that
says, "Health is indeed better than wealth." Sadly, too many people
lead their lives as if their net worth is a final accounting that will be
carved on their tombstones. Nationally known financial planner and
breast cancer survivor Deena Katz reminds us that we don't see a
Brinks truck in a funeral procession. We need to strike a healthy balance between the accumulation, consumption, and transfer of wealth
if we are to lead truly rich lives.

The great Benjamin Franklin, brilliant inventor, statesmen and
founding father, was an early advocate of the virtues of thrift, saving,
and avoidance of debt. Writing in *Poor Richard's Almanac*, he gave
us a wealth of common sense admonishments that are as relevant
today, if not more so, than when he started printing and publishing
that periodical in 1733.

"If you would be wealthy, think of saving as well as getting."
This advice is not at all revolutionary; yet our national rate of saving
in 2005 was actually negative, as we Americans consumed and spent
more than we saved.

I contend that Stephen Covey's mega-bestseller, *The 7 Habits of
Highly Effective People,* kick-started the burgeoning life planning

movement. However, I have found his follow-up and less acclaimed book, *First Things First,* a superior read.

My habit when meeting with clients is to start off with FTF (first things first) by inquiring how they and their families are faring. This reordering of priorities to address the qualitative aspects of clients' lives before we get into the numbers game of quantitative financial analysis seems greatly appreciated. Sharing enthusiasm for the news of a birth of a grandchild is more gratifying than discussing how the Dow average finished the quarter. To illustrate, early in *First Things First,* Covey poses the provocative life-balance question, "How many people on their deathbed wished they'd spent more time at the office?"

Frequently, some catalyst draws new clients to our planning firm. Some event occurs that has a direct impact on their financial lives, with significant changes to their income, outgo, assets, and debts. The triggering event used to be retirement. In more recent years, the catalyst has widened to involve a variety of life events. A few examples follow.

Six of our women clients in their forties suddenly and tragically lost their husbands and must carry on without their life partners. Many of our clients fall into this suddenly single category and find themselves coping, midlife, with the emotional and financial devastation wreaked by death or by separation or divorce.

Al, another representative client, had been a collegiate wrestler and was a highly successful chief information officer at a distribution firm. This active fellow's life is now slowed by the cruel effects of Parkinson's disease. Reluctantly, he was forced to give up his work and accept disability income. As the workforce gets older, an increasing number of health-related issues cause unfortunate changes in peoples' lives.

In addition, economic cycles can adversely affect family businesses. One such example is that of a couple who shut down their third-generation operation because of a depression in the domestic machine tool industry. This unfortunate turn of events affected not only their own opportunities but also those of future generations in their family.

Financial and life planning means recognizing, anticipating, and adapting to transformational economic forces of change. The emergence of China as a global economic powerhouse is having a profound influence on us as job seekers, business owners, investors, and consumers. At only 49, John Thornton left the presidency of the prestigious Wall Street firm Goldman Sachs to accept a position in China as a university professor to teach business. His decision had nothing to do with money. It came from his strongly held belief that "the single most important thing to happen in our lifetime will be the emergence of China." We would be wise to develop a personal China policy to respond to the daunting challenges and exciting opportunities China presents in both business and investing.

Many planning issues are multigenerational in scope. I counseled a client in her mid-sixties who was both planning her own retirement and arranging for the care of her 92-year-old mother, who lives 300 miles away and suffers from dementia. The client confided that selling her mother's house and moving her mother to a long-term care facility for her own well-being was by far the hardest decision she ever had to make.

Personal values can conflict with financial security. Another client recently admitted that she was going to sell some holdings, against the wishes of her husband, to pay for an expensive drug rehabilitation program for her granddaughter, believing it was a good investment.

Last summer my wife, Cathy, and I felt honored to be invited to a twenty-fifth wedding celebration for Sue and Shel. What made this event special for this fun-loving couple in their seventies was that both had been married before, and for 25 years each. After the premature deaths of their first spouses, friends had played matchmaker and linked these two together.

Like many of our clients, Sue and Shel have lived a life rich with experiences. Now residing comfortably in a gated community in Florida, Shel talks movingly about growing up poor on 12th Street in Milwaukee, the son of Eastern European immigrant Jewish parents. When Sue was a young girl, she lived above her father's grocery store in London during the Nazi bombing blitz of WWII. Sue reflected on that terrifying time 65 years earlier after a night she and Shel spent huddled in the dark in a closet of their condominium during a hurricane.

Planning often involves an unanticipated turn of events, some pleasant and some not. Such was the case of a couple I encountered after they relocated to Milwaukee following the husband's acceptance of a professional position. They had just learned they were beneficiaries of a somewhat unexpected inheritance. During this same time, the childless, late-thirties, two-income couple discovered they were to become parents of triplets. Talk about major changes in the course of their lives and finances, these folks had them in spades!

Experience has taught me that psychology plays the biggest role in investment decision-making and that investors are often their own worst enemies. This phenomenon is not just my observation. Daniel Kahneman was awarded the Nobel Prize for Economics in 2002 for his work on the subject. Over the past decade, I have come to know two highly respected professors of finance, John Nofsinger of Washington State University and Werner Deboldt at DePaul University. Interestingly, both of these PhDs started their careers as engineers but gravitated to behavioral finance because of their intellectual curiosity for how things in that field really work.

Throughout the following chapters, I bring attention to examples of irrational investment behavior—or what Nofsinger describes in the title of one of his books as *Investment Madness*. I spotlight destructive investment actions that can sabotage the best laid financial plan, and call upon noted academics such as Kahneman, Nofsinger, Deboldt, and Jeremy Siegel to add credence to my contentions.

The last decade has taken stock market investors on a roller coaster ride, with the bulls and the bears taking turns pulling the momentum in different directions. The five years from 1995 to the end of 1999 were unprecedented, as the S&P 500 index turned in successive average annual performance returns of 20 percent and more. The rollicking party came to an abrupt end as the dot-com-fueled technology bubble burst in the first quarter of 2000, causing the Nasdaq index to cough up all of its heady five-year gains and then some. What followed was a wrenching three-year bear market (2000-2002) as severe in its way as the period following the Great Depression of 1929.

When aiming for investment success, it makes sense to model one's behavior after proven winners. In the course of this book, I share common sense investment wisdom from many astute major-league investors such as John Templeton, Peter Lynch, Bill Gross and Ralph Wanger. In the current field of investing, there is no bigger superstar than Warren Buffett. He has amassed personal wealth in the neighborhood of 53 billion dollars (note: that's *billion* with a "b"), and built this incredible fortune entirely through his superior investing prowess.

Commonly referred to as the sage from Omaha, Buffett offers two rules to live by in investing. Rule number one, don't lose money. Rule number two, never forget rule number one. Preservation of capital is a bedrock principle of successful investing. A long-term, patient investor, Buffett is on record as saying that once he makes a stock purchase, he would not be bothered by the stock market shutting down for the next ten years. Contrast this sound buy-and-hold approach with the suicide course of day traders and the frantic, high-turnover activity of investors who, at best, are minor leaguers in the investment world.

I am a long-time fan and admirer of John Bogle, founder and retired chairman of the respected Vanguard Group. I have read all his books and buy into his common sense approach to investing. Bogle is well-known as the father of and loudest advocate for the wisdom of indexing. Serving as the conscience of the mutual fund industry, he constantly reminds us that costs really do matter in investing. Look for a recounting of his wisdom in the course of this book.

I like to also emphasize a lesser-known Bogle premise, what his successor at Vanguard, John Brennan, refers to as the "elegance of simplicity." To quote from Bogle's book *Common Sense on Mutual Funds*, in a section titled, "When All Else Fails Fall Back on Simplicity," Bogle says, "Never underestimate either the majesty of simplicity or its proven effectiveness as a long-term strategy for productive investing. Simplicity indeed is the master key to financial success." No less an authority than Warren Buffett tops the list in endorsing Bogle's common sense approach.

In keeping with my major themes of common sense investing, namely simplicity and avoidance of the big mistake, I do not recommend the ownership of individual securities, be they stocks or bonds. The lone exception is ultra-safe United States Treasury notes, which are the most liquid investment in the world and do not carry the risk of default.

Single-issue holdings are risky and therefore imprudent. To not diversify is to speculate. Those who got caught holding onto Enron stock too long were supposedly sophisticated investment experts. Enron employees, many with heavy concentrations of their once high-flying company stock inside their 401(k) retirement plans, were crushed financially. In WorldCom's case, its corporate bonds cratered when it declared bankruptcy.

I am a long-time proponent of mutual fund investing, believing fervently this should be the investment vehicle of choice for investors. The greatest benefit of mutual fund investing is that investors achieve instant and continuous diversification. Make no mistake about it, diversification is the most effective and prudent form of risk reduction.

In the first years of the twenty-first century, the forces of change have proven dramatic on both life and finances. Chief among these was the horror of 9/11 and the specter of terror that clouds predictability; the severe three-year bear market of 2000-2002; the collapse of Enron and subsequent swift demise of the venerable accounting firm Arthur Andersen; the war in Iraq; and the mutual fund scandal.

On a personal level, the shocks to our family were both health-related: my own cancer ordeal and our oldest daughter's neurological disease diagnosis. Listen to the words of the late love doctor, Leo Buscaglia, writing in *Living, Loving and Learning:* "An investment in life is an investment in change. When you are changing all the time, you've got to continue to keep adjusting to change, which means you are going to constantly face new obstacles." As we venture forth and life goes on, the pace of change can only be expected to accelerate.

Part of living and living well is possessing what the French refer to as *joie de vivre*, or joy of life. Former president George H. W. Bush exhibited this zest on his eightieth birthday when he repeated a stunt from his seventy-fifth birthday, parachuting from an airplane. What makes a life special is the pursuit of passion. An avid fisherman, Warren Knowles suffered a fatal heart attack at age 83 while enjoying the Governor's annual fishing opener, a tradition he had started and a fitting end to a long and productive life. Knowles embraced the Native American proverb that says, "God does not charge time spent fishing against a man's allotted life span."

My acquaintance with another octogenarian began when she was 83. One of our favorite clients is Ruth, now in her mid-nineties and aging gracefully. At the start of our client relationship, she asked how long I planned to look after her personal finances. I hesitated before responding, and she observed she knew what I was thinking. "After all, I am 83, and I know you know that. But what you don't know is that my mother lived to 104—and, John, I am healthier than she was."

Her daughter-in-law has since confirmed Ruth's assessment of her health status. Ruth is adamant that the only way she will leave the independence of her modest white-frame house, where she tends her garden and continues to handle lawn-keeping chores and snow removal, is feet first. Another admirer of this extraordinary woman recently shared with me that Ruth was warned by her doctor to put away her bicycle, or, if she insisted on cycling, to move full circle to a tricycle. Ruth shunned the advice from her physician, who has lived just one-third of the life she has. Instead, Ruth boldly continues to tempt fate on two wheels.

Financial services company Nationwide ran a print ad of an old photo of a 5-year-old girl perched on a scooter next to a now 65-year-old woman striking the same pose on a motor bike. The tag line stated, "Life comes at you fast." Time does indeed seem to fly, as Ruth would attest.

Harking back to John Bogle, in my mind the most amazing thing about this financial icon is that a heart transplant gave him a new lease on life, and he has been driving life hard these past 13 years since.

The financial press keeps badgering Warren Buffett, 77 years old as of this writing, about his plans for retirement. After all, he doesn't need the paycheck. Buffett obviously enjoys managing Berkshire Hathaway, an investment holding company. He coyly told an inquiring reporter, "You'll be interviewing me twenty years from now. If enjoying life promotes longevity, Methuselah's record is in jeopardy."

Throughout *Embrace the Journey: Stories of Life and Finance,* I make many references to athletics. In the world of sports, life is played out in ultimate reality, with identified winners and losers, and a contest and a season decided in real time. Athletes such as Lance Armstrong have genuine stories to tell us, primarily outside the sport that defines them.

Athletic coaches at all levels are really teachers. The legendary football coach Vince Lombardi, of Green Bay Packers fame, saw a direct analogy between sports and life. Speaking to his players, Lombardi stressed that success in football and life is built on perseverance and hard work: "There are three things that are important to every man in this room. His religion, his family, and the Green Bay Packers, in that order." After being diagnosed at age 58 with the colon cancer that would take his life, the deeply religious Lombardi said: "I'm not afraid to meet my God now. But what I do regret is that there is so damn much left to be done on earth."

Like Lombardi, another native New Yorker who made his mark in my adopted home state of Wisconsin was the late Al McGuire. I am a loyal fan of the former winning basketball coach at Marquette University, my alma mater. A distinguished sports broadcaster as well, McGuire succeeded in both careers. Having led Marquette to an NCAA championship in 1977, he left college basketball at the summit. He reached the top again as a colorful network television commentator.

McGuire was also a homespun philosopher, full of Irish wit and grounded by his New York City upbringing. He once declared, "I'm an Einstein of the streets and an Oxford scholar of common sense." He followed this comment with sage investment advice: "If somebody offers to double your money, move away. But if they are talking of earning a 20 percent return, hear them out." McGuire grew up poor. Asked if he was financially set at the height of his lucrative speaking and broadcasting career, he replied, "I have so much now I don't even count it. I weigh it."

In 1997, I attended a Marquette basketball game to see my hero McGuire and relive the 1977 championship at a half-time ceremony commemorating that joyful win 20 years before. McGuire recalled the final moments of that championship game, when an unexpected victory over a favored North Carolina team became assured. At that moment, McGuire's emotions gave way and tears streamed down his face.

Recalling that time, McGuire said he expected to live an additional 15 years. He promised the crowd that "the next time I will cry is when I die. My life has been that beautiful."

My friend John Cary, student manager for Marquette basketball in the McGuire years, was one of those hospice visitors in the final days of Al's life as he fought his losing battle with leukemia, a bloodborne cancer, at age 72. He shared with me that Al's final parting message to his grief-stricken friends was, "Fellows, I'll see you down the road." The final buzzer had sounded for McGuire. He had embraced his journey.

CELEBRATING THE LIFE OF CASSIE

My aunt Cassie and I were very close. I was truly blessed to have her in my life in a special way for 51 years, until she lost out to colon cancer. I was the first-born child of Peggy, her older sister.

Cassie also was my godmother, a relationship she took seriously and carried out in exemplary fashion. Being a godmother defined her philosophy of life. To her, a child was a gift from God and the description of mother was a dispenser of love.

Cassie's life was simple to read, because it was centered on the twin roles of devoted wife and nurturing mother. When you entered her fashionably decorated home you noted a prominently displayed portrait of Cassie in her bridal gown. A beautiful bride with flowing red hair, she started down the aisle of married life with her mate, Dan, a decent, good-looking, hard-working, and proud Polish-American attorney. Their union lasted 50 years, before cancer took Dan a year before his wife's death.

Aunt Cassie's mission in life was defined by their four blue-eyed, golden curly-haired children: Danny, Mimi, David, and Brian. It was her unlimited capacity, courage, and strength to care for and love her youngest child that defined her as Mother with a capital "M."

My cousin Brian started life with a very difficult birth. His was a constant struggle living with a cognitive disability. Brian also endured a string of hospitalizations related to Crohn's disease and assorted health problems. When you met Brian, you found a well-mannered, well-dressed, special young man, quick with a handshake and genuine greeting. Brian died at the tender age of 33 from kidney failure. Cathy and I learned first-hand from Aunt Cassie how to love and care for our own special child.

Cassie was always there for me and for her large, extended family. She was continually rooting for us, and proud of our accomplishments. She and Uncle Danny attended my college graduation. She hosted a shower and engagement party for Cathy and me at her home and joyously celebrated the births of our children with beautiful, handmade gifts. When her sister and best friend, my mother, fought a losing but courageous battle against cancer, my godmother was a constant comfort and provided a shoulder to cry on. When I was dealing with my own cancer, it was Cassie who responded to my letter to family and close friends sharing the condition of my health with a *bravo!* for my attitude and determination to fight and win out against the disease that was prevalent in our family.

My last visit with Aunt Cassie took place at her home one month before her death, a few days short of Mother's Day. Although weak, thin, and pale, her personality was sparkling. I thought she looked as radiant as ever wrapped in her white robe.

Next to her bed stood a small picture of her own beloved mother, my maternal grandmother. When Grandma was in her late nineties and not long for this world, Cassie had confided to me that she would miss her mother dearly when she was gone.

Aunt Cassie survived only about six months after her cancer diagnosis. The deadly cancer had already spread from her colon to her liver, and the doctors held out not even a glimmer of hope. During this time Cassie's well-meaning friends pressed her as to when she would start chemotherapy treatment. In discussing this matter with me and her son Dan, she stated she didn't want to undergo this tough treatment if it would prove futile. She didn't want to be viewed as giving up or afraid, but reasoned that her last months could be spent in the comfort of her own home and in the warm embrace of family.

As I assured her, I wholeheartedly supported her approach. A course of toxic chemotherapy or some other experimental procedure might prolong her life a mere month or two, at best. She decided the tradeoff was not worth the price of losing precious quality time, such as we spent just a few weeks before her death.

I felt honored that Cassie, through her children, asked me to deliver the reflections at her church funeral service. She also instructed that I read *A Parable for Mothers* by Temple Bailey. This parable is a simple, earthly story with a powerful, heavenly meaning. Cassie's message to all of us gathered there was to celebrate her life, but was especially directed to her children and grandchildren that her parting was okay. Her work here was complete, and we should be assured she rests in heaven.

When I read this moving parable, not a dry eye remained in the church. I managed to get through the delivery of this reflection, having shed many tears in preparing to memorialize Cassie.

I was at work when I learned of the passing of my aunt and godmother. Filled with sadness, I went home. Upon entering my house I immediately felt her presence, because in our front hall hangs a beautiful work of art she crafted for us of the *Madonna with Child*. Looking at this piece I can visualize Cassie with Brian cradled in her arms. On another wall in our home hangs *An Old Irish Blessing* she made, which I cherish. From her daughter Mimi, I learned that Cassie thought of her needlepoint as a good tranquilizer to cope with the many health problems faced by Brian.

AN OLD IRISH BLESSING

May the road rise to meet you.
May the wind be always at your back.
May the sun shine warm upon your face,
the rains fall soft upon your fields and,
until we meet again. . . may God hold you
in the palm of his hand.

When I finished the reflection at my aunt's funeral service by repeating the final lines of this heartfelt blessing, Cassie seemed to be speaking to those celebrating her life on that bittersweet June day in 2002.

CHAPTER 2

THE JOURNEY

Life is currently described as one of four ways: as a
journey, as a battle, as a pilgrimage, and as a race. Select
your own metaphor, but the finishing necessity is all the
same. For if life is a journey, it must be completed. If life
is a battle, it must be finished. If life is a pilgrimage, it
must be concluded.
And if life is a race, it must be won.

J. Richard Sneed

The life of one sports celebrity can be spoken of using all these metaphors. The Lance Armstrong story is truly inspirational —even miraculous. The only child of a teenaged, single mother, Armstrong grew up in football-crazy Texas in the seventies. He stood out as an athlete by displaying a prodigious talent for the then little-known sport of the triathlon, which combines long-distance swimming, biking and running. Young Armstrong developed into a world-class cyclist. By the age of 25, this self-assured, cocky young man appeared to have it all, with annual earnings of $2 million, a showplace home, and a sleek Porsche in the driveway to complement a carefree, bachelor lifestyle.

But fate intervened. On October 2, 1996, this seemingly invincible young athlete was humbled by a diagnosis of cancer. For the first time in his life Armstrong knew real fear as he faced an uphill race simply to live. However, his winning discipline and resolve stayed with him throughout his ordeal. He beat incredible odds to defeat a highly aggressive form of testicular cancer that had spread to his abdomen, lungs, and brain. He endured three surgeries, including a delicate brain operation and five courses of toxic chemotherapy, and he pulled through. After fighting so hard for his life, Armstrong harbored no real expectation of ever getting on his bike to race again.

He struggled back to health, fell in love, married, and settled down. He began to train again. After some false starts and self-doubt, while cycling in the mountains of North Carolina he experienced an epiphany about his future. With a renewed passion and a singular focus, he set the audacious goal of winning the *Tour de France*, the Super Bowl competition of bike racing. Armstrong not only triumphed in the three-week, 2,300-mile ultimate test of endurance, courage, and perseverance, but also shattered a record, achieving this astounding feat for seven consecutive years.

Flush with his first victory, he witnessed the miracle of birth with the arrival of a baby son. Although cancer had left Armstrong sterile, he had shown the foresight to have his sperm frozen before treatment. More good news followed with the addition of twin daughters. Hollywood could not have created a more feel-good script.

May 2, 2000, marked my own life-changing anniversary, the day a doctor told me those three chilling words, "You have cancer." In the recovery room following my surgery, the nurse taking my blood pressure noted it was high. She asked, "Is that normal for you?"

"No," I answered. I had enjoyed excellent health to that point. The high reading was likely due to my prolonged state of shock as I continued trying to come to grips with this dreaded diagnosis. Although my blood pressure would return to "better than textbook" readings at a later date, my life story would forever contain this unwelcome chapter.

When I was being wheeled from recovery to the oncology floor of the hospital, accompanied by my loving, brave, but equally scared wife, Cathy, we passed a wall poster featuring a man I instantly recognized. Lance Armstrong was pictured wearing the yellow jersey of the *Tour de France* winner and proudly cradling in his arms his infant son, Luke. The poster was an advertisement for Bristol-Myers Squibb's life-saving cancer medicines. Having followed this athlete's remarkable comeback, I took it as an omen of hope, triumph, and survival.

My own cancer ordeal, although less dire than Armstrong's, was no walk in the park. I had squamous cell carcinoma, a head and neck cancer that my oncologist referred to ominously as major league, with a survival rate of just 50 percent.

Following surgery to remove the tumors that confirmed the diagnosis of malignancy, I knew my survival depended on the best medical care possible. I was fortunate to have as my neighbor Dr. Michael Keelan, a member of my church, a highly respected cardiologist at Milwaukee's Froedtert Hospital, and a faculty member of the Medical College of Wisconsin.

With a bandaged neck and, I suspect, a deer-caught-in-the-headlights look, I crossed the street to share with Mike Keelan my diagnosis and to seek his professional guidance. He told me it was critically important to, in his words, "jump on" this particularly serious form of cancer. He immediately phoned a faculty colleague and oncology specialist, Dr. Thomas Anderson.

Later that day in my initial phone consultation with the oncologist, he asked about the stage of my cancer. I replied, "Stage four." Although the cancer deaths of both my parents had touched me deeply, I had been unfamiliar with head and neck cancers—until my wife, a nurse, educated me that stage four cancer was the worst possible case. Dr. Anderson listened, then gave me some cryptic advice until he could see me to evaluate the best course of treatment: "Hang tough." During a routine annual physical the following year, my internist reminded me that I was indeed lucky to have "dodged a bullet." I will always be grateful that my neighbor, Dr. Michael Keelan, took a personal interest in my case and in my life.

In June of 2000, when I began seven weeks of intensive radiation to destroy the rogue microscopic cells that had invaded my body, Lance Armstrong's book was released. I bought a copy of *It's Not About the Bike: My Journey Back to Life* and eagerly read it cover-to-cover in one sitting. I felt reassured by knowing that a public figure had so successfully conquered the same dark disease I was battling in private. I vividly recall being comforted by Armstrong's assertion that despite the hardships he suffered, he believes cancer was the best thing that ever happened to him.

For one thing, he is fairly certain he never would have won the *Tour de France*. He writes:

The illness forced me to survey my life with an unforgiving eye. Cancer forced me to develop a plan for living, and that, in turn, taught me how to develop a plan for smaller goals like each stage of the Tour. It also taught me that sometimes the experience of losing things, whether health or a home, or an old sense of self, has its own value in the scheme of life.

Hamilton Jordan, best known as former President Jimmy Carter's Chief of Staff, reemerged from relative obscurity because he survived three different bouts of cancer: non-Hodgkin's lymphoma, melanoma, and prostate cancer, all before the age of 50. He penned his personal journey in *No Such Thing as a Bad Day*. In the postscript to this worthwhile read, Jordan sums up his experience in a positive light: "A life-threatening disease like cancer is a strange blessing that casts our life and purpose in sharp relief."

I found comfort in reading the accounts of these two survivors during my darkest days in the summer of 2000 and prayed that I, too, would join the ranks of the cured.

A newer member of my own cancer survivor network, Judy, phoned me in the fall of 2004 to share her good news. She had successfully completed 35 radiation treatments to combat breast cancer, a scourge that strikes the lives of millions of women every year.

Cancer not only affects the life of the patient but also has a profound impact on those we love and who love us. Judy, for example, is a new grandmother, nurturing mother, loving wife, and only child of aging parents.

In the course of our uplifting talk, this wonderful woman echoed a theme similar to Armstrong's and Hamilton's, referring to cancer as a gift and a significant waystation on her life's journey. She expressed heartfelt appreciation for the love and support of her family and gratitude for her friends and the medical personnel she came to embrace as family. She has a renewed sense of joy. Her family is even more precious; and, like Hamilton Jordan, Judy now believes there is no such thing as a bad day. Judy's optimism made my day. Her positive outlook on life that parallels an excellent prognosis is life affirming.

THE BEAT GOES ON

Heart disease is another health challenge that takes many lives each year. To me, the most amazing thing about John Bogle, investment industry icon and heart patient, is that he has been driving life hard these past years since receiving a heart transplant in February 1996. Bogle refers to his second chance at life as his "extra" years and marvels that his donated heart beats with the vigor of a 34-year-old.

Bogle was born with a rare genetic heart disease that caused him decades of trauma. His heart stopped beating eight times. He had five heart attacks and frequent hospitalizations. In his thirties and early in his career, this father to four young children was told he would not live to see 40, and he should cease working, give up playing tennis and squash, and not father any more children. He elected to take none of this advice.

Bogle is a survivor. He lives life with the motto to "press on regardless." As Abraham Lincoln, whose own failures ran deep, put it, "Your own resolution to succeed is more important than any other." This tenacity has served Bogle well in good times and through tough stretches.

He credits the medical care and humanism of cardiologist Dr.

Bernard Lown of Havard Medical School with extending his life and allowing him to press on. Dr. Lown, speaking of his most persistent heart patient, observed how Bogle reached "a point where most people would have panicked, been exercised beyond measure, and frightened." Instead, Bogle characteristically refused to give in. By 1992, barely able to climb stairs, he realized that a heart transplant was his only hope.

Faced with death knocking at his door, he endured 128 days of hospitalization, kept alive by life-prolonging drugs administered by his guardian angel nurses and doctors. He was sustained by the love of his wife, Eve, and a nightly reading of the twenty-third psalm, which ends, "not my will but Thy will be done."

On February 21, 1996, he was blessed with a miracle of rebirth. The transplant performed that day proved a success, and his aging body accepted this priceless new heart.

John Bogle muses in his writing that life is never easy and that he experienced his full share of dark days. Bogle credits his inspiration to the Greek philosopher Cicero, who said, "It is the character of a brave and resolute man not to be ruffled by adversity and not to desert his post."

Before his heart condition began to threaten his life, Bogle had scrambled to attain a college education at Princeton. A family business failure during the Great Depression meant juggling a series of part-time jobs and competing for a scholarship.

After seven years as chief executive of Wellington Management Company, a large investment management firm, he was, to use his own words, "fired with enthusiasm." Out of this low point of losing his job, he started Vanguard in 1974. Bogle's overriding philosophy was to give fund shareholders a fair shake. The bold experiment that would become Vanguard was first enunciated in his senior thesis written at Princeton in 1949.

Vanguard was far from an instant success. Its first four years it teetered on the brink of failure, as assets under management declined precipitously. Bogle fathered the first index fund in 1976, but it, too, was slow to catch on, attracting a mere $11 million in its first year.

No one in the late 1970s considered Bogle a visionary. If anything, he was thought of as foolish. Yet, in spite of the naysayers, the noble Vanguard experiment succeeded beyond his wildest dreams, eventually becoming the fastest growing of all mutual fund firms. The Vanguard 500 Index fund brought the concept of passive investment management to the forefront and evolved to claim the mantel as the largest mutual fund in terms of asset size.

After his successful heart transplant in 1996, Bogle was able to return to a lifestyle that included rigorous exercise, including plenty of walking with his wife and semi-weekly games of squash—which he resumed with passion.

At the age of 70, having devoted 25 years to building Vanguard's success, Bogle was unceremoniously pushed out as its chairman and director. Bogle moved on, pouring himself into running the Bogle Financial Markets Research Center. This continues to give him a platform for speaking out, writing, lecturing, and furthering his overriding mission to bring reform to the mutual fund industry and investing simplicity to American families.

John Bogle strongly believes that the industry's marketing and asset gathering has superseded its investment stewardship, to the detriment of fund shareholders. His zeal and outspoken criticism did not sit well with a supremely prosperous industry content with the status quo. Often, other mutual fund industry leaders derisively labeled Jack Bogle "St. Jack," for what they viewed as his holier-than-thou preaching. Time, however, has proven Bogle right. He was vindicated in the wake of the mutual fund scandal that exposed the very problems St. Jack had been harping on for decades. I am glad he has lived long enough to see his once-radical thinking become accepted.

In seeking to explain his obvious passion for life, Bogle refers to a *New York Times* article he once read.

When confronted with a life-threatening disease, most people want to do precisely what they were doing before that awful day when the doctor gave them the news…some collapse under the pressure, but most want to be the way they were. George Bernard Shaw called it a life force—what you experience as a human being, a determination to get back into life, to be part of life.

I have observed Bogle's passion for life first-hand. Jack, as he refers to himself in correspondence between us, wrote, "My schedule is unbelievably busy, especially for someone who is my age, but I'm having a lot of trouble slowing down. My mission is large and my energy is unbelievably high." Despite the variable winds of change, and in keeping with the nautical theme of Vanguard, Jack signed off a personal note with the life planning advice to "stay the course."

MEET OUR MAGGIE

The oldest of our three children goes through life carrying the burden of the cognitive disability of mental retardation. Yet anyone who has ever met Maggie realizes there is something truly special about her. I like the description of special, believing it is particularly apt for Maggie.

Our son, Jack, is nine years Maggie's junior. When his second grade classmates asked him what was wrong with his sister, Jack explained matter-of-factly that she was "special needs." He continues the role of "younger" big brother, championing her efforts and progress. Maggie possesses the best of childlike qualities. She is unconditional in her love, genuine in her feelings, lacking any prejudices and totally unconcerned with status, material possessions, or appearances. Her American Girl doll, Samantha, holds a favored place with her, sharing a pillow as a cherished friend.

After her younger sister, Martha, started driving, young Jack suggested aloud that his sister could now drive him to his soccer games. "Not this sister," Maggie reminded him in all seriousness.

Life for Maggie is simple, honest, and straightforward. Her sense of humor seems to be at a heightened developmental level, and, on occasion, she displays incredible insight. Maggie likes music and sing-alongs, and drawing in her sketch book. She loves babies, and she speaks softly to them, gently touches them, and lightly holds their little hands. Once a mother asked our special teenager if she would like to babysit sometime. "Oh no, that would not be a good idea," Maggie replied with insight.

Life with Maggie does have its heartache but is never dull. She possesses the enviable gift of never having outgrown childhood and all its wonder. She believes in Santa Claus and the whole magical experience he represents. Not only is Santa real, but his home is the North Pole, he comes down the chimney, and he enjoys the milk and cookies we put out for him.

After the death of her grandfathers, we informed Maggie that her grandpas were now in heaven. She understood that heaven is far up in the clouds and she could no longer see them. She told us how these old and sick men were transported to heaven. According to her, there is a giant and fast escalator that took them to the pearly gates.

Heaven aside, Maggie is blessed to have angels come into her life on a regular basis. One such person is Vanesssa, with whom she was partnered in a circle of friends in sixth grade. The two girls were brought together by Miss Krahn, another angel and Maggie's special education teacher in middle school.

After a time of separation following high school, these true friends joyously renewed their friendship. Maggie has her own language. When Vanessa heard her old friend using the description goofanage for a major goof, she knew right away everything would be like old times.

Heidi Krahn was a recent graduate of the University of Wisconsin, and our daughter was her very first student in a new program instituted in our school district. The arrangement was not without its challenges—such as the time Maggie pulled the fire alarm and the entire school had to be evacuated.

Heidi and Maggie developed a truly unique bond. To this day Maggie refers to her as her favorite teacher. Heidi married while Maggie was in eighth grade, taking the name of Mrs. Markes. In

Maggie's bedroom hangs a picture at the wedding showing the beautiful bride huddling with her beaming, prize student.

Heidi is now a very busy mother of three young children of her own, all of whom are known by Maggie. Although they see one another occasionally, this pair continues to hold a special place in each other's heart.

If Maggie likes you, she tends to shorten your name. Brother Jack is bro, sister Martha is sissy, her doll Samantha is Sammi, and next-door neighbor Michelle is Shelly. Mrs. Markes is simply Markes. Vanessa she calls Nessa.

These days Vanessa and Maggie look forward to enjoying a weekly girls' night out. Their activities include shopping at the mall, stopping for pizza, baking cookies, and doing their nails. One evening while hanging out at Vanessa's they made a music CD titled "Maggie's Mix." Maggie recounted how they burned this CD using Nessa's computer, but there was no fire involved.

Whenever these two young women return to our house after these dates, their shared happiness and wide glowing smiles are intoxicating to see. Recently, I watched a typical, touching goodbye between them. Maggie told Nessa she loved her and Vanessa replied in kind. Maggie countered that she loved her first, so Vanessa countered she loved her second. Maggie then responded she loved her last, and Vanessa conceded.

In many ways Maggie's life is full. Each night as she heads up to bed, Maggie says "I love you, Dad," and I know for certain she means it. Taken with emotion, I ask her if I can have a goodnight kiss. Her standard reply in the sweetest voice is, "Of course you can!"

Toward the end of the Academy Award-winning movie *Forrest Gump,* a poignant scene occurs. Forrest, the fictional lead character played superbly by Tom Hanks, expresses his desire to marry Jenny, the beautiful but deeply troubled victim of abuse he has known since childhood. When Jenny, as expected, does not agree to his heartfelt proposal, the slow-witted Forrest says, "I might not be smart—but I do know how to love."

Our Maggie clearly knows how to love, which is a great gift not everyone possesses.

Allow me to abruptly change gears here and move from talk of Maggie to the subject of estate planning.

THE IMPORTANCE OF PLANNING YOUR ESTATE

There is no area within the financial and retirement planning field where more misconceptions are held, mistakes are made, and myths abound than in estate planning. This is unfortunate, because estate planning is integral to a sound financial and retirement plan, and much value can be derived from the estate-planning process. Too many people look upon estate planning as unimportant, unpleasant, or unnecessary. Virtually everyone can benefit from undertaking some form of estate planning; yet, far too many ignore or avoid it.

Often, the major impediment is procrastination brought on by inertia, indecision, or unwillingness to make decisions. Many of us simply do not wish to confront our own mortality. As estate planning attorney William Zabel discovered, "You would be shocked that many people think that doing a will hastens their death." Estate planning can be clouded in emotional issues and family relationships. But those who choose to ignore or delay planning foster a legacy of turmoil and disharmony after death or in the event of incapacity. Making no decision is a decision by default.

Founding father Thomas Jefferson died at the age of 83 on July 4, 1826, the fiftieth anniversary of the Declaration of Independence, the famous document he so eloquently authored. His passing marked another personal tragedy. His beloved Monticello estate was put up for auction, because Jefferson was mired in debt of $100,000, the equivalent of several million in today's dollars.

We know from his correspondence with former President James Monroe that Jefferson was deeply depressed about his financial predicament and lamented his lack of attention to estate planning. "To keep a Virginia estate together," in Jefferson's words, "requires in the owner both skill and attention, skill I never had and attention I could not have, and really when I reflect on all the circumstances, my wonder is that I should have been so long as 60 years in reaching the result to which I am now reduced."

We should step back and note that in Jefferson's era there was no life insurance option to help save his property for the generations that followed. On the other hand, in 1826 there was no federal estate taxation, a twentieth century burden that would have been contrary to Jefferson's philosophy.

I had an enlightening experience while presenting a joint seminar with an attorney on retirement and estate planning. The attorney started his part of our presentation by asking members of the audience to raise their hands if they had an estate plan. Observing the response, I noted a lot of puzzled looks, open-mouthed glances between spouses, and other body language indicating that these seminar participants did not know how to respond. If they had a will, did that qualify them to nod in the affirmative? What about a trust? Did the sheaf of documents they had paid an attorney a generous fee to prepare qualify as an estate plan?

My co-presenter answered his own query, stating that anyone confused about whether they had an estate plan obviously had not been proactive in creating a plan. Estate planning is an active endeavor, a lifetime process of wealth accumulation, conservation, control, and transfer.

He said, your estate is a storehouse of wealth and includes all assets, property, life insurance, and other financial interests. If you have a dollar that you don't plan to spend, you have an estate. The attorney then went on to say that whether they realized it or not, everyone in attendance had an estate plan.

When someone dies without a will, it is referred to as dying *intestate*, and the state of residence (domicile) steps in to apply the rules of intestacy to determine how any minor children will be provided for and how property will be distributed. The point is, by not accepting responsibility for one's own estate, the person is abdicating control. As a result, heirs could suffer a delay in the transfer of assets, unnecessary expenses, taxes, and other negative consequences. In fact, the very individuals we wish to protect may not benefit at all.

A critical part of any estate plan is to name beneficiaries on retirement plans, life insurance, and annuity contracts, and to choose the appropriate type of ownership (titling) of one's residence and other financial assets.

Billionaire Howard Hughes died intestate in 1976. Like too many Americans without a will, his oversight resulted in a particularly thorny mess. William Rice Lummis, a lawyer and distant relative of Hughes, ruefully observed, "No one knew who owned the estate or where Hughes was domiciled."

Once it became known there was no claim on file to Hughes' vast fortune, bogus wills appeared out of nowhere. For example, the tabloid press spent much ink on the tale of a trucker who picked up a stranger stranded on a remote desert highway. To thank him for his act of kindness, the stranger—Hughes—purportedly made this Good Samaritan the sole beneficiary of his wealth.

Hughes' estate consisted of a mishmash of holdings, much of it illiquid or not fully valued. Claims ranged from an $80 judgment against Hughes to the IRS's demand for a whopping 77 percent piece of the total pie. State revenue departments in California and Texas also eyed a tax bounty. Hughes probably was a resident of Nevada, which imposes no state death taxes, but he never bothered to declare Nevada his domicile (home state). Reportedly, it took a full 20 years to untangle this complicated estate—at an unnecessary cost of some $100 million in legal fees.

Perhaps an eccentric recluse like Howard Hughes can be excused for not putting his affairs in order, but the same slack is not as likely to be accorded the former top-ranked judge in the land.

Retired Supreme Court Chief Justice Warren Burger passed away in June 1996 at the age of 87. A widower, Justice Burger did leave a will, but not an estate plan appropriate for his $1.8 million estate. He apparently decided against outside expertise. Typographical errors suggest that he drafted and probably typed the three-line document himself. For whatever reason, he did not feel it worthwhile to seek more sophisticated estate planning counsel, which could have secured additional assets for his son and daughter and might have reduced or eliminated the $450,000 estate tax that was imposed.

A prime objective of estate planning is the minimization and elimination of estate taxation. However, some people seem to believe that tax avoidance is unpatriotic. Perhaps Justice Burger should have reviewed the 1945 U.S. Supreme Court ruling that upheld the "legal right of a taxpayer to decrease the amount of what otherwise would have been his (or her) taxes or to avoid them altogether, by means which the law permits."

Judge Learned Hand—a great moniker for a justice—once elaborated, "Nobody owes any public duty to pay more than the law demands; taxes are enforced extractions, not voluntary contributions. To demand more in the name of mortals is mere cant."

When Elvis Presley died prematurely in 1977 at the age of 42, he left an estate in excess of $10 million. The King may have assumed he was immortal, because it appears he did little in the way of estate planning. How else can one explain why the government tax coffers ended up with 73 percent of his accumulated wealth, and his heirs got the short end?

We know this information from fully accessible probate records. One of Presley's signature renditions, "Don't Be Cruel," could serve well as the title of a song lamenting why substantial estates leave more money to Uncle Sam than to actual relatives.

There is much to be learned by contrasting the lack of proper estate planning of these celebrities with the model estate plan of the late Jacqueline Kennedy Onassis. The famous widow of a slain U.S. president, and later of a Greek shipping tycoon, left a detailed estate plan. Her will alone ran 36 pages. It was so well done, it is now used as a case study in law schools. When this very private public figure, mother, grandmother, and sister died from cancer at age 64 in 1994, she left an estate valued in the vicinity of $200 million.

Jackie Onassis, with the aid of a prestigious New York law firm's estate planning attorneys, matched her personal wishes with a carefully crafted estate plan. A byproduct of the plan was the effective minimization of taxes on the transfer of wealth at her death. In reference to this objective, Susan E. Kuhn in the magazine *Fortune* concluded, "In a world where supposedly nothing is inevitable except death and taxes, a good will and a sound estate plan are valuable gifts."

Planning dictates managing and adapting to change. All financial planning, especially estate planning, is conducted in a dynamic environment. We must be prepared to respond to changes in our personal and family situations, changes in our financial condition, and the inevitable changes in tax legislation.

In our personal lives we experience marriage, divorce, remarriage, the birth of children and grandchildren, adoption, stepchildren and death. Our health and that of one's spouse and beneficiaries eventually deteriorates. Employment changes may result in possible relocation to other states with different tax laws. One's personal financial condition and net worth are constantly fluctuating. Additionally, the depletion or alteration of an estate through a lifetime gifting program or the sale of a business has an impact on all other financial and estate matters.

Estate planning is technical, complex, and shrouded in legal jargon. It is also highly personal and confidential. My advice is to consult with an estate planning attorney. Estate planning is a highly specialized field. Not just any attorney is qualified or trained to handle an estate plan. Find someone with whom you feel comfortable and confident. Many people put off obtaining this professional service because they think it will be too expensive. Often, I find that clients expect to pay more than the charges they actually incur. In my opinion, carefully drafted and properly executed estate planning documents represent a valuable investment.

Understand that life insurance is likely to play a significant role in one's estate planning. Life insurance is a unique product, capable of providing liquid cash to coincide with the time of death.

The need for life insurance changes dramatically over a life span. In your pre-retirement accumulation stage, your priority is likely to be for insurance that provides an instant, sustainable estate for surviving dependents. Looking at your post-retirement stage, life insurance might be used to leverage a charitable bequest, pay estate taxes, complement an illiquid portfolio, or perhaps keep a business in the family. Therefore, life insurance policy needs and objectives should be reviewed regularly.

Estate planning is often driven by the legitimate desire to minimize personal income taxes and estate and gift taxation. Through proper planning, tax-minimization strategies can be highly valuable and save hundreds of thousands of dollars. Minimizing taxes is a prime motivation for initiating planning efforts. As popular entertainer Arthur Godfrey often told us in the 1940s, fifties and sixties, "I feel very honored to pay taxes in America. The thing is, I could probably feel just as honored for about half the price."

Realize that estate taxation, which is the toll for passing wealth at death, is a moving target that makes planning challenging. As of 2007, the federal estate tax exemption (tax-free transfer amount) is $2 million, scheduled to increase to a substantial $3.5 million by 2009. As it now stands, there is zero estate tax in 2010, but in 2011 the exemption amount backs down to $1 million.

Because of the exemption amount, and owing to talk of the complete elimination of the so-called death tax, many people believe it is no longer necessary to do estate planning. My retort paraphrases Mark Twain: "Reports of the death of the estate tax have been greatly exaggerated." While its present structure will likely change, it's highly unlikely that lawmakers (politicians that they are) will dispense with all taxes related to estate transfers.

To illustrate the point, listen to Congressman Bill Archer speaking to a *Wall Street Journal* reporter on the subject of the elimination of the estate tax: "The ancient Egyptians built elaborate fortresses and tunnels and even posted guards at tombs to stop grave robbers. In today's America, we call that estate planning."

Politicians aside, it is important to appreciate the fact that estate planning encompasses much more than the reduction or elimination of taxes. Put another way, if there were no estate tax, it would still be necessary to attend to estate planning. Additionally, although the federal estate tax may not currently be as much of a factor, revenue-hungry states such as my home state of Wisconsin have recently reinstituted a state inheritance tax that needs to be accounted for in the planning process.

As a financial planning practitioner, I have come to share the belief of my family's personal estate planning attorney Gerard J. Flood when he says, "Estate planning is often needlessly complex; simplicity is clearly better." John Bogle, in his book *Common Sense on Mutual Funds*, preaches us to return to simplicity. "The great paradox of this remarkable age is that the more complex the world around us becomes, the more simplicity we must seek in order to realize our financial goals."

As proof of estate planning complexity, I offer the IDGT, or intentionally defective grantor trust. It is called intentionally defective because it is flawed in a manner that results in an income tax inclusion, but not an estate tax. This concept doesn't sound simple to me.

When the subject of trusts is raised, some individuals assume they are unlikely candidates to employ these mysterious documents in their own estate planning. They visualize marble-columned financial institutions and think Rockefeller rich and stuffy. Trusts are really not mysterious, nor are they only for the rich.

A trust merely establishes a fiduciary relationship whereby a grantor (creator) transfers property (assets) to a trustee who agrees to hold, manage, and distribute property for the benefit of specified individuals (beneficiaries). The provisions of a trust are spelled out in a written agreement.

An example of a useful and flexible planning tool is a revocable living trust. *Revocable* as opposed to irrevocable means it can be changed and even terminated. *Living* means it is operating during one's lifetime (as opposed to testamentary, operating after death). A revocable living trust can in many cases be the centerpiece of an estate plan, because it has many advantages. It allows your named trustee complete control over your assets, along with disposition of trust assets after your death without probate. It also allows for professional asset management during your lifetime and avoids legal guardianship in the event of incapacity. It can provide a mechanism, if properly drafted, for the minimization of transfer taxes.

I should point out that living trusts, even with their many advantages, are not for everyone. They have too often been oversold. A living trust does not negate the need for a will nor does it by itself reduce estate taxes, and it has no impact on income taxes. There is a cost involved in drafting documents and possibly for maintaining the trust.

Note that probate does not have to be the horror story some make it out to be.

The state has an interest in protecting citizens and minors who cannot protect themselves. When our daughter Maggie reached age 18, her mother and I had to go through a formal guardianship process to be legally named her caretakers. Incredibly, this procedure required an administrative judge—a total stranger—to grant us the authority to care for our first-born child.

During the administrative hearing the court-appointed attorney interviewing Maggie asked if she was okay with her mom and dad making decisions for her. Without missing a beat, she quickly responded in a confident voice, "Oh, no! I don't want that."

Taken aback, the attorney probed further. Was she able to take the bus and go on her own to the shopping mall. "Yeah, sure I could," she convincingly stated.

It was not until he asked her address and she offered her phone number that her capacity was brought to light.

A too-often overlooked estate planning matter is to not name guardians in a will to provide care for minor children—those under the age of 18. I have always been confounded by parents who purchase insurance on their own lives to protect the family, but do not draw up a will naming guardians for minor children or specifying investment management for these same life insurance proceeds.

The seriousness of this lack of planning is exemplified by a tragic accident I heard of in which young parents were killed by a drunk driver who crossed the median and hit them head-on. Miraculously, this couple's two young children—a son aged two and a baby daughter barely two months old—were buckled up in the back seat and survived this deadly crash with only minor injuries. Unfortunately, the tragedy for these orphaned children continues with a nasty fight over legal guardianship. Part of the motivation for the suit may be attributable to funds made available from life insurance and settlement proceeds. Had the parents drawn up a will to name a guardian for their minor children, this legal anguish could have been minimized.

On a personal note, my wife and I have named my sister Colleen to act and make decisions for the care and well-being of our children, should this nightmare ever befall our family. A bank trust company has been named to provide investment management of the financial assets of our estate.

Owing to increasing life expectancies and a greater probability for mental or physical deterioration, at some point you might be unable to manage your financial affairs. Think for a minute of the situation faced by former president Ronald Reagan and his family. Alzheimer's disease attacked this formerly powerful world leader, and he lived for many years with increasing incapacity.

We might not want to contemplate our own disability, but it is a distinct possibility. In a worst-case scenario, you could be dragged through the indignity of a legal process to prove your competency to manage your own affairs, which could result in court supervision of your estate and the appointment of a guardian. Guardianships can be expensive and cause a rift or feud among family members. Neal E. Cutler of the American Institute of Financial Gerontology wants us to know that "one of the last things people want to give up, even if they need to, is control over their money." The durable power of attorney (DPOA) provides one solution. Another option is the revocable trust, discussed previously.

Advances in medical science have reached the point at which a once-imminent death can be postponed. The most celebrated recent case involved tragically brain-dead Terri Schiavo, whose estranged husband and parents fought bitterly and publicly over whether to pull her feeding tube. Many individuals would like more control over these very personal and literally life-and-death matters. The law provides for formalizing such choices.

A health care power of attorney is an important legal document that allows for decision-making by an appointed representative. A living will, on the other hand, is a directive for treatment. While you are fully capable, and after careful thought, you can indicate your intentions in writing and give directions for what you want done in the event of a terminal condition.

Returning to our girl Maggie, like millions of concerned parents of children with disabilities we realize she will probably outlive us. We worry about her care and general well-being after we—her caregivers and guardians—are no longer here. Working with our estate planning attorney, we established a special needs trust. An important part of special needs planning is to make certain that a loved one's long-term financial security is met.

Because this trust is properly drafted, it gives us peace of mind while maintaining Maggie's eligibility for important government services, such as supplemental Social Security income (SSI) and Medicaid. Sometimes known as a supplemental trust, this vehicle, once funded, will afford Maggie's trustee to cover her non-essential expenses that will make for a more comfortable and dignified lifestyle.

From my experience, it is generally a good idea to have an intergenerational family meeting to address estate planning issues. In our practice we have arranged for adult children and parents to come together for an open discussion. It is beneficial to involve the estate planning attorney in this type of meeting. Robert Whitman, professor of estate law at the University of Connecticut, has stated,

"Parents who refuse to open up and discuss estate planning with their children are going down the wrong road." It is extremely important that one's plans, wishes and fears are on the table; for, as Whitman observed, "you don't want surprises at the end."

Humorist Mark Twain spoke from experience when he observed, "You never really know a man until you divide an estate with him."

The author of *Winning the Tax Game*, Tim Cestnick, wrote a column for the *Toronto Globe & Mail* in which he points out that one of the challenges of getting older is dealing with your adult children in your will.

In his experience, it is wise to treat all children equally in the distribution of an estate. "When money is at stake, treating the kids differently will result in hurt feelings at best, and litigation and alienation at worst." He says that to do differently, even for good reasons, can leave your children hurt and wondering why you waited till death to play favorites or to "punish" them. Cestnick believes it is better, if you want to treat your children unequally, to do so during your lifetime. That way you can explain why you're doing what you're doing.

KISS

We are all familiar with the KISS acronym for Keep It Simple, Stupid. I am a big believer in the power of simplicity, finding it especially practical in personal finance and investment matters. However, because I am the father of a mentally impaired child, perhaps you can understand my sensitivity about referring to someone as "stupid" and my discomfort with book titles for dummies.

A frequent word in Maggie's vocabulary is to refer to someone or something as silly. I have been on the receiving end myself. Just the other day she referred to me as the "silliest guy on earth." I took it as a compliment.

I once made the error of casually asking Maggie what she learned at Sunday school religious education.

She replied, "About God, silly. Hello, dad."

I would like—at least in this book—to have KISS stand for Keep It Simple Silly. My friend and editor Jan Lennon suggested Keep Investing Simple and Sane. Either way, when it comes to investment behavior, it is always silly season out there, and we would be better off practicing good sense and simplicity.

Over 30 years ago, in 1974, the now-renowned sage of Omaha—Warren Buffett—said, "You're dealing with a lot of silly people in the marketplace; it's like a great big casino and everyone else is boozing. If you can stick with Pepsi, you should be o.k." At the time, the country was faced with a treacherous financial environment. Those who heeded Buffett's financial advice and the KISS approach came out ahead.

The best-selling business book *Good to Great* by Jim Collins gives repeated examples of successful companies and individual leaders who disdain complicated strategies. Instead they favor simple, straightforward concepts.

Carl Reichardt, former CEO of Wells Fargo, was quoted in an interview describing how his bank successfully navigated the new competitive landscape wrought by deregulation. Rather than listen to the gurus who said the smart response was to adopt sophisticated models, the interviewer wrote, "Reichardt stripped everything down to its essential simplicity." Reichardt was quoted as saying, "It's not space science stuff. What we did was so simple, and we kept it simple. It was so straightforward and obvious that it sounds almost ridiculous to talk about it."

Robert Bartley, former editor of *The Wall Street Journal,* lost his life to cancer at the age of 66 in 2003. Editor-in-chief Steve Forbes described Bartley in *Forbes* as "one of the most influential journalists in American history." A colleague of Bartley at the *Journal,* Daniel Henninger, sought to explain the source of this brilliant man's success. "Indeed, simplicity, to use one of Bob's favorite words, was his lodestar."

Henninger's article reintroduces us to "the fourteenth-century English philosopher William of Occam, who posited the principle that the best and sturdiest solution to a problem is often the least complicated." *Occam's Razor* is a favorite reference of both Robert Bartley and John Bogle.

The recently departed economist John Kenneth Galbraith wryly observed, "The study of money, above all other fields in economics, is one in which complexity is used to disguise truth or to evade truth, not to reveal it."

Further support for this strong view comes from David F. Swensen, chief investment officer for Yale University. "As a general rule of thumb, the more complexity that exists in a Wall Street creation, the faster and farther investors should run."

From the world of sports, basketball great Bob Cousy makes the point, "It's not so much what you do, it's how well you do it. Keep it simple."

It is well accepted that simplicity and common sense go hand-in-hand. This is especially true with respect to investing. Sir John Templeton is unequivocal in his contention, "I believe that successful investing is mainly common sense."

As you may know, John Templeton is a distinguished gentleman with a 1912 birth date who is now a full-time philanthropist and founder of the John Templeton Foundation. He started his remarkable investment career in 1937. *Money* magazine has called him "arguably the greatest global stock picker of the century."

Warren Buffett is quick to admit that he owes his phenomenal investment and financial success to common sense. Unfortunately, as pointed out by Zig Ziglar, sales and motivational guru with a great name and interesting life story, "Common sense is not always common practice."

Common sense is a very democratic quality. It requires no large sums of money, no prerequisite knowledge, and no physical prowess. It has nothing to do with gender, race, age, social position, education, or the commitment of an inordinate amount of time. "Common sense," said the nineteenth-century poet and essayist Ralph Waldo Emerson, "is genius dressed in its working clothes."

MUTUAL FUNDS—SIMPLE INVESTMENT TOOLS

John Bogle, Warren Buffett, and John Templeton, along with countless other knowledgeable and successful investors, fully support the view that mutual funds offer a simple, common sense way to invest. While he was chairman of the Securities and Exchange Commission, Arthur Levitt was quoted as saying, "In the fullness of time, the mutual fund will come to be regarded among the greatest financial innovations of the modern era."

Add Ralph Wanger to those in the know who believe mutual funds are the common sense route to follow. Wanger, now retired, built a well-deserved reputation as a master investor while guiding the Acorn mutual fund group. During his long tenure managing these small-cap equity funds, Wanger was known, as Warren Buffett was, for differentiating his investor reports from the usual dull, uninspiring reports. He regularly spiced his communications to shareholders with wit and wisdom. He admits to being drawn to the investment business because the pay is good and no heavy lifting is required. He combined his investment knowledge and writing ability in a book he authored, *A Zebra in Lion Country*.

A quote from that book illustrates this philosophy: "Considering the time, discipline, skills, knowledge, resources, and personality that investing demands, mutual funds are the sensible course for 95 percent of the public. All things considered, then, mutual funds make sense for most people."

Mutual funds are derided by product hawkers as boring and unsophisticated. This may well be, but since when does investing need to be sexy and exciting in order to be successful.

Let's learn from the real-life experience of Virginia Moehring, whose stock portfolio was devastated early in 2000 by the tech wreck and mauled in the preceding three-year bear market. *The Wall Street Journal* profiled the sorry experience of this 57-year-old Californian, who readily admits to having been caught up in the raging bull market of the late 1990s. She was "playing" the market. Her portfolio of stock picks swelled to $180,000 at the peak in March 2000. She tracked her holdings daily and watched the tickers on CNBC at lunch, admitting that "stock symbols were my personal friends." After three years, her portfolio had shriveled to $80,000. Her prized holdings in such speculative names as Bsquare and Biotransplant, worth at their top $2,185 and $1,300, respectively, shrunk to just $78 and $10.

A panel of experts assembled by the *Journal* suggested Mrs. Moehring should shun individual stocks and opt instead for mutual funds. Yet she resisted this sensible advice, remaining stubbornly committed, as she admitted, to the "adrenaline and excitement of stocks." She was bored by mutual funds, "because they move too slow and I don't have much time left."

Mutual funds by design bring democracy to the investment masses by offering affordability, convenience, and liquidity to Main Street investors and retirement plan participants. By making an investment in a mutual fund, ordinary investors gain access to professional money managers and entrust to them the difficult and perplexing buy-sell-hold decisions. But the greatest benefit of mutual fund investing is that investors achieve instant and continuous diversification from the first dollar invested.

Investors are wooed with a barrage of alternatives to mutual funds, be it hedge funds, private placements, separate accounts, structured products, limited partnerships, equity-indexed and variable annuities, and thousands of tempting, thinly traded stocks.

Jonathan Clements, in his column for *The Wall Street Journal,* asserts that funds offer three substantial advantages over that of alternatives, namely low cost, low risk, and a low-investment minimum.

In spite of these advantages, the greatest growth in assets these past few years has been in hedge funds. Billions have flowed into these exotic investment vehicles by the promise of the holy grail of higher returns and lower risk. The anticipated result is often illusory, because these investments are poorly regulated, high risk, expensive, and illiquid. When considering venturing into hedge funds, keep in mind a favorite John Bogle maxim: *caveat emptor*, buyer beware.

I first became aware of the dark side of the hedge fund industry when reading *When Genius Failed* by John Lowenstein. This chilling tale recounts the spectacular rise and fall of a company with the name Long-Term Capital Management (LTCM). LTCM boasted two Nobel laureates in economics among its brainy partners; hence, the book title's reference to genius. For a couple of years, this high-octane hedge fund posted tremendous returns. It did so by employing a black box computer model that spewed out high-risk, leveraged strategies. Its success attracted billions from investors eager to share in this seemingly sure thing.

This massive fund soon failed spectacularly. Between October 1997 and September 1998 it lost 92 percent of its capital and hundreds of millions of dollars. In fact, it almost collapsed before being bailed out by a group of large banks—a remedy instigated by the Federal Reserve Bank of New York. Federal regulators were very concerned about the shock to the global financial system that could result from a failure of this magnitude.

A myth shrouds hedge funds and makes them alluring to investors, so much so that a trillion dollars is currently invested in these mysterious investment vehicles. Investors at all levels are eager to play in the exclusive sandbox of the rich, believing this is where the secret to riches can be found.

Yet academic and independent industry research has pulled back the cover to reveal that hedge funds are far riskier and provide lower returns than has been commonly assumed. In fact, hedge fund investors would be distressed to learn from Morningstar, the fund analysis firm, that in 2004, returns for mutual funds exceeded, on average, those of hedge funds. Further research by Citigroup and others found that average hedge fund returns are exaggerated by about a percentage point annually. Unlike mutual funds, whose past performance reporting is strictly regulated and therefore to be trusted, hedge fund returns are often illusionary, bloated, unverifiable, or missing.

Separate accounts is another alternative to mutual funds, with a certain cachet. Brokerage firms have sold investors on the promise of customized portfolios and access to top-performing money managers. The brokers do collect a healthy annual revenue stream, but in many cases investors have been short-changed with little, if any, true portfolio customization, no direct access to portfolio managers, and limited tax management. In other words, long on promise but short on delivery.

Equity-indexed annuities (EIAs) are a hybrid insurance and security product that is one of the biggest sellers in financial services today. Unwary, unsophisticated savers and novice investors are attracted by its combination of stock market returns with guarantees of no risk to principal. Consequently, investment and insurance reps find it an easy sell and covet its high commissions. Not surprisingly, federal and state regulators have charged some brokerages with misleading investors into buying complex insurance products, which carry steep commissions and penalize investors severely for early withdrawals.

Along this line, syndicated personal finance columnist Humberto Cruz felt safe making the bold prediction for calendar year 2005 that insurance companies will come out with even more mind-numbingly complex annuity products, so difficult to understand that even the people selling them often don't understand them, or if they do, they fail to explain them properly.

When investing, I follow two simple rules that have served our advisory clients well and may steer you away from a lot of trouble.

Rule number one. Never invest in anything you don't fully understand. This is especially important if you are unable to assess the risk inside and out.

To illustrate, I met with a veteran attorney who, if the truth be known, did not understand the investment he purchased the previous year from a broker. This despite the fact that he had bothered to read the dense 20 pages of the offering prospectus.

This intelligent and sophisticated investor had purchased a product, which used options, in the belief that it was conservative and low risk. He sought my counsel after having second thoughts on this souring investment. He was embarrassed not being able to explain to his inquiring wife what they owned and why. I found that he was pretty much stuck with this perplexing investment, as there is no market in which to sell this illiquid investment until a 10-year term is up. He would have been better served by following the course of Peter Lynch, who wrote in his book, *One Up on Wall Street*, "I've never bought an option in my entire investing career, and I can't imagine buying one now. Actually, I do know a few things about options. I know that the large potential return is attractive to many small investors who are dissatisfied with getting rich slow. Instead, they opt for getting poor quick."

Which brings us to *rule number two*. Never make an investment unless you can find it listed and readily marketable, like any mutual fund, in the financial section of *The Wall Street Journal*. Rules number one and two both knock out hedge funds and their alternative ilk, such as separate accounts, limited partnerships, and private placements. Following these tenets would have saved the attorney from making a costly mistake. Rule number two and the marketability feature also eliminate individual municipal and corporate bonds, equity-indexed annuities, and thinly traded, non-listed stocks.

THE FOLLY OF MARKET TIMING

An alarming example of poor decision-making by mutual fund investors is found by looking at research put out annually by Dalbar, Inc. Over the 20-year period from 1986 through 2005, the annualized return of the S&P 500 stock index was a healthy 11.9 percent. However, over this identical period, the average equity (stock) mutual fund investor earned just 3.9 percent.

How can this be, you ask? There is a simple explanation. The majority of mutual fund investors are terrible market timers. The close to 12 percent average annual return was earned by patient, long-term investors who remained in a passively-managed S&P 500 stock index fund each and every day over the same 20-year period.

The wild herd of investors is driven by powerful emotions of fear and greed. In a futile attempt to do better and outperform, and by thinking they are somehow smarter than the market, the herd restlessly trades among funds. They routinely chase after the latest hot-performing funds and impatiently flee those funds posting more pedestrian performance numbers. By attempting to *time the market*, these investors suffered a "lost opportunity" of 77 percent (3.9 percent compared to 11.9 percent).

Perhaps the most familiar and simple mantra of intelligent investing is to buy low and sell high. The Dalbar study confirms that our actions demonstrate that most investors regularly ignore this piece of basic advice. Instead, we do precisely the opposite, buying funds performing the best at the high and selling the laggards at the low.

Money magazine, says Peter Bernstein, may know more about investing than anyone alive. In an article in the November 2004 issue, Bernstein—a Harvard classmate of John F. Kennedy—defines the most common mistake investors make: "Extrapolation. Leaving fund managers in a down year to go with whoever's hot. The refusal to believe that shock lies in wait." He went on to say, "Believe me, individual investors are not the only ones who mire themselves in this mistake. It is endemic throughout the investing community."

The futility of chasing performance by buying high and selling low should not be difficult to comprehend. Some might well call this behavior silly. A personal incident illustrates my point. Once, while driving with my daughter Maggie, my front windshield suddenly fogged up with a change in weather conditions. I registered some alarm and mildly panicked because the defroster was not working. I pulled off the highway and stopped the car. Maggie asked, "What's the matter, Dad, can't you see?"

I like to refer to this silly behavior of buy high, sell low as the "rear view mirror" approach to investing. Some investors believe blindly that whatever went on in the past will continue the same momentum in the future. This is a dangerous way to drive as well as to invest. Bernstein says, shock—like a bad accident—may lie in wait.

As you have no doubt seen, all mutual funds are required to note in their reporting and in their promoting of historical performance that "past performance is no guarantee of future results." This warning should probably be more blunt and say, "past performance is a lousy predictor." Better yet: past performance is often a contrary indicator. Then again, the serious health warning on cigarette packs is sadly and blatantly ignored by those electing to light up. Investors determined to go full speed ahead might not heed sterner warnings either.

Attempting to time the market by jumping in and buying before the market heads upward—and getting out by selling before a downturn—is a risky proposition at best. To succeed you would have to be right twice, at the top and again at the bottom, and your timing calls would have to be impeccable.

How this performance-chasing plays out can be instructive. For calendar year 1999, funds that followed a growth investment style, primarily tech, ruled the very top of the performance pyramid. The Russell 2000 Growth index of small- and medium-sized stocks turned in a sterling performance, gaining 43 percent that year. Large-cap growth stocks (think Cisco and Sun Microsystems) as measured by the S&P/Barra 500 Growth index, turned in a not-too-shabby 28 percent return.

As the stock market and especially growth stock funds soared in the years from 1995 through March 2000, investors' natural fear of losing money was replaced by the fear of missing out on outsized returns—and, in some cases, by envy. Thus, it should not be surprising that some 79 percent of all new money invested in the first quarter of 2000 piled into growth funds.

In 1999 when large-cap growth was up 28 percent, small-cap value stocks such as an obscure cement, casket, or pet food company were actually in the red, losing 1.5 percent. However, the tide does turn, as the very next year, in 2000, large-cap growth lost a steep 22 percent while small-cap value names vaulted back, gaining 22.8 percent.

The stock market is uncertain, rarely moving in a straight line. Neither does it signal when it is going to turn. Market rallies are apt to occur in bursts, so being on the sidelines and missing out on even a few strong "up" days means missing out on substantial gains. In fact, missing out on the 30 best days of the total 5,323 trading days in the 20-year period from 1986 to 2005 resulted in an annualized return of the S&P 500 of 6.2 percent, compared to the 12.8 percent of staying fully invested.

Research by Ibbotson Associates adds further credence to the folly of stock market timing. Ibbotson found that missing out on just the best performing month in any given calendar year 1970 to 2000 resulted in a 7.5 percent average decline of annual total returns. Further, five times during this 31-year period, the best performing month's return kept stocks from ending negative for the year.

Market timing is a poor substitute for a long-term investment plan. It can severely penalize you for missing out on market returns. As I demonstrate, several "risks" are associated with getting in or being out of the market. To keep up, you have to invest through thick and thin, because no one can predict future performance.

Peter Lynch, maintaining a visible presence as a vice-chairman at Fidelity, tells us, "I'm always fully invested at the market top and at the bottom. I don't try to time the market." Near the very bottom of the wrenching bear market of September 2002, Lynch said in an AARP Bulletin, "When (the market) comes back, it comes back fast. So people who are out the bad months, are out for the good months. I personally suffer the bad months along with the good months, and have been very happy with the results." Prophetically, the market roared back in 2003.

Fund manager Ralph Wanger cuts to the chase regarding the futility of market timing in *A Zebra in Lion Country.* He writes: "But we know market timing doesn't work. A market may indeed be 'overpriced,' but it can stay overpriced for years. Bull markets come in all lengths. Your only defense against any sort of market jitters is to think like a long-term investor. If you stare the monster down with focus, patience, and a calm eye, you will be rewarded in the end."

Forbes, my favorite magazine, in a December 2003 story titled "*Your Own Worst Enemy*" in reference to mutual fund investors, quantifies the losses from what it calls "stupid timing." According to the article, "Something very close to $1 trillion is missing by dint of investors' own folly over the past decade, as they rushed into the market at the top and sold after the crash."

PRODUCING A DESIRED RESULT

Whenever my work involves discussing investment diversification, I borrow an insight gleaned from my own cancer ordeal. I remember as if it were yesterday. Nervously I sat in the small examining room of Dr. Elizabeth Gore, a respected radiation oncologist who specializes in head and neck cancers. I was scheduled to start seven weeks of daily radiation treatment the following Monday—a procedure necessary to destroy the deadly microscopic rogue cells that had invaded my body. In this prelude meeting the doctor would spell out what I might expect from the cumulative, damaging effects of such intensive treatment.

In her professional manner, she proceeded to recite 10 side effects. Months later, I figured I had indeed experienced each of them: skin burn and rashes, permanent dry mouth, fatigue, dramatic weight loss, swollen tongue, mouth sores, difficulty swallowing, jaw tightening, temporary loss of taste, and a general loss of appetite.

When I listened to the doctor tick off this list I thought none of these sounded like something I couldn't *live* with. Because I did not have to undergo chemo I was spared the nausea and hair loss that frequently accompanies those toxic drugs.

What I chose to focus my full attention on was Dr. Gore's assertion, at the conclusion of our discussion, "But I believe this treatment will be effective."

Ever since that particular office visit, I have come to believe that *effective* must be among the most beautiful and powerful words in the whole English language.

Webster's dictionary defines "effective" as that producing a desired result. My spirits soared, focusing like a laser on the message that despite many unpleasant side effects, this radiation treatment, in Dr. Gore's professional medical opinion, would work. What I took from her words was thank God, she expected me to survive and go on with my life.

Another definition of effective is to be "equipped and ready for battle." Bring on the battle, I thought, eager for the following Monday morning to arrive so we could engage the enemy.

Since that time, whenever my work involves discussing investment diversification, I emphasize and underline *effective* diversification. Diversification is a valuable and indeed essential ally to reduce and manage the risks found in investing. Too many investors naïvely believe their portfolio is adequately diversified, when in fact it is not. To produce the desired result, one needs to be *effectively* diversified.

Mutual funds by design provide an important level of diversification simply by the quantity of the holdings comprising a fund portfolio.

Contrast this safety to the following facts drawn from hundreds of examples of individual stocks that suffered from single-issue risk. A startling case in point is the price of United Airlines stock, which flew to a high of $101.75 a share in October 1997. By mid-January of 2003, it was practically grounded at $1.51 per share.

While leading an investment program in late summer of 2006, I asked the assembled group of 40 student physicians at a medical school, "How many of you own Dell computers?" Fully three-quarters of their hands shot up. Clearly, this glamour growth stock enjoyed a dominant market position within this tech-savvy group of young professionals. Yet in a quarter when the overall stock market was experiencing a steady rise in value, tech heavyweight Dell was floundering against the tide, having dropped 25 percent in the value of its share price in the previous three months.

To be truly diversified in stocks dictates not being overly concentrated in any industry or sector, such as energy, pharmaceutical, or technology stocks. Sectors have been known to drop in tandem, even in otherwise rising or stable markets. During the tech mania of the late 1990s, hordes of investors made the costly mistake of loading up on the then-soaring technology stocks. They were under the erroneous assumption they were adequately diversified by owning a half-dozen aggressive growth stock mutual funds. Trouble was, these funds were all heavy in technology issues and got slammed hard in the tech wreck that occurred early in 2000.

Sixteenth-century philosopher Francis Bacon told us, "Money is like muck, not good unless spread." To repeat, there is no better risk reduction technique than effective diversification.

An effectively diversified portfolio is achieved by commingling assets (investments) whose returns don't always move in the same direction. A good example is the zig and zag of stocks and bonds. In the language of investment professionals, stock and bonds possess low market correlation. As with a teeter-totter, one asset class moves opposite to the other. The lower the market correlation, the higher (better) the portfolio diversification. To conclude, *effective* diversification is powerful and actually works to reduce risk.

I am also very happy and relieved to report the radiation treatment I received was indeed effective, just like the good doctor said. It produced the desired result.

The important point to emphasize and constantly follow is that intelligently managing an investment portfolio requires the investor to diversify, diversify, diversify.

AN INVESTMENT IN KNOWLEDGE

I have long admired Peter Lynch, legendary mutual fund manager whose stock-picking powered Fidelity Magellan to prominence. I am impressed with the courage he showed to walk away from fame and fortune at Fidelity by retiring at age 44, at the height of his career. He decided to escape the constant stress and the time demands of active money management in order to devote more of his life to his wife and young daughters. Lynch realized life is indeed short, having experienced at age 10 the loss of his father from cancer. This premature death left the Lynch family in financial straits. His mother went to work at a manufacturing company, and young Peter moved from a private to a public school.

Lynch and I, in addition to being fellow Irishmen, were both fortunate to attend college on a caddy golf scholarship awarded on a combination of economic need and academic achievement. We both went the Jesuit college route. Peter went to Boston College and I attended Marquette University on an Evans Scholarship. The Evans Scholars Foundation is the nation's largest privately funded college scholarship program. It was started by Charles "Chick" Evans and the Western Golf Association.

Chick Evans was an accomplished golfer in the WWI era, becoming in 1916 the first to win both the U.S. Amateur and the U.S. Open in the same year. He wanted to maintain his amateur status and took the advice of his mother, who suggested he place his tournament money in escrow. This helped fund his dream of providing college scholarships for deserving caddies. From this act of generosity grew the Evans Scholars Foundation, which today has over 800 caddies attending colleges at schools throughout the Midwest, plus some 8,400 Evans program graduates—including me.

My scholarship paid every dime of tuition and rooming for four years at Marquette. I am very grateful. As the oldest of seven children, with my dad toiling at two jobs to support his family, I was not in a financial position to otherwise gain this level of education.

On the subject of education funding, the October 2005 issue of *Money* magazine brought us some eye-opening numbers regarding college costs: Included in these figures is $9,000 for "pizza money." These sobering amounts are in today's dollars, with costs expected to rise dramatically over the next 18 years. So it makes sense to start early on a college savings plan.

Money magazine goes as far as to suggest starting while the future graduate is *in utero*, pointing out that the time from cradle to campus amounts to 216 months, $171,384 to send a child to a top private college and $71,508 for four years at a state university. The value of education goes far beyond its hefty price tag. Remember what Benjamin Franklin had to say on the subject: "If a man empties his purse into his head, no one can take it away from him. An investment in knowledge always pays the best interest." If Franklin were here with us today, we can assume he would expand his thought to include women.

POWER OF SIMPLICITY

Nobel Prize winner in economics Daniel Kahneman told a group of financial advisors that "we would all be better off if we made fewer financial decisions." Following Kahneman's simplicity theme, I have narrowed the vast universe of mutual funds to concentrate on just two fund families, Vanguard and T. Rowe Price.

Truthfully, there are too many funds and fund groups. Investors are drowning in a sea of choices, overwhelmed by confusion and complexity. *Forbes* magazine in a 1988 cover story referred to "the maddening multiplicity of funds." At that time some 2,000 fund choices beckoned, a number that nine years later mushroomed to 8,000, and by 2005 multiplied to 13,000 funds. This tremendous over-capacity lies at the root of many of the industry's ills.

Investing is made much more complicated than it needs to be. Hence, it makes sense to limit fund recommendations to a select few. To be sure, other quality fund groups exist, but the two I focus on here are recognized as among the cream of the crop. Mutual fund authority Morningstar gives its highest overall marks to pro-investor stalwarts Vanguard and T. Rowe Price, using criteria such as expense costs, five-year-return averages, and guiding investment principles.

Invoking the keep-it-simple precepts, Vanguard and T. Rowe Price easily make the final cut for mutual fund choices. These elite fund groups are no-load and low-cost. Ranked among the very largest fund complexes, Vanguard second, and T. Rowe Price seventh, they survived unscathed from the wide-reaching mutual fund scandal. Most importantly, during the silliness at the peak of the bull market after

1999, each fund company demonstrated a responsible and disciplined approach to investing.

Vanguard ranks second only to the largest fund family in the world, Fidelity Investments. It was founded by venerable industry icon John Bogle, father of indexing and champion of low-cost investing. It is differentiated by a unique corporate structure, somewhat like a credit union. Vanguard is a cooperative, owned by fund shareholders, rather than run as a profit-making enterprise.

In existence since 1937, Baltimore-based T. Rowe Price is named after its founder, legendary growth stock investor Thomas Rowe Price. It is a publicly listed and traded stock. Tellingly, its own stock price rose at the height of the mutual fund scandal, after Merrill Lynch analysts and others noted this firm was free of the regulatory problems that plagued many asset managers.

T. Rowe Price has lived up to its trademark slogan, "Invest with Confidence." Its managers bravely went against the popular tech craze tide of the late 1990s, staying the course with a cautiously balanced risk/reward approach, while resisting the allure of short-term market fads. Although this sane, conservative investment policy proved a poor marketing choice, because assets fled into the spectacular returns found at high-flying growth fund groups such as Janus, the 2000-2002 bear market ultimately proved the wisdom of T. Rowe Price's patient and prudent attention to risk-adjusted returns. Many other funds badly underperformed or flamed out, leaving their performance-chasing investors burned and sadly disappointed.

Both fund groups are pure no-loads and carry annual expense ratios (charges) substantially below industry norms. Vanguard is well-known for imposing the lowest costs in the entire mutual fund universe, often just one-sixth of the industry average. T. Rowe Price touts responsible management of fund expenses. In comparison to other large family competitors, T. Rowe Price looks pretty good. It is a simple matter of investment math that any money expended on investment costs directly reduces both current yields and overall returns. Costs really do matter. As John Bogle reminds us, "Never forget that costs, like weeds, impede the garden's growth." The always-perceptive Benjamin Franklin also weighed in on costs: "Beware of small expenses; a small leak will sink a great ship."

Both fund groups (Vanguard.com and Troweprice.com) have offerings to meet every investment need, including retirement accounts, cash management, brokerage and even annuities. Staying within one family carries no extra risk. For one thing, multiple accounts are likely to be more costly to maintain and more difficult to manage distributions, beneficiary designations, and asset allocation. Both fund groups offer free educational resources and web tools to help investors intelligently manage their investment portfolio and plan their finances. The T. Rowe Price Retirement Income Calculator has won awards as a useful tool to help map out and chart retirement planning.

I have seen plenty of examples of individuals having a half dozen IRA accounts or more spread all over the place. Typically, people have a couple of accounts from previous employers, maybe a bank CD, and a brokerage and mutual fund account or two. Some justify this collection for the seeming diversification it affords. In truth, this hodgepodge tends to complicate matters. Better to organize and consolidate in a single IRA with a no-load fund group such as Vanguard or T. Rowe Price. As the genius Albert Einstein asserted, "Out of clutter, find simplicity."

TOTAL STOCK MARKET INDEX

There is an investment vehicle that neatly brings together common sense, prudent and effective diversification, and simplicity. Both Vanguard and T. Rowe Price offer total stock market index funds for investors looking for broad exposure to stocks. They are: Vanguard Total Stock Market Index (VTSMX), and T. Rowe Price Total Equity Market Index (POMIX).

As index funds, these choices are virtually identical, except for expenses, .20 percent at Vanguard and .40 percent at T. Rowe Price. Index funds are broadly diversified and benefit from being tax efficient, with a very low turnover.

Index pioneer John Bogle considers the total market index to be the perfect investment. The term "index fund" is often thought of in its most popular form, that of the Standard and Poors (S&P) 500 index, which comprises and tracks the 500 largest stocks in market capitalization. However, the large cap S&P 500 index misses about 25 percent of the total stock market, omitting small- and mid-cap stocks. This failure to capture the broader market misses the benefits derived from wider diversification.

Bogle, writing in *Common Sense On Mutual Funds*, states, "Theoretically, the preferred standard for the basic index mutual fund would be the Wilshire 5000 Equity Index of all publicly held stocks in the United States." The total market index offerings provide investors a broader market choice.

Sheldon Jacobs, publisher of *The No-Load Fund Investor,* touts the Vanguard Total Stock Market Index as his favorite investment. "This fund is the ultimate 'no-brainer.' The only way you can go wrong is if the market goes down and never recovers. It is difficult at this time to forecast which sectors of the market will beat the overall market. It's far more certain just to buy the overall market."

Burton Malkiel is best known for authoring the million-copy bestseller, *A Random Walk Down Wall Street.* In his 1973 investment classic, this distinguished Princeton economics professor lays out a compelling case for the wisdom of indexing. Malkiel sounded off in the 2005 edition of the *Vanguard Voyager*: "I believe more strongly in indexing today than I did in 1973. I can't think of any investment idea spawned in academia that has had as much empirical support."

The basic premise of his book is that the market itself prices stocks so efficiently that investment managers as a group can't outperform the broad market. The professor contends that "someone who drops a napkin over a newspaper's stock pages—and then buys and holds the stocks it covers up—could get a portfolio that performs as well as those managed by experts."

Malkiel famously theorizes that the market is so efficient that a blindfolded chimpanzee throwing darts at *The Wall Street Journal* could do as well as the smartest stock professionals. Starting in 1988, the *Journal* took Malkiel's idea and ran with it by holding contests. As a safety precaution, instead of the monkeys, staff members threw darts at a list of symbols. Malkiel suspected there was more to it, saying, "Financial analysts in pinstriped suits don't like being compared to bare-ass monkeys." Over the years, the pros' picks have held a winning percentage over the dart throwers; yet, it is embarrassingly narrow, barely edging out the Dow average and not enough of a margin to justify their fees.

Nevertheless, according to *Wall Street Journal* columnist Jonathan Clements, unabashed champion of indexing, there still exists a widespread belief that "picking winning funds is easy." In his *Getting Going* column he says, "Whenever I tout market-tracking funds, I get a slew of dissenting e-mails talking about how easy it is to select market-beating funds. All you have to do, my correspondents suggest, is buy funds that have fared well in the past."

The esteemed investor Benjamin Graham, author of *The Intelligent Investor* and mentor to Warren Buffett, gets to the heart of the matter. "The investor's chief problem—and even his worst enemy— is likely to be himself."

"There's nothing like a bull market to make everyone think they're a genius," says another professor of economics, Robert Strauss of Carnegie Mellon.

Returning to author Malkiel, "The odds against finding the winning mutual fund in the stock market haystack are demonstrably long, so I conclude: don't bother looking. Just buy the all-market haystack."

When it comes to the wisdom of indexing, great minds do think alike. No less an authority than Warren Buffett wrote the following in 1996 in his report to shareholders of Berkshire Hathaway: "Most investors, both institutional and individual, will find that the best way to own common stocks is through an index fund that charges minimal fees. Those following this path are sure to beat the net results (after fees and expenses) delivered by the great majority of investment professionals."

Add professor Terrance Odean of the University of California at Davis to the wisdom-of-indexing chorus: "My serious advice to people is that they should take most of the money they have to invest and buy a low-risk mutual fund such as an index fund." Academic research done by Odean, a recognized specialist in behavioral finance, and by fellow professor Brad Barber, found that the 20 percent of investors who traded most actively earned an average net annual return a startling 5.5 percent lower than that of the least active, or patient buy-and-hold, passive investors.

INVEST GLOBALLY

Over half of the stock market capitalization and an even larger share of promising growth opportunities exist outside the borders of the United States. Yet the vast majority of investors have too little, if any, money allocated to foreign stocks. This is a mistake, as international investing adds another valuable level of diversification to a portfolio. Additionally, there have been periods including the five years (6/1/01–5/30/06) when international stocks (EAFE index) outperformed domestic (S&P 500 index) by a large (32 percent) margin.

For a long time, many astute investors, including Warren Buffett, felt that by investing in top multinational U.S. companies, they did not need to flavor portfolios further by adding international. Recently, he and others have changed their tune and now sing the benefits of global investing. This broader approach is part of a trend that is unlikely to change. According to portfolio manager Susan Byrne of Westwood Funds, "The world is in a long-term development boom that will go through multiple phases and demands investor attention."

Similarly, the face of the world of sport is changing, dramatically illustrating there is talent to be found all over the globe. Americans have long rightly believed that the world's best basketball players were products of the USA. However, the rosters of NBA professional teams have become increasingly stocked with quality foreign players. The top player chosen in the 2005 NBA draft was from Australia and in 2006 from Italy. Steve Nash, the two-time league MVP is a product of Canada.

Whereas America's national pastime is baseball, the 2006 annual All-Star game lineups are filled with players from around the world. The 2006 Wimbledon tennis tournament in England was notable by the absence of American men and women among the contenders for this prestigious championship. Russians have risen to the top of this sport, once held by the likes of America's Chris Evert, Jimmy Connors, Pete Sampras, and John McEnroe. The leader board on the U.S. Ladies Professional Golf (LPGA) Tour is chock full of golfers from Asia, Europe, Mexico, and South America.

Sports reveal to us that the world is indeed shrinking, becoming more of a global village. Americans continue to be spectators of baseball with its abundance of foreign-grown talent. At the same time, our children are enthusiastically playing soccer, the game of the world. Little League is now sadly foreign to most American children, and the youth baseball diamonds are virtually empty, while soccer fields are jam-packed. The game is changing in the sphere of investing as well. We Americans would be smart to drop some of our isolation and instead look outside our borders and overseas for exciting and profitable stock investment opportunities.

As a personal aside, our soccer-crazy son, Jack, and I are toying with the idea of attending the 2010 World Cup to be held in South Africa. This location is yet more evidence that the world has indeed changed, and for the better. South Africa discarded its backward and repulsive notion of apartheid and was subsequently welcomed back to the world community, as shown by its being selected to host this huge international quadrennial event. It was reported that a billion people on the planet witnessed the telecast of the final of this "beautiful game" won in 2006 by Italy.

By far the simplest way to invest internationally is through a mutual fund. Again, both Vanguard and T. Rowe Price have index funds that sensibly fit the bill.

Vanguard Total International Stock Index (VGTSX) and T. Rowe

Price International Equity Index (PIEQX) receive high marks (four stars) from Morningstar, are broadly diversified (1,307 holdings in the T. Rowe Price fund), and cover both the west and Greater Europe and the east and Greater Asia. As expected of index funds, each imposes very reasonable expenses, especially for international funds, of .31 percent (Vanguard) and .50 percent (T. Rowe Price). This amounts to less than a third of what actively managed international mutual funds typically cost.

The next question becomes how much of your equity (stock) money should be allocated abroad. *Wall Street Journal* columnist Jonathan Clements, who also believes Americans should invest overseas, recommends 75 percent domestic U.S. balanced with 25 percent foreign. My partners and our investment committee basically concur with this allocation, as we typically place between 20 percent and 33 percent of total stock funds investments internationally.

In promoting international investing, Fidelity Investments says, "the world is your oyster." So I add, take advantage of the opportunities available.

CHAPTER 3

ON THE PATH

Do not follow where the path may lead—go instead
where there is no path and leave a trail.

Ralph Waldo Emerson

Two roads diverged in a wood, and I—
I took the one less traveled by,
and that has made all the difference.

Robert Frost

PLANNING PAYS OFF

Procrastination and inertia are two of the biggest obstacles to success, in both life and finances. Looked at another way, being proactive is the number one habit of *The Seven Habits of Highly Effective People,* according to Steven Covey, author of the groundbreaking, perennial bestseller by that name.

Covey goes on to describe definiteness of purpose, taking initiative, and making things happen as other valuable habits in the pursuit of success.

Why don't more individuals undertake some form of planning for a better future? The answer is difficult to pinpoint, but I believe it flows from our basic human nature.

Individuals by nature are reactive rather than proactive, especially when it comes to personal financial planning. Many express frustration when discussing their personal finances, often describing themselves as feeling lost, on a treadmill, spinning their wheels, or slipping backward. A good road map (financial life plan) would assist them greatly in reaching their hoped-for destination or goal.

When done effectively, planning is an important tool to increase the probability of achieving one's financial objectives and mapping out a route to successfully reach a destination. What is called for is a bias toward action. James Stowers is founder and chairman of mutual fund firm American Century. His philosophy for success is to just get started. According to Stowers, "The best time to plant an oak was twenty years ago. The second best time is now."

Anyone who has ever contemplated writing a book knows it is a daunting task. There are far more people who dream of writing a book than there are authors with completed manuscripts. Poet Robert Frost observed, "Most men die with their music inside them."

Look to the accomplished author of such American classics as *The Adventures of Huck Finn* and *The Adventures of Tom Sawyer* for sound advice on succeeding. As Mark Twain said, "The secret of getting ahead is getting started. The secret of getting started is breaking your complex, overwhelming tasks into small manageable tasks, and then starting on the first one."

The book you are now reading would never have been written had I not put pen to paper and scratched out an introductory chapter. In the immortal words of Chinese philosopher Lao-Tzu, "The journey of a thousand miles begins with one step." I'm the one who had to take that first step—and follow through.

Nike Corporation built a hugely successful advertising campaign around the activist life-planning slogan, "Just do it." This sports apparel and international marketing powerhouse sponsors such high-profile sports celebrities as Michael Jordan, Mia Hamm, Tiger Woods, and Lance Armstrong to endorse its products and promote its ubiquitous swoosh brand.

I am convinced my book would not have been completed had I not had a vision of the finish line. Habit number two of *The Seven Habits of Highly Effective People* expresses it well: "Begin with the end in mind."

As my writing process was being completed and the final editing underway, I took to heart this learned advice from Mark Twain: "A successful book is not made of what is in it, but what is left out of it."

THINK AND GROW RICH

The motivational message of Napoleon Hill's classic *Think and Grow Rich* reinforces the theme of the value of financial planning in the successful pursuit of financial independence.

Hill's book was inspired by steel baron and philanthropist Andrew Carnegie, who challenged the young journalist to undertake a lifelong pursuit of interviewing and chronicling 500 successful individuals, including such giants as Thomas Edison and Henry Ford.

From this comprehensive life study, Hill discovered certain secrets and formulas that he distilled into principles and steps. When rigorously applied, these steps were said to enable individuals to achieve financial and life goals. According to Hill, the starting point is to know what one is looking to accomplish. He frequently refers to this notion in his book as a definiteness of purpose.

Other traits common to the makeup of successful individuals include having a willingness to take control, setting clearly identified goals—financial or otherwise—developing a definite, organized plan, and mastering procrastination. Hill believes we need a vision and the courage born of self-confidence. He writes, "There are no limitations to the mind except those we acknowledge. Both poverty and riches are the offspring of thought."

Actor, lawyer, and author Ben Stein echoes this observation in saying, "The indispensable first step to getting the things you want out of life is this: Decide what you want."

Hill was a contemporary of Thomas Edison, who succeeded in producing the electric light only after he conducted 10,000 failed experiments. Hill claims the inventor finally achieved success when he committed his objective to writing and formulated an organized plan for proceeding. Like Edison, auto titan Henry Ford possessed very little formal education, yet succeeded due to vision, persistence, and a plan. A Japanese proverb sums it up well. "Vision without action is a daydream. Action without vision is a nightmare."

Two of the great Winston Churchill's favorite pastimes were planning and preparation, with a premium placed on execution.

Although *Think and Grow Rich* has been in print since 1926 and its success stories detail lives from a bygone era, its material and advice have withstood the passage of time.

Planning often does not come naturally. As an unfortunate result, too many people put off until tomorrow that which is better tackled today. Noting this propensity, British actor Sir John Harvey once quipped, "The nicest thing about not planning is that failure comes as a complete surprise, rather than being preceded by a period of worry and depression."

Planning deals with the uncertainty inherent in the future. The act of planning or strategizing the future provides us with a comfortable sense that we are exerting some control over that uncertainty. Influential financial planning industry observer Bob Veres notes, "All we can hope for is to tame the chaos." Industry leader Merrill Lynch, in promoting its planning services, ran a print ad with the tag line, "Is it true that people with a financial plan sleep better at night?"

Strategic planning is a necessity in achieving the desired outcome of any worthwhile pursuit. As I mapped out in my own first chapter, there is a movement within the financial planning community, which I fully embrace, called life planning. In reality, life planning is nothing more than financial planning done with breadth as well as depth. In practical terms, it balances the management of one's wealth with the hopes, dreams, and values that go into making a happy and productive life.

Investment management and performance are important, but to make a truly positive difference in the quality of our lives, we must take a more wide-reaching approach and encompass qualitative issues as well.

From my perspective as an advisor, marrying life goals with financial and investment planning pays off in a richer and more rewarding life. There is transformative power in the financial life planning process that—along with the richness of family, friends, and good health—makes life worth living.

Life planning is the qualitative (soft) side of planning, as contrasted with the quantitative (hard) side. It is the heart of the planning process and overlaps the investment, tax, estate, and retirement planning areas.

Financial planning often revolves around individuals dealing with major life events and change, be it the happy events of marriage, the birth of a child, and traditional retirement, or the sad challenges such as the loss of a job or a loved one, a divorce, or declining health. One recent industry study showed that over the course of a lifetime, approximately 55 potential triggering events may need addressing from a financial standpoint. Each event has an impact on net worth, making some change to either the asset or liability column and/or the income statement.

When I first met Mr. and Mrs. Smith they were in their late thirties and had recently relocated to Milwaukee. Mr. Smith had accepted a professional assignment and his wife had secured a managerial position. Because Mr. Smith was also inheriting proceeds from his parents' estate, the catalyst for our meeting was their enhanced financial condition

A further development and exciting topic of discussion was that they were about to become parents after many childless years, and the expectation was that they were having triplets. Consequently, Mrs. Smith was shortly to resign her position and become a stay-at-home, extremely busy mother. The talk progressed to the need for a larger home, childcare help, life insurance protection, college funding, and putting their own estate plan in place. Theirs is a marvelous example of many life planning stages compressed into a short period of time.

As a postscript, I recently became reacquainted with this nice couple, now a family of five. The triplets, two boys and a girl, are enrolled in preschool. Mom has her hands full with these three energetic five-year-olds, each demanding attention and exercising their unique personalities. Mom instituted "leader of the day" with some success to bring a sense of order to daily activities. A devoted dad is extremely busy with a demanding professional practice.

After five years, they felt able to come up for air and revisit personal financial matters. It appears the children are likely to go the more expensive private school route, and college times three looms just 13 years away. By putting into operation life planning techniques, this family will be able to better meet its goals.

Just recently, an estate planning attorney referred a 48-year-old couple receiving an inheritance to our financial planning and investment advisory firm. These inheritances are part of an estimated $7 trillion to $10 trillion of wealth transfer passing from the WWII generation to their baby-boomer children. This couple was in town from a neighboring state, as the husband was the sole beneficiary of a Wisconsin estate. His 83-year-old father, after six months of failing health, had died two weeks earlier from congestive heart failure. Six years earlier his mother had passed away from lung cancer.

Planning is often multigenerational in scope. These college sweethearts have four college-aged children and admit they have been stretched financially. Even though their children are going the more affordable state college route, the costs accumulate rapidly with four tuition payments. The couple also did not want to burden their children with much, if any, student loan debt.

It is becoming increasingly more common for recent college grads—or worse, dropouts—to become saddled with tens of thousands of dollars in student loan debt. This quote from an anonymous source seems to ring too true: "A major problem these days is how to save money for your children's college education while still paying for your own."

As is the case with the 48-year-old couple, it is common to want to fund a retirement saving program, yet be torn with the other goal of providing for the costs of higher education. Just think how old you will be when your youngest child enters college. In my case, it is an eye-opening 62.

It is important for this couple to responsibly manage their inheritance. Their first order of business is to completely pay off their accumulated credit card debt, mortgage balance, and car loans. In that way, they will free up thousands of dollars in monthly cash flow. They can then calculate how to cover their children's remaining college expenses out of earned income.

This inheritance dramatically improves their financial condition and net worth. After paying off their debt, they wisely plan to invest the bulk of this sum for long-term growth and to improve their own retirement security. Should his employment situation change, the husband wants to be in a position in seven years at age 55 to have options. As a long-time employee of a large, multinational, publicly traded company, he realizes that the fortunes of such firms have a way of changing.

From a life-planning perspective, I recommended they earmark a portion of this inherited sum and take a special trip with the whole family. I consider this an investment in family unity rather than an expense, as they can use this trip to remember mom and dad and the children's grandparents. As we parted, they decided to give this further thought, believing it a great idea. The children are all gifted musicians, and a dream trip to Vienna, Austria, and the birthplace of Mozart has strong appeal to them.

Regarding my personal situation, in a short seven years our youngest child, Jack, will be heading to college. I will be 62 years old and eligible to draw Social Security benefits, though I do not plan to do so. Our plan is to be completely debt free and have our mortgage paid off by my age 60. We have been prepaying $1,000 a month in additional principal payments on our 15-year, fixed-rate mortgage. In about five years, while our son is still in high school, the mortgage will be paid off. This plan will free up $3,000 a month that now goes to the prepayment and the regular principal and interest payment. A tidy $36,000 a year can be redirected to Jack's college expenses. Coupled with some money in an education savings account, future savings, and Jack's part-time jobs, this should be sufficient.

Jack has his heart set on going to Notre Dame. He has it all figured out that he will attend this great school on an athletic scholarship, based on his prowess in playing soccer. He is a good student and a very good soccer player, so we don't want to burst his bubble. However, as parents we believe it is prudent to have a Plan B in place. We like to adhere to the wisdom of Charles Buxton, who said, "In life, as in chess, forethought wins."

DOWN THE PATH

Following my own graduation from college in 1973 I visited Ireland. In the central part of that beautiful country, in Tullamore, famous for producing Tullamore Dew Irish whiskey, I stopped at a petrol station to ask directions to a family friend's farm on the outskirts of town.

A pipe-smoking, rosy-cheeked, mature gentleman sized me up as a young Yank and declared, "If I was you, and I was headed to where you're headed, I wouldn't be starting from where you're starting from to get there!"

He proceeded to draw me a crude map that included a tree marker where someone supposedly was lynched some 300 years earlier. Needless to say, I still got lost.

I use this example to illustrate the importance of knowing where you are before attempting to reach your destination. In the retirement planning process, it is difficult to determine where you are going if you don't know where you are. As former Secretary of State and diplomat Henry Kissinger pointed out, "If you don't know where you are going, every road will get you nowhere."

It might help to think of yourself as the CFO or chief financial officer of your own personal enterprise. To help you identify where you are and assess your financial strengths and weaknesses, you can utilize the same analytical tools that businesses use; namely, the personal balance sheet and income statement.

STATEMENT OF FINANCIAL CONDITION

The first part of any plan is to identify the current status or condition. I recommend that you put together a net worth statement, also known as a balance sheet. This most basic of personal finance statements is simple to construct and interpret. A net worth statement, also referred to as a statement of financial condition, can be thought of as a snapshot of your financial condition on any given date.

A net worth statement is a freeze-frame of your finances, accounting for both assets and debts and yielding a figure representing the difference. Put simply, what you own minus what you owe equals what you are worth. Alternately, assets minus liabilities (debt) equals net worth.

To gain a graphic perspective of your net worth statement or balance sheet, think in terms of the scales of justice, where both sides are in balance. The asset side of your ledger is balanced against the sum of your liabilities plus net worth. Say, for example, that total assets equal 100 and total liabilities equal 50. Net worth then computes to 50, providing for balance on both sides of the ledger of 100.

In a business, the net worth figure is referred to as a book (bookkeeping) value for valuation purposes. Book value is taken into account in any financial analysis to determine the wisdom of buying stock in a company or valuing a business for sale. As individuals, we submit our financial condition to analysis whenever we apply for credit, a loan, or a mortgage.

The net worth figure is critical in a personal analysis because it provides a clear measurement of financial wealth, a quick read on your financial condition, and a means of keeping score and measuring progress.

Your net worth is synonymous with your retirement nest egg. For estate planning purposes, add in any life insurance to arrive at an estate value.

INCOME STATEMENT

Another essential financial document is the income statement. This statement is the same analytical tool on which any for-profit or nonprofit business places considerable emphasis. It complements your net worth statement by offering a different perspective of your financial condition. Unlike the net worth statement that measures your worth as of a given day, an income statement charts cash inflows and outflows over a calendar year.

If the net worth statement represents a snapshot of your financial condition, the income statement is like a motion picture. An individual's 12-month calendar year corresponds to the fiscal or tax year of a business.

The top section identifies the income or, in business terms, revenue that flowed in during the preceding year. The middle section pinpoints the outgo or expense items for the year. A common question from individuals looking at their total income is: "Where in the world did all that money go?" Or, as Roger W. Babson opined, "More people should learn to tell their dollars where to go instead of asking them where they went." All serious planners need to get a handle on where their money is spent.

The third section of the income statement tells the story. The difference between inflows and outflows equals net income. In business jargon, the net income is referred to as the bottom line and is looked on as the measure of success or failure. If net is positive, the business has a profit and is operating in the black.

Having a positive bottom line is just as important to an individual. If income exceeds outgo, you are living within your means. Surplus dollars are available for savings and investment purposes. This sum can be converted into an asset in your drive to build your net worth. As comedian Art Buck told us, "If you're only making ends meet, you're running in circles."

On a personal finance level, you need to quantify in dollars your desired lifestyle. Income is a less significant factor, because the cost of lifestyle expenditures drives decision-making. Most of us have more wants than the income to provide for them. This creates the challenge of deciding which wants have priority.

No one can hope to enjoy real financial independence unless expenditures are kept well within the limits of income.

The opening lines of Chapter 12 in Charles Dickens' classic novel *David Copperfield* promotes living within your means for a happy life in Olde England. "Annual income twenty pounds, annual expenditure nineteen six, result happiness. Annual income twenty pounds, annual expenditure twenty pounds ought and six, result misery."

Think in terms of a spending plan instead of a budget. A properly structured plan trims fat but allows you to have what you really want while you enjoy the peace of mind that comes from knowing you are achieving your financial goals. Do you want short-term gratification or long-term financial security?

NET WORTH AND INCOME STATEMENTS COMPARED

The early 1980s movie *Country* portrayed the struggles of a modern-day Iowa farm family. I was struck by the way the movie's theme illustrated the relationship between net worth and income statements.

In the film a local banker informs the farmer, played by actor Sam Sheppard, that he has a high net worth based on the market value of his farmland. Because of that perceived financial strength, money is lent. In fact, the assumption of debt is encouraged, and the farmer is given loans so he can plant the land "fence post to fence post." From an income standpoint, however, the farmer soon finds himself operating at a loss. The outgo for fuel, fertilizer, loan interest, and other expenses exceeds the revenues due to declining farm commodity prices. It cost $2.20 a bushel to produce corn that yields a depressed $2 per bushel when sold.

In the movie, land prices fall as a direct result of crop revenue losses. The banker becomes anxious as his customer's net worth (collateral) rapidly declines. The farmer is forced to liquidate the farm (sell off the assets and turn them into cash) to meet his bank debt. The drama culminates as family members, including the farm wife, played by actress Jessica Lange, stand by watching their home and livelihood auctioned at distressed prices.

From a net worth standpoint the farm family had been considered wealthy because of the value of their land. But when that land no longer generated a profit, its value was driven down, throwing them into a severe financial reversal.

Farmers, ranchers, and small business owners share the plight of having their wealth locked up in illiquid assets such as real estate, inventory, and receivables. Though they might appear wealthy on paper, they face financial hardship unless those assets are capable of producing sustainable cash flow and income levels.

It's not how much you make, but how you manage debt and allocate the income you have that determines your net worth. Earmark a generous portion of your earned income for the purchase of investments that appreciate in value.

SAVINGS-FIRST APPROACH

Economically speaking, savings is income that's not spent. Accumulating savings is a prudent necessity if you are to reach your financial goals, and its importance cannot be overemphasized in building wealth, planning for retirement, or funding an education.

In many instances it is reasonable to target a savings rate in the range of 10 percent to 25 percent of gross pay. Substantial capital put aside regularly can provide handsomely for the future. The real key to wealth accumulation is compounded savings.

According to *The Wealthy Barber*, "Wealth beyond your wildest dreams is possible if you follow the golden rule: Invest 10 percent of all you make for long-term growth. If you follow that one simple guideline, some day you'll be very rich."

It is crucial to develop a systematic savings program as the foundation of your long-term wealth-building effort. As fundamental as saving is to financial success, it is not universally practiced. Failure to take this basic step can doom most planning efforts.

People fail to save for a host of reasons, chief among them procrastination. What is called for is a sense of urgency and a saving mindset that recognizes the importance of diligent, regular saving.

PYF is a helpful acronym for "pay yourself first." It suggests a saving mindset. Simply put, PYF means that when you allocate your income, you place the highest priority on saving. Adhering to PYF, you would channel X percent of each dollar into a savings program before meting out funds for your other obligations. PYF automatically regulates your spending without requiring you to draw up a formal budget.

According to surveys, PYF is contrary to the spending habits of most Americans, who admit to saving only "whatever is left over." However, most of us place demands on our income that make it unlikely to have surplus funds at the end of the month. Paying yourself *last*—or PYL—awards the lowest priority to your savings dollars.

PYF, if exercised conscientiously, programs us to save even before we meet the mortgage payment. To aid in the process of PYF, I like to add discipline. The secret of financial independence is not brilliance, luck, or some complicated strategy, but rather a common sense discipline to save a part of all you earn and put it to work for you.

One common sense method to increase your nest egg is to simply boost your rate of saving. Instead of saving 10 percent of your income, strive to save an additional 5 percent—a 50 percent increase. The rate of investing is often more crucial than the rate of return.

PROTECTING YOUR RESOURCES: INCOME & ASSETS

In the 1983 movie *Places of the Heart*, Oscar-nominated actress Sally Fields portrays a gritty young woman facing hardships in the cotton fields of Georgia in the thirties.

Field's character must cope with the tragic killing of her husband, the local sheriff. She is left alone to raise her young children without their father, a breadwinner, or manager of their farm. To keep her family intact, she is forced to bring in a cotton crop alone, all the while dealing with the prejudices directed against her as a woman.

She perseveres to save her home and farm from demanding creditors. The added peril of a tornado that destroys the property doesn't diminish her resolve.

To survive and hold on to the farm and home, she takes in boarders, including a blind man and a destitute farmhand played by Danny Glover, who suffers the indignity of KKK-targeted terrorism.

What struck me about this movie was how much better her fate would have been if she'd had insurance protection.

Risk is a way of life. Substantial risks are associated with asset ownership and income production. Managing these risks is a fundamental planning need. Of course, had our heroine had the benefit of an insurance plan, there would be no sad tale to tell.

In the financial planning field, we refer to risk management as the vital defensive component of any sound financial plan. Insurance planning and risk management are placid topics compared to the excitement of investing or the challenges of dealing with taxes.

Insurance is a means of protecting your assets and income against the unexpected.

We need to think in terms of a contingency plan, asking ourselves some pointed "what if" questions. What if you die prematurely, become disabled and incapable of earning an income, injure someone through the operation of your car, see your house and contents destroyed by fire or other disaster, need long-term convalescent care, or have heart disease that requires a transplant? How would any of these possibilities affect the makeup of your net worth and income statement?

Each of us should take the role of personal risk manager, identifying our risk exposure, searching for gaps or overlapping coverage, and determining the most effective way to provide adequate protection.

Any risk that cannot be handled from personal financial resources qualifies as an insurable need. One primary method for managing risk is to transfer that risk to an insurance company through the purchase of policies designed to cover specified exposures. Insurance premiums represent the cost of this protection and amount to a significant expense outlay.

Every time you pay an insurance premium, ask yourself what you are protecting. Adding up the costs of health, life, auto, home, long-term care, and disability insurance will open your eyes to this expense. What percentage of your annual income is expended on this defensive protection?

The objective in a properly secured risk management program is to marry the best value for your premium dollars with the most effective coverage. Understand that insurance does not improve or enhance your financial condition. Rather, it makes you whole after suffering a loss. Dollars overspent on insurance represent money diverted from investment purposes.

Returning to the plight of our fictional movie widow, she and her family and the quality of their life would have benefited greatly from a risk management plan. The death of her husband was emotionally devastating, but the economic loss of his income caused the pain to continue long after.

Life insurance in its most basic form is protection in the event of premature death and the financial hardship the loss of earning would impose on the dependents of an insured. Not everyone needs life insurance, although in the case of this film family, a clearly identified need for protection existed. The provider/father left young children, a wife with limited income capacity, no financial reserves, and a heavy mortgage on the house and farm.

A major goal in retirement planning is to build up a sizable living estate (net worth). If this financial independence is not reached, a plan needs to be in place to provide for survivors dependent on the insured. Life insurance is unique in that it provides an instant liquid estate at precisely the time of need.

I can tell you that in the darkest hours of my brush with life-threatening cancer, I was comforted somewhat to know that I had substantial life insurance in place. Life insurance is one of those products you cannot purchase once you really need it.

Had I lost out to cancer, or for that matter if I were struck by lightning, I could face the worst knowing that I made arrangements to protect my loved ones' financial security. Fortunately, I was prepared, because much earlier I had conducted a capital needs analysis comparing our family's available assets and resources against housing, education, and income needs. The shortfall between what we have and what we anticipate needing would be replaced by a life insurance settlement check. This would allow Cathy and our children the ability to pretty much carry on as is—financially, if not emotionally.

Disability insurance protects against the loss of earned income that results from a disabling injury or sickness. For this reason, such insurance is often referred to as income protection or income replacement. Some planners refer to a serious long-term disability as economic death. Although many individuals have a plan in place in the event of premature death, they are exposed to the much more prevalent risk of disability. Protection against income disruption is vital, although too often it represents the black hole in insurance protection plans. This coverage is costly and the provisions complex. Many employees are fortunate to have some protection as a fringe benefit.

For retired individuals or those on the verge of retirement, the single biggest fear is likely the financial devastation that would result from expensive long-term convalescent care.

With the aging of America, hundreds of thousands of people will suffer the cruelty of Alzheimer's or an incapacitating stroke. There is a legitimate concern that one's financial resources could be wiped out, perhaps leaving a survivor in dire financial circumstances. In the case of a single individual, a devastating illness could mean not being able to afford a level of dignified care. Another often-expressed concern is that of a proud parent who desperately does not want to be a burden to offspring.

One increasingly popular solution to this dilemma is to purchase a long-term care (LTC) insurance policy. As the name implies, these policies kick in with supplemental income in the event of a catastrophic illness and its resulting expense. Many policies also cover expenses associated with home health care. Some practitioners in the LTC insurance field refer to these policies as an estate-planning product because they effectively place a padlock on estate assets.

For many of us, the most important protection is health insurance. Even the wealthiest could be bankrupted without adequate coverage. A severe illness makes an impact on both the income statement and net worth condition, and it raises havoc with the financial health of the affected individual or family.

Health care costs have accelerated at rates much faster than the general level of inflation. For many people, health insurance premiums exceed the mortgage payment. Often the real concern is not affordability but availability. Much attention is being focused lately on such issues as portability of coverage, insurability, and the onus of pre-existing conditions.

One common sense piece of insurance advice is not to sweat the small stuff. Rather, turn your attention to those risks that would be most harmful to you. For example, you might be able to "self-insure" against certain risks by "going naked" (without coverage), or by increasing your deductibles or extending the waiting periods on certain policies. In these ways, you reduce the cost of insurance to better spend the same premium protection dollars somewhere else.

CARRY ON, CARMEN

I had the pleasure of meeting Dick and Carmen in 1986 when they came to my office to discuss a pressing financial and life planning matter. The previous year, at the height of his business career, Dick had been diagnosed with amyotrophic lateral sclerosis (ALS). This incurable, always fatal neuromuscular disease has to be one of the cruelest fates to hit anyone.

Dick had been a lifelong athlete who lived to play a robust game of racquetball three times every week. He noticed something was terribly wrong when he routinely became unable to return the ball. Frustrated by this inability, he shocked his wife by announcing he was going to give up playing. Knowing his love and passion for these regular games, Carmen urged him not to do something so radical.

ALS sufferers, of which there are some 30,000 throughout the United States, experience progressive muscle weakness, leading eventually to paralysis and death. Yankee baseball great Lou Gehrig was struck by ALS at the peak of his illustrious Hall of Fame career. Since then, ALS has commonly been known as Lou Gehrig's disease.

Lou Gehrig's talent earned him the nickname the Iron Horse. This muscular power hitter played in more consecutive baseball games than any other player, until being surpassed 60 years later by Cal Ripken. It was a big deal, then, when in the 1939 season Gehrig took himself out of the line-up. Inexplicably, he could no longer perform at the game he had mastered so skillfully over many all-star years.

Gehrig's accomplishments on the baseball field made him an authentic American hero, and his tragic early death in 1941 at 38 made him a legend. His number 4 jersey was retired in a ceremony at Yankee Stadium, the first number retired in American professional sports. He also was immortalized in the movie *The Pride of the Yankees*, with Gary Cooper portraying a stricken Gehrig as he proclaimed at that emotional farewell ceremony, "Today, I am the luckiest man on the face of the earth."

Jonathan Eig is the author of the new book, *Luckiest Man: The Life and Death of Lou Gehrig*. Putting more gloss on Gehrig's already illustrious baseball career, Eig reminds us, "when Lou Gehrig hit .295 with 29 home runs in 1938, some writers took swings at the Iron Horse, saying that he had worn himself out by working too hard over the course of his career."

The author shines a light on these statistics, saying, "Today some of the neurologists I've spoken to consider Gehrig's achievement in 1938—when he already displayed symptoms of ALS—one of the greatest athletic feats of all time." Like many diseases, ALS remains a mystery to doctors and medical researchers. Ironically, it does seem to strike athletic men.

Returning to Dick and Carmen, this couple found themselves challenged financially, living as they were under the terrible cloud of Dick's health predicament. Life insurance coverage was eyed with the hard reality that these policies would inevitably be paid out to Carmen, as beneficiary, a few short years down the line.

True to the sad course of this disease's brutal nature, Dick's body steadily degenerated, forcing him to give up working. Distressingly, the company he worked for was sold, and the new ownership did not honor some of the employment benefits Dick should have had.

Unlike the finality of death, the economic facts of life can be harder with a long-term disability such as Dick's, where the breadwinner is no longer able to provide support. Unfortunately, Dick had no private disability insurance—which serves to illustrate the need for this valuable income replacement protection to augment job benefits.

As the months went by, the couple needed to scramble to pay the mortgage and keep pace with living expenses, so they tapped savings and investments. Finances were tight, but they managed somehow to keep the house and even to cover college tuition costs at the local public university for two of the boys. Carmen took a part-time office position, and with the help of Social Security disability payments, they managed to stay above water financially.

Sometimes in life, when it rains it pours. In the middle of Dick's struggle with his life-robbing disease, Carmen's brother Carl lost his life to liver cancer. Ten years younger than Carmen, he had been cared for and raised by his older sister. Carl's premature death left his wife a widow, and two bright and energetic sons, ages 7 and 16, fatherless. Profound grief overtook this close-knit Sicilian family. Liver cancer often is a swift death sentence, and so it had been for this 46-year-old father, husband, brother, uncle, and son.

I don't mind admitting I was terrified early in my own cancer treatment when the oncologist informed me that a full-body MRI exam had uncovered something irregular, and she would need to order an ultrasound of my liver. I knew enough to realize that if my cancer had spread to the liver, I would have just months to live. My doctor attempted to calm my expressed fears by telling me that an MRI detects even insignificant abnormalities. I was comforted by her assurance, until I got home from the hospital and reported this latest news to my wife.

Until that point, Cathy had been a rock, but the prospect of liver cancer pushed her over the edge. Cancer patients know this roller-coaster existence between hope and fear is part of the ordeal they ride. I tossed, turned, and sweated the nights leading up to the ultra-sound. As my physician expected, my liver and the adjoining pancreas were normal. Greatly relieved, we were back on a definite high. We were far more fortunate than Carl and his family.

After Carmen's tragic loss of her brother to liver cancer, and with ALS extracting its toll on her husband, the family needed healing. They decided the best medicine would be a long road trip to Arizona to visit with their uncles who lived there.

Because I was their financial advisor, Carmen phoned me to say they were considering buying a full-sized van as transportation but were torn over the cost and how they would pay for it. As she talked, it occurred to me that such a vehicle was not a luxury but a necessity for this weary family, and I encouraged her to purchase the van.

Their trip included Carmen, Dick, two of their sons, her recently widowed sister-in-law, and her two boys. Carmen prevailed in a hard fight with the insurance company to pay for the electric scooter Dick came to rely on for mobility, and the new van was large enough to adapt to fit the scooter and accommodate this band of seven travelers. They took many memorable trips with Dick in that van.

Carmen gives me undue credit for unequivocally encouraging the purchase of the van. I viewed it as a quality-of-life investment, not as a frivolous expense. I am thrilled this non-financial advice paid off in such happy dividends for their family.

During the long course of Dick's illness, Carmen determined to make a happy home for her loving husband. To do this, she attempted to hold her emotions in check, and only let down when she was alone in her car. Outside the family, the wonder was how they would manage, since their bedrooms were on the second floor of their house. Carmen recalls with pride that somehow they managed so Dick never had to sleep anywhere other than in their own bedroom.

Carmen credits the twin pillars of her faith in God and her tightly knit family with giving her strength to carry on. Dick and Carmen fervently hoped and prayed for a miracle cure. As part of their quest, they journeyed every Friday for over seven years to Holy Hill, a church and shrine set in the picturesque Kettle Moraine countryside of southeastern Wisconsin, just a half hour's ride from their home.

Some 150 years ago, a French hermit experienced a miraculous cure after worshipping at a cross some local residents had erected atop what became known as Holy Hill. Dick and Carmen followed in the wake of hopefuls who made the pilgrimage to this special place.

Thankfully, Dick's sight was unaffected by ALS, and after feeding her husband in the privacy of the van, she would position him so he could view and admire the spectacular countryside. Carmen then trudged up the steep steps to the chapel to pray, light a candle, and ask God for strength and to look after her dear husband. During one of these weekly visits they experienced some excitement they would never forget. While sitting in the parking area waiting for Carmen to return, Dick was startled to see a large man get out of a car completely naked and take off in the direction of the chapel.

In his weakened condition, Dick felt helpless to do anything and was afraid this obviously deranged fellow could do harm to his petite wife. As luck would have it, the police soon arrived, having answered a call about a naked man cavorting on the grounds of Holy Hill. Carmen was busy chatting with a friend and oblivious to all the activity going on until a woman came up to her to ask if she was Carmen, saying her husband had described her and wanted to find her.

Carmen's first thought was that Dick must be having medical trouble. She ran to the van. Breathless, she arrived to find police cars and a small crowd, but no ambulance. Somehow, the big, naked guy had managed to put on some clothes and was now proclaiming his innocence. Dick was able to finger him to the authorities and was also very relieved to find Carmen safe. Later, they enjoyed a good laugh shared with their friends and family.

Dr. Richard K. Olney is a 57-year-old neurologist who lists as his proudest professional achievement the founding of the ALS center at the University of California-San Francisco. What makes this compassionate physician's story cruelly ironic is that after treating some 1,000 ALS patients, he was diagnosed in 2004 with this same baffling disease. Dr. Olney's goal had been to help cure this disease, but now he courageously says, "I've learned to focus on things I can influence and accept those I can't."

Carmen's husband, Dick, died January 26, 1993, but the couple did experience a miracle of sorts. Most ALS victims survive between two and five years from diagnoses. Dick's disease was atypical, and he lived close to eight years. In addition, his capacity to speak and intelligently communicate with his loved ones, and his ability to eat and swallow, stayed with him until the very end. On the morning of his death, Dick was able to tell Carmen that he was losing his ability to breathe. Both of them recognized what this foretold. Carmen asked Dick if he wanted to go on life support. In a final act of love, he bravely said no. He reasoned it would be too hard on her, and instead bade Carmen a final goodbye. Dr. Olney, speaking of the mystery of ALS, had observed, "One of the good things about this disease is that it gives you the chance to say goodbye." Dick and Carmen were grateful for that opportunity.

Carmen's saga continues, with her sister-in-law and school-age nephews moving in to share her home. She went back to work full-time as an office manager, where she soon became indispensable. At age 69 she retired, not due to age but because symptoms of Parkinson's disease forced her to slow down. Because Carmen and Dick had faced the challenge of his disease with a life plan, Carmen was able to persevere.

Carmen is very proud of her four sons, characterizing each of them as a hard worker. I contend this was learned from observing and being mentored by their hardworking parents. After raising four boys, Carmen feels blessed to have three precious granddaughters, all of whom do well in school, display musical talent, and play the piano. She is thrilled her youngest son and daughter-in-law, after many years of trying to start a family, have adopted and taken into their hearts and home an infant daughter. Carmen downsized to a condominium a few years ago, and she remains close to her family. Her personal finances are in good shape, which makes her feel secure financially. Her two nephews excelled as students. The oldest is now a physician, and his younger brother is studying to be an engineer.

Led by her son, Curt, Carmen's family helps in an annual golf event, "Hit It and Hope," to raise money and awareness to combat ALS. Carmen's Parkinson's is well controlled. To prove her point to herself and others, she energetically jitterbugged at a recent class reunion. Carmen credits her regular chiropractic treatments, and a great doctor who has headed a Parkinson's clinic for 35 years, with her ability to stay ahead of her own tough disease. Those of us who know this remarkable woman would add that her positive attitude makes a difference and propels her forward.

Carmen's story line is now bright because her sister-in-law remarried, and a new man entered Carmen's life, too. Each couple had met in high school. Bob and Carmen married, and they are excited about their life together. I recently learned from Carmen's oldest son, Dennis, that his mom and Bob are embarking on a trip to Italy—the first visit for this woman of Italian ancestry and the fulfillment of a lifelong dream. Reading my account of her life, Carmen modestly said I make her look like a saint—which, she says emphatically, she is not.

LIFE'S ULTIMATE LESSON

Fox TV's financial journalist Neil Cavuto is author of the book *More Than Money*. The subtitle of this inspirational read is *True Stories of People Who Learned Life's Ultimate Lesson*.

Cavuto leads off by telling of his personal battle with an advanced form of Hodgkin's cancer that left a tumor in his chest the size of a football. Cavuto pulled through, putting up with what he recalls as one year of bad stuff. Similar to fellow authors and survivors Lance Armstrong and Hamilton Jordan, Cavuto believes his brush with death made him a better person. For this, and for life itself, Neil considers himself "a lucky bastard."

He tested this self-description to the limit when, soon after recovering from cancer, he was jolted with a diagnosis of multiple sclerosis. Referring to the title of his book, Cavuto writes, "Tools we use to measure financial success fail miserably when used to define deeper success."

It is worth reminding ourselves that financial life planning involves measuring quality of life as well as quantity of treasure. As nineteenth-century essayist and physician Oliver Wendell Holmes Sr. wrote, "I find the greatest thing in this world is not so much where we stand as in what direction we are going."

Economists found that although our society has become wealthier, we are not necessarily happier. As Aristotle said many centuries ago, "Happiness is the meaning and purpose of life, the whole aim of human existence."

Researchers identify 10 dimensions of what constitutes true wealth. At the top of this list is physical health—the best predictor of overall happiness—not income. Other characteristics of happiness are family, work, love life, location, friends, spirituality, learning, and outside interests.

We are familiar with the bumper sticker philosophy that says, "He Who Dies With The Most Toys Wins." Investment advisor/journalist Steve Moeller points out the obvious: "But he who dies with the most toys still is dead."

Moeller, the author of a book on the science of happiness, queries, "Shouldn't life be about more than toys?" According to him, lawyers are now America's highest paid professionals, with incomes surpassing that of physicians. Yet, in spite of this level of affluence, they are by their own admission "dissatisfied" and more at risk of major depression than other professions.

President Abraham Lincoln told us, "Most people are about as happy as they make up their minds to be." Lincoln had many reasons over the course of his life to be depressed and unhappy, but he always managed to pick himself up and move forward. His mother died when he was only eight, his sister died in childhood. As a young man, his first love, Ann Rutledge, died suddenly. His election as president caused the southern states to secede from the union. The great Civil War that soon erupted added to his already heavy burden the onerous role of Commander-in-Chief. While he was in the White House, his cherished son Willie perished and his wife, Mary, fell into deep depression.

It is safe to say that no American political leader faced darker, bleaker times than did Lincoln. Yet throughout the turmoil he remained resolute, as evidenced by his statement, "The best thing about the future is that it only comes one day at a time." With all this great man endured, he looked to a better tomorrow. Before he was felled by an assassin, he succeeded in reuniting the nation and ending the moral outrage of slavery.

I find many similarities between Pope John Paul and President Lincoln. Both came from humble circumstances, with no expectation that greatness lay in their future. Like the President, the future Pope suffered the heart-wrenching loss of his mother when he was just eight years old. Whereas Abraham Lincoln actually was born and raised in a log cabin, a young Karol Wojtyla was raised in a modest, drafty flat in dreary Krakow, Poland. Nonetheless, each of these great men was optimistic by nature and each believed unconditionally in a higher power.

POSITIVE MENTAL ATTITUDE (PMA)

I have become a true believer in the beneficial role that a positive attitude plays when someone deals with the unwelcome in life, such as cancer. In this belief I find support from J. Frank Wilson, M.D., a renowned cancer specialist at the Medical College of Wisconsin. From his observations of thousands of patients over the years, he goes on record to say that a positive attitude is vital, and indeed necessary, to cope successfully with a life-threatening disease such as cancer.

Interestingly, a growing body of scientific observation agrees that the emotional approach to a serious medical condition can make a measurable difference.

Referring to his many patients, Dr. Wilson says, "I've seen a lot of different situations that are encouraging and inspiring to me." He speaks of viewing most surprises in life, such as a cancer diagnosis, as opportunities for improvement. Recall this oft-quoted saying from philosopher Friedrich Nietzsche: "Whatever does not destroy me makes me stronger."

Another physician and a client of our firm wrote me the following uplifting words in response to my letter announcing the condition of my health. "Your wonderful, positive attitude and family support will be the most important asset in achieving complete recovery."

Echoing this, actress Patricia Neal is quoted as saying, "A strong positive mental attitude will create more miracles than any wonder drug."

FACING A BUMP IN THE ROAD

It was a Friday night in the winter at the end of a long work week when my son, Jack, handed me the phone. "John, this is Shirley." I sensed immediately by her voice that something was terribly wrong.

My first thought was that her husband and my good friend Tony had died. I knew he had been coping with some health issues. This strong, big-hearted fellow carries more weight than he should, though it's manageable.

Instead, Shirley was calling to confide that she had been diagnosed with multiple myeloma, a particularly painful blood-borne cancer that attacks the bones. I was aware of the seriousness of this cancer, having lost Cathy's dad to it nine years before. Shirley was reaching out to me as a friend, but also as someone who experienced cancer first-hand, and just as importantly beaten it.

Only six weeks before, I had spent a wonderful five days as a guest of our former backyard neighbors Tony and Shirley at their winter home in sunny Arizona. I left feeling even closer to my friends and again witnessed the special bond and love these high-school sweethearts have for each other.

Shirley has long looked to take charge of her health. She showed me a prescription written by her primary physician that read, "Walk a half an hour a day, every day, for a healthy life." As it was, we did take daily walks during my visit and even a hike with friends on a county park trail.

Looking back, I knew something was not right with Shirley. She became easily fatigued during these walks and was periodically forced to stop and rest. On the hike she couldn't keep up with the group. Frustrated, she did not want any of us to wait for her. Six weeks later the extent of her condition came to light when she passed out in her home and had to be rushed by ambulance to the hospital.

Tony was angry the same doctor who had wisely prescribed walking did not detect anything wrong months earlier, despite Shirley's complaining of not feeling right and having taken multiple diagnostic blood tests.

Listening to Shirley discuss her health predicament, I realized what a determined fighter she is. She has a whole lot to live for, and at age 57 hopes and prays to be able to grow old and enjoy a well-earned retirement with Tony. I always felt Shirley would make a terrific grandmother some day, as they have two marvelous adult children in Jenny and Tim.

Shirley knows all too well the dark side of cancer, having lost both her father and mother to this deadly disease. Yet her positive attitude and steely resolve to do whatever it takes to overcome what she stoically refers to as "a bump in the road" is truly inspirational. Her courageous story is a case study in life lessons and a how-to guide on waging a fierce battle against a formidable enemy.

Over the months of her ordeal, Shirley continues to communicate with her many friends and family members through a series of touching e-mail letters. I suspect these beautifully written and personal messages are part of her therapy. In them she gives us a candid account of what she is going through, such as her pain level and blood counts. Still, she makes a point of always emphasizing the positive and putting a positive spin on matters.

For example, she states in one note, "The pain is being managed and I am tolerating the chemo fairly well." She has taken to numbering what she refers to as good news bulletins, which she addresses to Dear Ones, her shorthand for loved ones. Most recently, as the battle is fully engaged with the effects of chemo treatments, she has upgraded these to great news bulletins.

In each letter Shirley leads off by quoting from an inspirational message. My personal favorite is one by Lebanese-born poet Kahil Gibran because it captures Shirley's indomitable spirit. "Your living is determined not so much by what life brings to you as by the attitude you bring to life; not so much by what happens to you as by the way your mind looks at what happens."

Shirley will need a bone marrow transplant. Her brother and two sisters unhesitatingly lined up to be tested, to see if they are a bone marrow match, each wanting to be her hero. Shirley already counts them as heroes and was thrilled to learn she had already beaten the odds by having two matches.

She admits to being knocked over and lifted up by the show of love and support from all quarters. As an example, her Hispanic gardener offered to be tested as a potential bone marrow donor.

Shirley has enlisted her vast army of friends in her personal battle, referring to us as partners and letting us know she is counting on us to keep the prayers coming. Shirley believes fervently in the power of prayer to heal and feels that prayers are being answered. She closed one of her letters to her partners with "If you worry, you didn't pray. If you pray, don't worry!" Her gift of faith has been strengthened by all she has endured. This is summed up in the biblical passage from

Romans 12:12. "Be joyful in hope, patient in application, faithful in prayer."

When my dear mother was facing lung cancer, she told me she was putting her faith in God and in the hands of her doctors. Shirley has great confidence in Dr. Shaw, her hematologist (blood) oncologist (cancer specialist). Her bulletins make it seem as if he is our doctor, because she lets us in on what he is finding ("numbers looking good"), thinking ("starting a second chemo drug") and planning ("two bone marrow transplants six months down the road").

Shirley's faith and optimism is warranted as new treatment options and advances are available today that were not there for my father-in-law when multiple myeloma attacked him a decade earlier. She is now receiving a drug that has just been approved, and she wants to be part of a clinical study. She also has the good fortune of sibling bone marrow all lined up.

As could be expected, Shirley admits to leaning on her family for support, starting with her mate, Tony, saying she could not survive without him. She describes Tony as her rock and strength, who picks her up whenever she gets a little down. "Our days are filled with appointments, bone scans, treatments, ultrasounds, MRIs, blood tests, IVs. But we're together."

I was fortunate to visit dear Shirley and her rock of a partner at their home a second time while on a business trip to Arizona. It was therapeutic for me to see and hug my good friends. As anticipated, I found Shirley thin, weak, and completely bald from the effects of chemo. Yet her eyes seemed to sparkle and her smile was as bright as ever. I took this as a very encouraging sign, which her doctor seconded at her next visit.

While Shirley napped, Tony and I sat and talked about life. He showed me the huge arsenal of prescription drugs Shirley takes and recounted the setbacks she stoically endured, including a severe allergic drug reaction that led to hospitalization. Eyes tearing, Tony told me how proud he is of his partner's willingness to sign up for any medical treatment, no matter how difficult or rife with suffering, if it holds any chance for her to come out on top of this cancer.

When I commented on the great job he was doing managing without complaint the care of his ailing Shirley, he shrugged it off. He reminded me that he is not doing anything heroic—only what needs to be done. He left no doubt that if the tables were turned, his bride would do the same for him.

Tony's response called to mind my Uncle Bob and Aunt Mary. As my late parents' closest friends, Bob and Mary were not blood relatives but true family nonetheless. At the age of 68, Mary suffered a major stroke, which resulted in a need for a wheelchair and constant care. Bob stepped in and provided high-quality care in their home for twelve years, until his spouse passed on.

At her church funeral service, the parish priest told of how Bob would bristle when referred to as a good caregiver to Mary. He would say, "I am not a caregiver, I am a husband."

My wife, Cathy, Uncle Bob, and friend Tony must be cut from the same fine cloth, for by their actions they demonstrate what a true marriage partnership means, in sickness and in health.

COMING OUT BETTER AND STRONGER

This next story has the happy ending I hope and pray Shirley's will have. I first met Joe during a basketball game in which each of us had a fifth-grade son playing. Just the week before, Cathy had told me that the father of one of Jack's classmates was dealing with a big-time cancer. As it came to pass, I found myself in the school gym on a Saturday morning sitting next to this new cancer patient. We spent the next hour talking not of hoops, which under other circumstances would have been our preference, as college basketball fans, but of our shared cancer experiences. We agreed to stay in touch, and I followed his case with interest. His wife, Lora, kept us updated regularly.

Joe, an economics professor in Marquette University's business school, suffered a rough semester, but survived with the love of Lora and their three children and the support of colleagues. During the peak of his health scare, he was informed by the Dean that he had earned a full professorship.

He elected to inform his students what he was up against with cancer. In a letter thanking me for reaching out and talking to him about the shock of such a health challenge, he wrote, "My hope is I will have the strength to show my students that with faith and support from family, friends, and community, we can handle life-changing events with grace and come out the other side a better and stronger person."

Joe succeeded, and the real-life lesson that he offered his students was more valuable and instructive than any these 20-year-olds might have received from textbooks. Lora's account of Joe's personal cancer odyssey is touching and worth sharing:

In January, when Joe was diagnosed, he was already at stage four (the highest stage) and he was presenting a poor IPI (International Prognosis Index) reading. According to our doctor, his situation was very serious. Joe has undergone six cycles of chemotherapy and six lumbar spinal chemo injections, CAT scans, PET scans, MUGA scans, two bone marrow biopsies, chest x-rays, countless blood draws, a six-day hospital stay (part of which was in isolation, due to the RSV virus), blood clots, a blood transfusion, pneumonia, hair loss, mouth sores, loss of feeling in his fingers and toes, and a great deal of fatigue. However, last week we received the fantastic news that he is now in remission!

Like Shirley, Joe shares the same Catholic faith and says he found praying the rosary helped him sail through spinal taps. Shirley wrote, "I received a beautiful John Paul II rosary from my dear sister-in-law, Catherine, that I pray during the night hours." Animal-lover Shirley suspects that her cat must be Catholic, for "She helps me pray the rosary during the night, pulling on my beads with me."

The late Pope possessed a strong Marian devotion and was captivated by the figure of Christ's mother. According to Peggy Noonan's book, the Pope believed that Mary interceded to save his life when an assassin shot him at point-blank range in St. Peter's Square. The

Pope went on record as saying, "One hand fired, and another guided the bullet"—a reference to the killer's bullet having missed fatally severing his artery by a razor-thin, one-tenth of an inch.

Fast forward to six months after my initial meeting with Joe. We found ourselves attending a Sunday night summer basketball game our sons Jack and Wes were playing in. Joe was wearing a telltale baseball cap but looked great, saying his hair and even eyebrows were growing back. He had just completed his final procedure, which involved the harvesting of stem cells. Joe was under the impression this would be, to use his words, "a piece of cake," but getting a sufficient amount of cells turned out to be problematic.

Joe's appetite had come roaring back, so we made arrangements to fulfill a joint dinner date with our wives—a date we had talked of when we first met, to be scheduled after Joe's treatment was complete. Not only is Joe's another inspiring story with a happy ending, but also Cathy and I have made new friends in the process.

While chatting during the boys' basketball game, Joe asked who number 15 on our team was, a point guard clearly making a positive difference in the game. This solid player was Tom, and it occurred to me that his father, Vince, also in attendance to watch his son play, was yet another survivor of cancer.

The boys played well and our team was victorious. At the end of the game I took the opportunity to introduce Joe to Vince, blessedly cancer-free himself five years after beating back Hodgkin's disease. It hit me that all three of us fathers of currently sixth-grade sons were sporting *Livestrong* wristbands.

LIVING STRONG

During Lance Armstrong's record sixth *Tour de France* victory race in July 2004, he sported a yellow rubber wristband with the life-affirming description *Livestrong*. A famous cancer survivor, he started a charitable foundation whose mission is to help the fortunate 50 percent of us survivors cope and continue to lead our lives at the highest level. Yellow is the jersey color of the Tour leader and winner, and this simple item spawned a national craze. Politicians in both parties, Hollywood actors and actresses, professional and Olympic athletes, as well as ordinary folks from all walks of life began wearing this symbol, raising the nation's consciousness about cancer victims and survivorship. I am particularly impressed by how school-children and teenagers embraced the wearing of these *Livestrong* bracelets. Included in this vast *Livestrong* army are our own son and daughter. For too long, cancer was a taboo subject. I believe it is a positive sign to bring discussion of this insidious disease out in the open.

Lance went on to win a record-shattering seventh *Tour de France* in 2005, then triumphantly retired from the sport that had made him a legend. Yet no life is without setbacks. Divorced from the mother of his three children, Armstrong enjoyed a celebrity romance with singer/songwriter Sheryl Crow. After his retirement, seemingly on top of the world, this happy and loving couple announced they were engaged to be married. Yet early in 2006 they broke off their engagement. Shortly came the news that Sheryl Crow had been diagnosed with breast cancer. Armstrong was reportedly devastated by this turn of events.

I feel privileged to have come to know and see in action clients such as Carmen who exhibit a positive attitude and are truly living strong because of having faced adversity.

MY BUDDY AL

Al is a prime example of someone living strong and carrying on in spite of health challenges. I first met this good guy in a client capacity, and our relationship has developed into that of good friends. A college wrestler and highly successful chief information officer at a distribution firm, this active fellow has seen his life slowed by the cruel effects of Parkinson's disease. Parkinson's is a progressive neurological disease whose visible symptoms can include shaking, hand tremors, rigidity, and difficulty walking. Despite Al's disability, his buddy Brian and I marvel at how he manages to regularly beat us at golf. He wastes no time or energy with practice swings, and after a shot well-played will flash us a happy grin. It is only when you notice him shuffle his feet in a slow jog back to the golf cart that you appreciate what he is up against.

Due to the heavy toll of the disease, Al was forced at age 50 to give up the job he loved and was so good at, and reluctantly retire on disability. If ever there was a clearcut disability claim it was for Al, whose doctors had categorized his Parkinson's as stage four. Yet the insurance company fought and balked at paying for his disability. For Al, this reaction was like pouring salt on his wound.

Rather than take the word of the doctors, the insurance company hired private investigators to follow Al and videotape his activities with friends, such as sailing. But the competitive athlete is still very much a part of Al's personality, so he fought back by hiring an attorney and ultimately winning his case and back benefits.

Actor John Wayne said, "Courage is about getting back on the horse after you have fallen." During Al's legal and health battles he was taking a boatload of pills daily in an attempt to control the worsening symptoms and fatigue of this disease. In a bid to get back on the horse and enjoy a better quality of life, Al courageously underwent a new surgical procedure in which electrodes were inserted deep in his brain on both sides of his skull. The electrodes are connected to pacemakers implanted in his chest. I have taken trips by air with Al, and it is something to see the special treatment he gets from airport security, since he cannot go through the usual screening owing to the pacemakers and metal tubes in his head.

His surgery, known as deep brain stimulation, was a remarkable success. Al relishes demonstrating how his tremors are gone and saying that for the most part he is off meds. He is not out of the woods, however, as he must still take a daily nap. Diminished eyesight limits his driving, and his voice is so soft that others sometimes have difficulty hearing him.

Al does not feel sorry for himself. Rather, he shows a zest for life. Anyone who spends time or plays golf with Al notices his joy.

Unlike many golfers, he never gets mad at himself for a bad shot or complains about the weather. My partner Mike Weil was golfing with Al recently during a steady rain. While setting up to tee off, Al suddenly fell backward. Concerned, Mike went over to help him up, asking if he was all right. Al got right up and nonchalantly said he was fine, other than being a little wet from the ground. To prove his point, he proceeded to blast his best drive of the day some 230 yards straight down the fairway.

Al has a true passion for sailing and lives to spend time on his sailboat. The backyard of his comfortable country home sits on a river, and Al savors the outdoors and camping and traveling.

Fighter that he is, Al has plans to travel to the Mayo Clinic. There he will be evaluated at this cutting-edge research institution. He is willing to go down any road that will allow him to live strong and at the top of his game, despite Parkinson's.

TWO SPIRITUAL GIANTS

Icon and evangelist Billy Graham continues to live strong at 87 despite Parkinson's and his generally declining health. After a series of falls he uses a walker. This great American has just penned a new book titled, appropriately, *The Journey*. In it he recounts his early days on a North Carolina dairy farm, his encounters with the powerful, including every modern-day U.S. president, his ministering to the humble, and his 65-year marriage to his wife, Ruth. Supposedly retired after 60 years of worldwide ministry, he remains at heart a preacher.

As I mentioned earlier, the late Pope John Paul II suffered with Parkinson's. Like the noted American religious leader, he too pressed on to the very end. Graham, referring to the then 84-year-old Pope, used him as a role model. "In fact, I've thought a number of times, the Pope is going on with his message to the world at his age. I can go on at my age with the gospel I've preached all over." In the last years of his papacy the Pope was repeatedly pressed to retire. His succinct reply, "Christ didn't come down from the cross."

Like Al, the late Pope was a robust athlete who loved to go hiking in the mountains. In the twilight of his long life, when the effects of age and Parkinson's left him unable to walk, the Pope was asked about his health. He replied, "I'm in good shape from the neck up. Not so good from the neck down." To see the frail Billy Graham participating in yet another of his celebrated crusades, I suspect he might respond in the same way.

Peggy Noonan, when discussing the Pope, could have been writing of Billy Graham when she said, "By dying in public the old Pope got us thinking about dying, which got us thinking about living, and life."

Obviously these two spiritual giants had a strong faith that helped them carry on and lead exemplary lives.

In my friend Shirley's most recent health update, number 17, she shared with all of us who care about her that the bone marrow transplant she so desperately needs to survive has been delayed for a second time. The first postponement was caused by an allergic reaction to a drug, resulting in hospitalization. Past that, she developed the bad timing of catching a cold.

To use her own words for what she describes as small roadblocks, "I guess I'm like a space shuttle…unless all systems are 100 percent, it's just not a blastoff." Shirley is anxious and "ready for the fight" that this chemo/transplant entails.

On the eve of what we hope is a life-saving procedure, Shirley lifts us with this quote from scientist Edward Teller. "When you come to the end of all the light you know, and it's time to step into the darkness of the unknown, faith is knowing that one of two things will happen: Either you will be given something solid to stand on or will be taught to fly." The late Pope and Billy Graham would surely applaud Shirley's spirit.

FATHER AND SON

Tim McGraw is one of country music's biggest and most successful stars. He is married to the talented and beautiful country singer

Faith Hill. By all appearances, this high-profile couple leads a charmed life. Yet Tim's early life was quite a struggle. He was abandoned by his biological father and raised by a single mother. Not until he grew into a young man did Tim learn who his father was.

Tug McGraw, when he fathered Tim, was a minor league baseball pitcher. He went on to success and fame as a World Series relief pitching ace for the Philadelphia Phillies and the New York Mets. Eventually the two reconciled and built a relationship. Ironically, it was Tim who took in and cared for his father in his Nashville home when Tug developed brain cancer. Tug McGraw lost his battle with cancer at age 59.

Speaking of the poignancy of life and music in an interview, Tim McGraw observed, "If there's one thing I've learned from country music, it's that you never know how the song of life is going to end."

In 2004, this superstar performer with the goatee, sideburns, and signature black cowboy hat had a monster hit, "Live Like You Were Dying." It is clear from images in the music video that Tim had his father on his mind when singing this moving ballad.

The lyrics tell the story of a friend, still in his early forties, who learns he has cancer and presumably only months to live. The singer asks his sentenced friend what do you do when you get that kind of news. The inspirational reply is that you live at a high level, as if you are dying. The chorus is, "I went sky diving, I went rocky mountain climbing." The dying man ends by telling his friend that tomorrow is a gift and "…one day I hope you get a chance to live like you were dying."

Warren Zevon was a composer and performer. He was also a philosopher, although he probably wouldn't describe himself as such. In the fall of 2002, while under a death watch with lung cancer, Zevon was interviewed by David Letterman. Letterman probingly asked, "From your perspective now, do you know something about life and death that maybe I don't know?" Zevon answered philosophically, "I know how much you're supposed to enjoy every sandwich." I take this to mean cherish every morsel of life.

STILL KICKING

Let me tell you about Diane. It was in the years right after college when I met and developed a friendship with her. You couldn't help but notice her resolute demeanor despite requiring hand crutches to get around. Being the same age, we are growing older in tandem and have managed occasionally to stay in touch over the years.

In August 1955 a polio epidemic broke out in Milwaukee and Diane, then 3$^1/_2$ years old, contracted this dreaded, disabling condition. Every mother of young children in the early 1950s was acutely aware of the real fear posed by polio epidemics. Years later when my mother met my friend, she realized that Diane was among the very last children to be stricken with this life-changing condition.

In 1954, the year before the epidemic hit, Jonas Salk developed the vaccine that would essentially eradicate polio. The problem was manufacturing sufficient amounts of this miracle vaccine. Consequently, the limited supply was rationed, with school-age children the first to receive it. Because Diane was of preschool age, she probably just missed being vaccinated. Knowing this, I asked Diane if she ever felt angry or cheated regarding her disability. She replied honestly that she harbors no bitterness, as this is the only life she has ever known.

These days Diane must use a wheelchair. Rather than feel sorry for herself, Diane has purposely elected to make lemonade out of the lemons in her life. She is executive director in residence of Welcome H.O.M.E. (House of Modification Examples). She runs a non-profit bed and breakfast nestled in 17 acres of rolling prairie and woodland, 35 miles northwest of Milwaukee in Newburg, Wisconsin.

As could be expected, the home is a wheelchair-friendly living laboratory. Its modifications include wide doorways, sloped floors, louvered doors, adapted countertops, and reachable faucets and controls that allow those with disabilities to live independently. Diane might not be able to ride a bike, but there is no doubt she is living strong and helping others to live strong, too.

Our Maggie has been fascinated by wheelchairs ever since she was a young girl. She even has a toy chair for her doll. Maggie routinely takes to people in chairs with her special touch.

Our family has attended and enjoyed many camp weekends staged by the Wisconsin Lions at their beautiful lake and woods property in the central part of the state. These spring and fall camp weekends bring together families that have a member living with a cognitive disability.

The camps have proven especially enriching and enlightening for our children Martha and Jack. On top of being fun, it allowed them to see they were far from alone in having a special sibling. As parents, we are reminded that many families cope with much more severe situations than we face with Maggie.

It was at Lions Camp that we met and befriended children Maggie affectionately refers to as "the wheelchair girls." Unfortunately, it has been more than a few years since we last saw or visited with these severely handicapped girls. Yet, out of the blue, Maggie will inquire about them, and quickly recall their names—Nikki and Jenny.

In the game of life, you never know where a connection will help open a door. Cathy and I worry about what the future holds for Maggie, considering her progressively disabling neurological condition. To see how Diane has learned to adapt and function so well despite not being able to walk gives us inspiration and a roadmap to follow.

During my most recent phone conversation with Diane I asked how she was holding up. "John," she responded, "I'm still kicking." Diane is definitely carrying on and living strong.

KISS—ASSET ALLOCATION IS THE KEY

Allow me to turn from stories of life to finances. In the seemingly bewildering and complex world of investment management, the consensus solution lies in the surprisingly simple concept of asset allocation. The roots of asset allocation lie in modern portfolio theory (MPT), built on a solid foundation of Nobel prize-winning economic analysis. Most experts come out firmly for asset allocation as an effective, long-term approach to investing.

To understand how asset allocation works, it helps to think of a silver dollar. This dollar coin equates to 100 cents, and the circular shape can depict a pie chart. Asset allocation has to do with the relative amount investors assign to various asset classes. Put another way, how many cents, what percent is allocated. Asset classes represent types of investments— stocks, bonds, and money markets (cash). Stocks are further classified into sub-classes: large and small, U.S. and foreign, and those with an orientation emphasizing value or growth.

Modern Portfolio Theory has convincingly demonstrated that the asset mix of a given portfolio is the primary determinant of investment return. In fact, studies have shown that more than 90 percent of investment performance is a direct function of how one allocates assets. The essence of successful investing is simply to seek to maximize (push up) return on one hand, while minimizing (pushing down) risk (volatility) on the other. By blending asset classes in a proper allocation, higher returns are possible along with some management of risk.

Modern Portfolio Theory uses statistics to demonstrate that asset classes behave differently. In layman's terms, bonds are likely to be zigging while stocks are zagging. Research shows that you can actually achieve a lower overall risk and higher return potential by adding a usually riskier asset class, such as international or small-cap stocks.

If you accept the compelling evidence in favor of asset allocation, it logically follows that is where your attention should be focused. Of course, this focus is contrary to that of the majority of the wild herd, which recklessly chases after the latest hot fund and attempts to beat the market.

Like many simple and workable concepts in the investment field, asset allocation is frequently misconstrued and made out to be more complicated and more difficult to execute than it really is.

Since asset allocation is the key to long-term investment success, you should develop your own personal investment policy. My goal is to show this process is not as difficult as it seems. The asset allocation weighting of stocks balanced with more stable bonds and money markets is the most important investment decision you will make. It is the starting point for designing a strategic asset allocation investment plan. By taking into account your personal circumstances such as age, investment expectations, and risk tolerance (stomach for losses), you can match your portfolio with the right overall mix for you.

Peter L. Bernstein, whom I mention earlier, is the acclaimed author of the investment tome *Against The Gods*. With his trademark bow tie, mustache, oversized glasses, and large nose, this still-active octogenarian has the appearance of a cartoon character. But in institutional and academic investment circles there is nothing funny about this brilliant and respected investment mind. So it is not surprising that an article Bernstein wrote in 2002 for *Bloomberg Personal Finance* magazine is perhaps the most cogent and valuable investment piece I have ever read.

In Bernstein's considered opinion, the ideal allocation is 60 percent stocks mixed with 40 percent bonds, known as 60/40. In his view, this mix represents the center of gravity and is "a good compromise for the long-run average balance between maximizing return and minimizing risk."

In the 75-year period from 1925 thru 2000, a portfolio invested 100 percent in stocks turned in an average return of 11 percent, while one split 60 percent stocks balanced by 40 percent bonds did 9.3 percent. Seeing as stocks have historically outperformed, why shouldn't long-term investors stick with all-stock portfolios and shun bonds completely? After all, investors were amply rewarded with this fully weighted allocation to stocks during the spectacular bull market of the 1990s.

The answer, according to Bernstein and perceptive others, is uncertainty, along with bear markets. We were still in the throes of a deep bear market when he wrote this article. Uncertainty comes in the form of the psychology of investors, who have shown no staying power whatsoever to ride out the volatile storms that occasionally rock the stock market, such as in the three-year bear market of 2000–2002.

Bonds might seem boring but are a necessary portfolio ingredient to dampen the inherent volatility of stocks. A bond component adds stability and smoothes the ups and downs in the market. Stability in turn helps nervous investors hang in there when the going gets rough.

The insightful Bernstein chooses to emphasize the important psychological or behavioral aspect of investing and investors. "In my real-world experience, investors with smaller allocations to stocks and with some anchors to windward have been the ones most likely to be the winners over the long haul."

In my opinion, the Vanguard Star (VGSTX) mutual fund might be the best and least complicated investment vehicle to be found. I can say with confidence it is an easy and inexpensive way to derive the benefits of broad-based diversification and the optimum 60/40 allocation split recommended by Peter Bernstein.

Mutual fund authority Morningstar calls this fund a real standout and an excellent option for moderate-allocation fans. In one neat package, this fund of funds combines 11 of Vanguard's highly regarded low-cost, actively managed fund offerings. These investments cover the full spectrum of stock categories and styles, including 15 percent in foreign stocks to go with 40 percent anchored in bond funds and cash.

Vanguard Star fund performance during the raging bull markets of 1998 (+12.3 percent) and 1999 (+7.1 percent) badly trailed the S&P 500 (+28.5 percent and +21 percent) in those years. It is safe to assume that staid investors did not brag about this performance at cocktail parties. If discussed at all, such stodgy performance was ridiculed by high-flying investors.

Nick Murray calls this prudently diversified and balanced approach during market manias the courage to underperform. According to Murray: "Diversification is the conscious choice not to make a killing, in return for the blessing of never getting killed."

Vanguard Star shareholders could quietly smile and relax with their slow-moving fund during the subsequent three-year bear market of 2000–2002. Over that period many stock investors got clocked, lost their shirts, or got cleaned out. The Vanguard Star fund *did not lose money.* In 2000 and 2001 it was in positive territory, posting returns of +10.96 percent and +.50 percent, respectively.

In 2002, while the S&P 500 stock index coughed up a loss of -22 percent, the Vanguard Star fund managed to keep its loss in the single digits at -9.87 percent.

This steady performance was accomplished during a tumultuous storm that battered the entire market. Yet Vanguard Star was designed to withstand even this severity without being shipwrecked. Its prudent strategy allowed its investors to stay the course and find safe harbor.

It helps to recall master investor Warren Buffett's two rules to live by. "Rule number one, don't lose money. Rule number two, never forget rule number one."

Vanguard Star is not necessarily an exciting investment to own, yet over time it has proven itself to actually work. Peter Bernstein would approve, as indicated by this statement:

Many aspects of investing are fun, but your future wealth isn't a game. You should manage it in the most cold-blooded fashion. Emotion, pride, ego, dreams, and nightmares have nothing to do with the process, although some investors rely on little else. It is in this sense that volatility really matters.

The T. Rowe Price fund group sports a similar offering that is definitely worthy of consideration: its T. Rowe Price Personal Balanced (TRPBX) fund. Morningstar's take is that Personal Balanced is a fine choice at a reasonable expense for getting one-step exposure to a diversified portfolio of stocks and bonds in a no-fuss way. Like Vanguard Star, this balanced fund takes a middle-of-the-road or all-weather approach, with a moderate allocation of 60/40. As such, it too survived the bear market with minimal damage while also participating in the good years.

Professor Perry Glasser of Salem State College, writing in *The North American Review,* said it like it is: "Underpinning the financial services industry is the dubious claim that finance is a complicated and ever-changing realm no layperson can hope to understand."

Fund-tracker Morningstar says about T. Rowe Price Personal Balanced: "Investors face the often inevitable task of selecting good investments, putting together a diversified group of holdings, and rejiggering their portfolios regularly to ensure no one piece of the portfolio comes to dominate. There's the option of doing all that on your own, of course, but this offering does all the work for you."

AN INVESTMENT IN A LIFETIME

The power of investing appropriately for the long haul can be illustrated by this case study. Dan and Sheila are bright, energetic teenagers, busy with school, activities, and part-time jobs. They are each encouraged by their parents to open a Roth IRA with $2,000 from their respective earnings and to continue annual investments going forward. Roth IRAs take their name from Senator William Roth, the primary proponent. Contributions to this back-loaded IRA are not deductible, but withdrawals, when taken, are tax-free.

The hope is that these impressionable 16-year-olds will start on a financial planning and investment course that will pay handsome dividends over their lifetimes. The lessons to be learned are many, including the value of saving, knowledge of investments, importance of goal-setting, power of compound growth, and tax awareness.

To get the ball rolling, each of these young people invests in a balanced asset allocation mutual fund. Commonly referred to as lifecycle, lifestage, or lifestyle, this all-purpose fund type offers a simple path to accumulating wealth and a substantial nest egg.

At this stage of their young lives these teenagers would wisely choose a ready-made asset allocation mutual fund weighted 80 percent in stocks for growth, capable of producing a double-digit, 10 percent, long-term average annual return.

Dan establishes his Roth IRA account at T. Rowe Price and uses its T. Rowe Price Personal Strategy Growth (TRSGX), while Sheila goes to Vanguard and taps its Vanguard Life Strategy Growth (VAGSGX). These no-load, low-cost balanced 80/20 funds are ideal for small investors, as they neatly provide one-step exposure to a wide variety of investments. A typical lifecycle/asset allocation fund is invested in as many as nine asset classes and 700 to 1,200 individual securities.

These Internet-savvy young people will track their investments online, reviewing their portfolio makeup and current allocation, checking their returns, and being brought up to speed by reading the annual reports and investment commentary on their holdings.

Our teenagers will benefit greatly from the extraordinary power of money to grow over time. Without a doubt, the best aid Dan and Sheila have in pursuit of financial success is to harness the tremendous power of compound growth. Compounding adds wind to your investment sail and provides the horsepower that drives your savings engine, thereby enabling you to reach your goal. An appreciation of the power of compound growth encourages the savings and investment efforts crucial to financial success.

Time truly is money, and the value of time forms the principle of the time value of money. As the brilliant Benjamin Franklin wrote in 1748, "Money is of a prolific generating nature. Money can beget money, and its offspring can beget more."

All financial planning is heavily influenced by the time value of money. Teenagers Dan and Sheila are following the wisdom of Vanguard's founder John Bogle when he advises, "Give yourself the benefit of all the time you can possibly afford."

Over the last 50 years, a portfolio weighted 80 percent in variable stocks and 20 percent in more stable bonds has averaged an annual return in excess of 10 percent. So, looking over the 50-year time horizon to age 66 for these 16-year-olds, this round-number, double-digit targeted return is a reasonable assumption. Their balanced growth portfolio also includes international and small-caps stocks to boost performance.

The genius Einstein, when asked to name the most amazing thing available to mankind, purportedly said, "compound growth." It doesn't take a genius to understand that money has the ability to grow. To comprehend the time value of money is to understand what is meant by compound growth or compound interest. Although frequently referred to as magic or a miracle, compounding is simply the ability to earn interest on your interest.

A handy formula that demonstrates the power of compound growth is the Rule of 72, which approximates how long it will take you to double your money using different rates of return. The number 72 divided by the rate of return gives you the approximate number of years it will take to double your money. For example, 72 divided by 10 percent = 7.2 years.

If you allow $1,000 to grow, or *compound*, over a period of 7+ years and if your rate of return holds steady at 10 percent, your total interest earned would equal the initial principal, virtually doubling your money. Over long periods of time, the interest contributions come to dwarf the original principal. It might help to visualize this snowball effect with each passing year. The sum grows at a greater speed over time, gaining momentum with each passing year. This geometric progression shows $1 doubling to $2, $4, $8, $16, $32, $64, $128, and so forth over the 50-year period.

The extraordinary power of compounding underscores the value of time. Whereas compounding a problem makes things worse, compounding *interest* makes one wealthy. An important part of financial planning involves the use of time-value-of-money calculations to make projections, test what-if assumptions, calculate needs, and construct financial planning models.

Billionaire Warren Buffett and his less visible right-hand man, Charlie Munger, are on record as sharing a deep appreciation for the awesome power of compounding. Munger is reported to have a compound rate-of-return table always handy. He says, "Understanding both the power of compound return and the difficulty of getting it is the heart and soul of understanding a lot of things."

Teenagers Dan and Sheila start on this half-century accumulation plan by putting $2,000 away each year in a tax-deferred Roth IRA and bumping this up every decade by $1,000 to $3,000 annually at age 26, $4,000 at age 36, $5,000 at age 46, and $6,000 at age 56. Over the course of the 50-year period they would contribute $200,000 to the kitty. At age 66, assuming a 10 percent average annual rate of return, each account would be valued at a cool $3.5 million.

T. Rowe Price and Vanguard each have a handy online calculator that can do time-value-of-money calculations for our young saver-investors. They can calculate what their accounts are projected to grow to by using various return assumptions. They might wish to graph their actual progress over the years.

It is often difficult to make a once-a-year lump sum contribution for investors such as these teenagers, whose earned income is spread over the calendar year. So Dan and Sheila divide their $2,000 investments into 12 equal monthly installments of $166.66, and they sign up with their respective mutual fund company's automatic monthly installment program. This disciplined approach will make their retirement years far brighter.

CHAPTER 4

RIVER OF LIFE

Every man is born to one possession which outvalues all
his others—his last breath.

Mark Twain

Samuel Langhorne Clemens, better known as Mark Twain, was
an American original—a master storyteller, a humorist, and
the best-known and greatest writer of the last half of the nineteenth century. Born in 1835 in the then-western outpost of Missouri,
his birth coincided with the appearance of Halley's Comet. Twain
led a long, rich, and interesting life, departing this world in 1910, a
year when the comet appeared once again.

As a young boy, Clemens was terrified by thunderstorms, believing that God would surely punish him for his misdeeds. Throughout
his life, whenever he was dealt a severe blow, he referred to it as a
thunderbolt. Over his lifetime, Clemens did seem to suffer more than
his share of heartbreak. His younger brother, Henry, tragically was
lost in a steamboat accident on the Mississippi. Three of his four
children predeceased him, as did his beloved wife, Livy.

His modest start in life did not presage his becoming the representative figure of a growing nation's emergence from the trauma of
the Civil War. Clemens was born two months premature, and it was
feared this sickly child would not survive.

But survive he did. When young Sam was just 14 years old his father died suddenly, and the family thereafter led a hardscrabble life.

As a 30-year-old at the conclusion of the Civil War, Mark Twain thought of himself as an utter failure. Penniless and friendless, he was a public drunkard, and he had been fired as a newspaper reporter in San Francisco. He harbored dark thoughts of suicide.

Fortunately, Twain carried on. His varied life experiences, from a stint as a steamboat pilot on the Mississippi River to worldwide traveler, coupled with his truly special gift with words, guaranteed for future generations a wealth of material—not the least of which are quotations covering both life and finances.

For example, an unsuccessful gold and silver prospector himself, Twain warns us in his typical folksy manner to beware of investment fraud: "A gold mine is a hole in the ground with a liar on top."

As a keen observer of the human condition, Twain gave us a timeless adage: "Why is it that we rejoice at a birth and grieve at a funeral? Is it because we are not the person involved?" My favorite Twainism is, "I believe our heavenly father invented man because he was disappointed with the monkey."

Twain lived high but suffered from a lifelong anxiety over money. Along with his wife Livy, he spared no expense on building and furnishing their showplace mansion in Hartford, Connecticut. Despite a sizeable income and royalties from his many books and a lucrative lecture circuit, Mark Twain found himself at age 58, at the height of his fabled career, facing the embarrassment of bankruptcy.

A cascade of events—including ill-fated business ventures, a series of tempting get-rich-quick schemes, and associations with incompetent and sometimes unscrupulous individuals—left Twain buried under a mountain of debt. The mindset of false hope that brought Twain down is represented in this statement by today's comic character philosopher-king Homer Simpson: "After years of disappointment with get-rich-quick schemes, I know I'm gonna get rich with this scheme…and quick."

A failed publishing partnership, coupled with his having thrown hundreds of thousands of dollars into a money pit of a supposedly high-tech typesetting machine, finally caught up with Twain and brought his financial undoing. Some 110 years later, investment manager Bill Gross sees similarities to Twain's time. "Today's winning technology is tomorrow's sinkhole."

Similar to Twain in his day as a celebrity, modern-day athletes and entertainers are capable of commanding astounding incomes at relatively young ages. Take the case of Las Vegas Casino headliner Wayne Newton, who filed for bankruptcy in 1992. At the time, he was pulling down over a quarter of a million dollars a week singing "Danke Schoen" and "Daddy, Don't Leave" to packed audiences. It is hard for anyone struggling to get by to sympathize with the financial plight of Newton, whose annual income at the height of his career exceeded $10 million.

Webster's New World dictionary defines *speculate* as "investing with higher than ordinary risk, taking part in risky ventures on the chance of making huge profits." The great stock market crashes of 1929 and 1987 both occurred in the month of October. In 1894, Mark Twain remarked wryly in *The Tragedy of Pudd'nhead Wilson*: "October. This is one of the peculiarly dangerous months to speculate in stocks. The others are July, January, September, April, November, May, March, June, December, August and February."

Twain also said, "There are two times in a man's life when he should not speculate: when he can't afford it, and when he can."

His and Livy's dire financial condition led them to flee the country to escape their creditors. They abandoned their cherished Hartford home and embarked on a grueling around-the-world trip, visiting such far-flung English Empire destinations as India, Australia, New Zealand, and South Africa with the express purpose of earning enough money from lecturing to pay off their huge debt.

Unlike individuals today who find no shame in personal bankruptcy, Twain considered repayment in full a moral imperative and a badge of honor. Although he could have gotten away without repayment, he felt obligated to—in his words—"not compromise for less than a hundred cents on the dollar." So he went on a mission to erase his debt by doing what he did best, writing and speaking. Almost ten years passed before he returned in triumph from his self-imposed exile.

Over time, Twain succeeded in satisfying his creditors in full. This worthy achievement was world news and made him a moral exemplar. With great relief he wrote, "I have abundant peace of mind again—no sense of burden. Work has become a pleasure again."

Throughout this ordeal, Twain never lost his marvelous sense of humor. To wile away the hours on board ship he participated in shuffleboard tournaments. Writing to his advisor back home Twain quipped, "[it] is rather violent exercise for me."

When the hard-nosed Mount Morris Bank abruptly called in his loan, Twain was prompted to pen the following cutting observation: "A banker is a fellow that lends you an umbrella when the sun is shining but wants it back the minute it begins to rain."

For a period of time while living in Europe, Twain attempted to keep a low profile. This effort proved futile, as an inquiring press worked to feed the American public's appetite for news of the exile. A rumor circulated that he was living destitute and near death in London. This led to one of the most well-known of all Mark Twain quotes. The obviously alive and healthy author told a young reporter checking the story, "The report of my death was greatly exaggerated."

Twain benefited mightily in his writing from having renowned editor William Dean Howells in his corner for over 40 years. This long association elevated the careers of both men. Without Howells' sound advice and counsel, Twain would not have achieved the literary success he did, and we likely would not know of his storytelling genius today. In stark contrast to his prodigious talent, Twain's myriad business and investment dealings were a horror story.

A TRUSTED ADVISOR

For your own financial security, nothing is more important than having a trusted and competent financial advisor guiding you, pointing out the pitfalls and clearing your path. This advisor should be someone you trust implicitly and who always places your own interests first. Ideally, the mission of this individual or advisory firm should be to make a positive impact not only on your investment portfolio but also on improving the quality of your life.

Dealing with an incompetent or dishonest individual, or someone concerned only with making a sale or transaction, is downright dangerous to your finances, security, and happiness. A mutually beneficial relationship with a trusted advisor is the most valuable investment you can make and will pay huge dividends over your lifetime.

Twain's sinking financial ship was rescued and righted on a proper course once Henry Rodgers, a successful businessman, entered the author's life as his advisor. Rodgers did not need Twain more than Twain needed him. The floundering debtor learned to respect Rodger's judgment. Importantly, he listened to and took the businessman's advice and counsel.

Henry Rodgers faced down Twain's hard-line creditors, advised Twain in dealings with his publishers, skillfully managed his cash flow, and prudently invested his money. He regularly communicated his progress to Twain and literally pulled him out of bankruptcy. Rodgers restored the author's reputation and financial well-being.

Mark Twain: A Life, is a fine biography by Ron Powers that I have read and heartily recommend. It is the source of much of my knowledge of this fascinating American figure. Powers notes Samuel Clemens' uncanny way of crossing paths with luminaries of his era, such as Ulysses S. Grant, a youthful Winston Churchill, and—to quote Twain—a "stone blind and deaf, and formerly dumb" 14-year-old Helen Keller. In many ways the blind girl and the middle-aged, mustachioed writer and humorist were kindred spirits, for each recognized the genius in the other.

After meeting Twain for the first time, Helen Keller was favorably impressed, confiding to her mentor that he "made us laugh 'til we cried" and referring perceptively to the "deep and beautiful things he has written."

At the age of 16, Helen Keller scored high enough on the Harvard entrance exam to gain admission to Radcliffe College. Twain, concerned about this remarkable young woman's financial ability to pursue this educational opportunity, took it upon himself to get titans John D. and William Rockefeller to cover her college expenses.

As he wrote to a friend, bringing his powers of persuasion and incredible insight to bear, "It won't do for America to allow this marvelous child to retire from her studies because of her poverty. If she can go on without them, she will make a fame that will endure in history for centuries." Helen Keller went on to graduate with honors, and her life story remains an inspiration to all of us.

Listen to the similar life affirmations in the words of these two very different giants on the American scene. For Helen Keller, "Life is either a daring adventure or nothing." Mark Twain implored, "Twenty years from now, you will be more disappointed with the things you didn't do than by the ones you did. So throw off the bowlines, sail away from the harbor. Catch the trade winds in your sails. Explore. Dream. Discover."

WINSTON THE GAMBLER

In many ways the financial proclivities of Winston Churchill were a lot like Mark Twain's. Both men earned considerable sums of money at an early age from their published works.

Churchill, though not bankrupt, nonetheless found himself, in his words, "stretched thin and financially embarrassed under a pile of debt." The British statesman possessed a speculative streak. He liked to gamble. His wife, Clementine, being more financially responsible, urged her husband to "err on the side of caution and exercise economy of spending." Having an American mother and loving

American history as he did, Churchill in 1929 toured the Pennsylvania Civil War battlefield and site of Lincoln's Gettysburg Address. He returned to New York City at the end of October, which coincided with the great Wall Street stock market crash. In fact, he claimed to have witnessed a suicide jumper, undoubtedly despondent over being wiped out in the market.

Churchill had likewise gotten caught up in the grossly speculative and inordinately optimistic frenzy of the American stock market. Hence, the great 1929 crash saw the loss, in today's dollars, of his own millions. According to Churchill's biographer, "He was both impoverished and on the edge of not being able to meet his obligations." Jumping out of a window was not in Churchill's makeup. Rather, he turned to his profitable writing career as a means of rebuilding his shaky finances.

MEN BEHAVING BADLY

Men are said to possess more investment knowledge than women. However, facts prove that women have more success as investors than their male counterparts. Experts in behavioral finance explain this gender difference as due to men's wild investment impulses. Chief on this list is overconfidence: males are apt to think they know more than they actually do. Overconfidence leads them to be overly aggressive and try to hit homeruns, instead making mistakes and frequently striking out. Men tend to trade too often, chase performance, try to time the market, and lack discipline and patience. It sounds to me that testosterone is the culprit.

According to a study commissioned by Merrill Lynch, women are more patient investors and more often seek financial advice. Compared with men, women are also more likely to learn from their mistakes.

Women tend to be much more concerned than men about their future financial security and dignity. In fact, many intelligent, educated, and financially comfortable women harbor a real fear of ending up as bag ladies. Perhaps this is because well over half of all

65-year-old women are currently single and alone. They think one major financial mishap could push them over the edge. Hence, they take notice of and have a special sympathy for the woman scrounging through garbage bins to collect cans in a shopping cart.

THE FAIRWAY OF LIFE

In searching for a way to emphasize avoiding the big mistakes and demonstrate how personal finances and life planning mesh, I found inspiration while attending the 2004 PGA golf championship in August of that year. This major professional golf event was held at the beautiful Whistling Straights golf course on the shores of Lake Michigan, north of Sheboygan, Wisconsin. The course had been built by Herb Kohler of the Kohler Company, who spared no expense in its creation.

Pro golfers Scott Simpson, Larry Mize, and Loren Roberts collaborated on a little-known book, *Focus—The Name of the Game.* In it they share their secrets of success in golf and life against the backdrop of their spiritual faith. To quote a representative phrase, "Golf, like life, is about discipline and struggle through the highs and lows of triumph and defeat. It is about focus. Focus on short-term lessons. Focus on long-term goals."

There are remarkable contrasts between professional golfers John Daly and Loren Roberts. These two men could not be farther apart, both on and off the course. Daly, known as "Long John," is one of the longest hitters on the tour, booming drives well in excess of 300 yards. Roberts is average, at best, in driving distance off the tee. The strength of his game lies on the green, where he has earned the moniker "boss of the moss" for his putting proficiency.

Daly, a self-described redneck, is overweight, a heavy smoker, an admitted alcoholic, and a problem gambler whose domestic life is a total mess. Roberts leads the life of a quiet family man. He is the picture of health and a committed Christian. According to Roberts, "I think you should try to live your life in such a manner that you mirror God's love."

There is no argument that Daly possesses the superior talent; yet, it is Roberts who has enjoyed more consistent success. Both golfers have won tour events. Daly won a major, the British Open, as a 25-year-old phenomenon. Roberts took a journeyman route, not posting his first win until age 39. Golf bears a similarity to investing in the sense that both endeavors carry a definite risk and reward factor. In golf, course management describes the approach taken and shots played on a particular hole. Daly and Roberts illustrate this factor in their approaches to play.

Daly is notoriously aggressive, taking high-risk gambles in an attempt to break par. On a par 5 hole, he will go for the green in two shots, looking to be rewarded with a birdie (1 under par) or an eagle (2 under par). On such a hole he is likely to out-drive Roberts by a substantial 80 yards. The risk side for Daly is the greatly increased possibility for an errant shot. The result could be out of bounds, deep in the rough, behind tree shots, or in-a-bunker hazard.

Golfers as well as investors would be wise to listen to professor Peter Bernstein, who says, "Whether you should take a risk depends not just on the probability that you are right but also on the consequences if you are wrong." On such a long and treacherous hole, Loren Roberts plays it smart and within his limitations, laying up his second shot in order to have a high-accuracy wedge shot to reach the green safely in a regulation 3. He then plays to his strength for a good chance to one-putt for his birdie.

John Daly's high-risk gambles frequently pay off and have made him a folk hero among the many golf fans who root for him to display his prodigious talent and overcome the demons in his personal life. The problem with this go-for-broke style is that he is prone to suffer the occasional "blow-up" hole. Such was the case on the first day of the 2004 PGA championship at the par 4 eighteenth finishing hole, where he posted a disastrous quadruple bogey (4 over) 8. This score basically put him out of contention.

Another figure famous for being aggressive and offense-minded was World War II General George Patton. Yet Patton was quoted as recommending this strategy: "Take calculated risks. That is quite different from being rash."

As things turned out, Daly failed to make the cut. Roberts did make the cut and he played on the weekend. Roberts' game is rarely spectacular, but it is consistently respectable. Although not among the leaders, he was in the second tier and earned a healthy paycheck.

There is an apt saying in competitive golf that you "drive for show, but you putt for dough." The essence of successful investing and financial security is to intelligently manage risk while avoiding the quadruple bogey mistakes that wreck your scorecard and/or portfolio. A reminder from former golf pro Gene Littler could be said to "hit the ball right down the middle" in its application to financial success: "Golf is not a game of great shots, it's a game of the most misses. The people who win make the smallest mistakes."

Jack Nicklaus, the Golden Bear, is widely considered the greatest golfer ever. This three-time winner of the British Open once summed up his phenomenal success by saying, "I think I just made fewer mistakes than the other golfers."

Chief among investing's "high risk" gambles, the quadruple bogey is a failure to adequately diversify. Remember, in investing as in golf, it is easier to *stay* out of trouble than to *get* out of trouble. Having a single stock too heavily represented in a portfolio is a big gamble.

A telling example is the bankruptcy of Enron, which became a large-scale corporate and personal finance tragedy. An important lesson can be learned from this debacle in terms of prudent investment management: the absolute need for diversification.

The most financially devastated Enron employees were those who had all of their retirement savings tied to the fortunes of this once high-flying stock. These folks either did not recognize the risk inherent in a heavy concentration of a single stock—or chose to ignore it.

This debacle involved both criminal wrongdoing by Enron corporate executives and a serious failing by the company's accountants at Arthur Andersen. Note, however, that participants in Enron's 401(k) program were allowed to freely choose among 30 diverse mutual fund offerings to direct their investment balances to. To load up on Enron stock was a conscious decision, made because it had been a star performer in previous years. Enron stock was seen as a ticket to riches, with no thought to the potential for ruin.

The reality is, no one foresaw Enron's plunge from a $90 stock price to pennies a share and sudden bankruptcy. "No one" includes Wall Street stock analysts, rating agencies, and supposedly sophisticated money managers. Enron was considered a glamour stock, ranking seventh largest in the stock universe, and a favorite holding for institutional pensions and mutual fund portfolios. The demise of Enron should dispel the myth that certain stocks are immune from a freefall. The risk of too much of a nest egg in a single stock, however touted, is simply too great.

Many similar tales abound. Employees held a full third of the total 401(k) assets in Kmart's retirement plan in the stock of Kmart when this once-proud retailer declared bankruptcy. They, too, were caught short.

Loading up in the stock of a company where you draw your paycheck is a particularly bad idea. If the stock plummets for whatever reason, you could also lose your job. This double-whammy happened to thousands of hard-luck employees at bankrupt Enron, Kmart, WorldCom, and Adelphia Communications.

All too often investors get crushed with too many eggs in one basket. They rationalize this risky behavior with a variety of reasons such as loyalty, familiarity, the company's having been in their words "good to them," or the capital gains tax hit they would incur if they sold. Others are blind to the risk or hold on from simple inertia. Professor and behavioral finance authority John Nofsinger tells us certain investors possess a strong attachment bias.

I am personally aware of investors who were comfortably overconcentrated, for all the above reasons, in the stock of blue chip stalwarts Merck, Procter & Gamble, and Marsh & McLennan. After all, what could happen?

Pharmaceutical giant Merck was hit by a thunderbolt in 2004

when the stock lost 24 percent in a single day. The cause was Merck's announced removal from the market of the drug Vioxx, thereby exposing the company to an onslaught of lawsuits.

Dow component and consumer heavyweight Procter & Gamble might well be the safest and most defensive stock in the entire market. Yet it, too, lost 28 percent in one day, and its stock price slid from $100 a share to $55 in a matter of weeks. This tumble occurred at a time when stocks in general were in the midst of a raging bull market.

Insurance broker Marsh & McLennan had been steadily climbing when it suddenly fell to earth, the result of regulators filing a lawsuit alleging payoffs and bid-rigging in the firm's insurance business.

Despite these shocking turns of events, some investors wearing rose-colored glasses actually viewed this fallback as a buying opportunity. As *Money* magazine's stock expert Walter Updegrave observed, "Just because a stock has fallen in price doesn't mean that it can't fall farther, or that a rebound is either imminent or inevitable."

With Enron down to just $4 a share, I recall a client asking me what he could lose by taking a chance on the stock. My quick answer was: $4 a share.

In March 2000, at the extreme of the tech-stock bubble, the star of networking firm Cisco Systems shone brightest as the world's most valuable company. Cisco was widely heralded as the ultimate one-decision, sure-bet stock, the ruler of the then-booming Internet kingdom. Thus, it came as a shock to see this star fall from the sky when Internet stocks imploded that same month. Cisco was not immune to this wreckage: its stock suffered an 80 percent decline in value.

Veteran financial industry journalist and author Nick Murray likes to say that people may well become wealthy in spite of under-diversifying, yet they cannot count on staying wealthy if not diversified. Think of Cisco and absorb this warning from Murray: "There is no more recklessly speculative strategy in this world than continuing to own far too much of a single great investment."

Cisco was just one among a long line of glamour stocks that lost their shine and sparkle—notably Enron, Krispy Kreme, WorldCom, Kmart, Polaroid, Kodak, Xerox, Wang Labs, and Control Data. My first job out of college in 1973 was with computer concern Burroughs, another member of the chorus line of fallen angels.

Tens of thousands of stories can be told, I imagine, of retirees whose financial security was shattered because they made the big mistake of being too aggressively invested in tech before the wreck.

Take the sad saga of a comfortably retired 65-year-old couple whose long-term retirement security was set, provided they did not lose 50 percent of their nest egg. When expressing concern about that possibility to their wet-behind-the-ears 26-year-old broker, he told them in no uncertain terms not to worry, because it couldn't happen. He reminded them of how well their portfolios were doing and said to trust him, as he knew what he was doing. He expressed complete confidence their portfolio would continue to grow.

In hindsight, they now kick themselves for being greedy, wanting to believe the good times would continue to roll. Devastated by a sudden change in fortunes when their worst fears were realized, they were forced to drastically scale back their standard of living and seek employment.

LESS IS MORE

Continuing with the analogy of golf and common sense investing, let me introduce you to Carl Unis.

Carl is in his late sixties, a husband, father, and grandfather, as well as a PGA teaching pro. His golf resume is impressive. Carl qualified and actually played in the U.S. Open championship in 1967, won that year by a fellow Ohioan, the great Jack Nicklaus.

This veteran instructor's constant refrain to his fledgling golf students, including yours truly, is "less is more, more is less."

By this Carl means high handicap (lousy) golfers routinely overswing, use more motion and effort than necessary, and put a death grip on the club. *More is less*. They achieve better results (better shots, lower scores) by allowing the club to do the work and drastically lightening up on the grip. *Less is more.*

Investors, be they amateurs or professionals, are likewise instructed to do *less* in search of better returns. This would take the form of exercising patience and trading less, paying less in investment expenses, and giving less attention to short-term performance.

A MAN FOR ALL SEASONS

Albert O. "Ab" Nicholas has managed money for 50 years. He founded the Nicholas Funds, the mutual fund family that bears his name. I have the good fortune of having gotten to know and respect this good man over the past 25 years. Ab Nicholas credits his memory of the go-go years of the late 1960s and the bracing bear market of 1973 and 1974 with teaching him hard yet valuable lessons. He learned the hard way to resist chasing after the current momentum of the market.

Nicholas does not make any pretense of his ability to time the market or discern its direction. He is fond of saying he is cautious and bearish for the short run, but confident and bullish for the long term. As such, he resisted following the pack and buying indiscriminately into the red-hot tech sector of the late 1990s. Like Warren Buffett, Nicholas felt the valuations were excessively high and couldn't see how the stock of these businesses were sustainable at their lofty levels.

Chief among the lessons Nicholas learned was how far one has to bounce back to get even, once a stock falls by a certain percentage. The math works out to show that a 25 percent rebound is needed to square up after a 20 percent loss. In the case of the 30 percent one-day losses of Merck, P&G, and Marsh & McLennan, the stocks had to recover 43 percent merely to bring an investment back to even.

To Nicholas, echoing pro golfers, it is far easier to *stay* out of trouble than to *get* out. An aggressive tech stock fund that gained 100 percent in 1999 and lost 50 percent in 2000 would be back to where it started. You might as well have tucked your investment money under a mattress. From its peak to its bottom, the Nasdaq composite lost 78 percent in value. In dollar terms, that's an astounding $2.5 trillion. Investors waiting for Cisco to climb back to its peak share price should plan on waiting a long time, as it takes a 400 percent recovery once 80 percent in value is lost.

Recently I was fortunate to spend some time catching up with Ab Nicholas. I found the now-70-something Ab looking fit and enjoying good health. I was privileged to have gotten to know him personally through a mutual connection with the late Warren Knowles, as Ab was a close friend of the former Wisconsin governor and mutual fund executive.

We started our conversation by fondly reminiscing about "the Guv," who was taken from us 12 years earlier. Ab said, with a sigh, that many of his circle of friends from that group are now in frail health, or, like Warren, have passed on.

In the pages of my previous book, *The New Millennium Guide to Managing Your Money*, published in 1998, I reported how disturbed Nicholas was by trouble he saw brewing in the mutual fund industry. In this early warning, Nicholas was like Vanguard's erstwhile chief John Bogle in publicly fretting that asset-gathering appeared to have superseded the interests of fund shareholders.

Both of these industry veterans led to my conviction, put in writing, that—contrary to public perception—marketing prowess, not investment skill, was the most important attribute of too many financially successful mutual fund companies at that time.

Bogle, never hesitant to raise his voice and share his strong opinions, had railed against fast-trading mutual fund companies that encouraged short-term investing, a practice he derisively labeled "casino capitalism." He disdained the mutual fund industry's promoting "two countervailing principles: switch and get rich, and pick hot managers."

Along this same line, I reported in my book Nicholas's being alarmed by the heavy advertising of mutual funds he saw taking place. In his opinion "the unfortunate fact is that the best time to advertise and promote past performance is actually the worst time for investors to buy."

Bogle had been more blunt, writing, "I think that advertising performance numbers should probably not be permitted. Advertising any performance numbers is misleading. The simple fact is, you put in performance numbers because they draw in money from investors who must believe returns will be repeated."

This widespread industry practice of promoting what is hot and bringing out fad funds conditioned gullible investors to unhealthy investment behaviors.

Those of us in the financial services industry cannot speak enough about the bedrock virtues of trust and integrity.

Ab Nicholas, a lanky former basketball star at his beloved University of Wisconsin alma mater, was born in Illinois. Like me, he is also a hero worshipper of Abraham Lincoln. Lincoln earned and deserved the moniker Honest Abe. A telling example is his mentoring advice to an aspiring young lawyer: "Resolve to be honest at all events, and if, in your judgment, you cannot be an honest lawyer, resolve to be honest without being a lawyer." This is vintage Lincoln; simple, succinct, straightforward, and right on.

The high-profile John Bogle is characterized in the press as a man with strong opinions and stringent ethical judgments. In recent correspondence between us concerning what I am writing here, he thanked me sincerely for my trust.

One of the major casualties of the mutual fund scandal that surfaced in 2003 happened to be another Milwaukee mutual fund firm bearing its chairman and founder's name. This fund family attracted billions in assets and grew rapidly, in large part by marketing its hot performers, as well as quickly introducing whatever style of fund was in vogue. Not surprisingly, this marketing strategy proved a financial success. It vaulted the founder onto the list ranked by *Forbes* of the 400 richest Americans.

However, as a result of being caught up in the scandal, this once high-flying mutual fund company was permanently grounded.

Government regulators imposed a hefty fine and forced its sale to an out-of-town financial institution, which quickly buried the fund's name. The chairman and founder, whose name had once been gold, was required to issue a public apology and was permanently banned from the securities industry.

THE BIGGEST MISTAKE OF ALL

One of those ubiquitous motivational success posters pictures an idyllic scene of a golf green and flag. Its caption is this inspirational message: "It matters how hard you drive, but it is more important to find yourself and enjoy life."

When I had my fiftieth birthday, a golfing buddy let me know I was now playing on the back nine of life, meaning the second or final half of my years. I found comfort in the fact that golf pro Loren Roberts turned 50 in 2005 and continued to have success on the Champions Tour, also known as the Seniors Tour, earning Rookie of the Year honors. Meanwhile, John Daly was continuing his erratic play, struggling and missing cuts. Lately he had to drop out of a couple of invitational tournaments because of a mysterious injury to his hand. The way Daly is going, this supremely talented golfer may not make it to the Champions Tour. After reading his autobiography, *My Life In & Out of the Rough*, I felt there is grave concern that Daly's unhealthy and destructive lifestyle will prematurely land him in that nineteenth hole in the sky.

Daly is one of the very few professional golfers ever caught on camera with a cigarette dangling from his lip. He would be smart to heed the latest U.S. Surgeon General's report, which again conclusively linked smoking to lung cancer and heart disease. If that wasn't bad enough, the report also presented a tie with cancers of the cervix, kidney, pancreas, and stomach.

When the King, golfing legend Arnold Palmer, smoked as a young man on tour, that was in the days before the surgeon general issued a stark warning. Arnie wisely stopped lighting up, and this well-known survivor of prostate cancer continues to tee it up in his seventies.

Chillingly, a 50-year study reported in the *British Medical Journal* found that up to two-thirds of all who take up smoking as teenagers will die from smoking-related illnesses. This same study found positively that those who kick this nasty habit can add years to their lives.

UP CLOSE WITH MICKEY

Mickey Mantle, switch-batting power hitter of the New York Yankees, was one of the greatest baseball players to ever play the game. This golden boy had a storied Hall of Fame career.

I spent the summer of 1967 as a visiting team batboy for the Chicago White Sox major league baseball team. To land this coveted spot, I entered an essay contest sponsored by the *Chicago Daily News*, a long-gone afternoon newspaper. As a runner-up winner, I worked that season in the dugout, field, and locker room of the opposing teams of the American League White Sox.

So it was that as a 15-year-old I was up close with such Hall of Fame baseball greats as the Tigers' Al Kaline, Brooks Robinson, and Frank Robinson of the Orioles, the Twins' towering home-run hitter Harmon Killebrew, the triple-crown winner and MVP that year, Carl Yastrzemski of the Boston Red Sox, and the immortal Mickey Mantle.

Mantle was hampered by serious knee injuries; yet, a lifestyle of excessive drinking and womanizing helped cut short his playing career, hurt his stats, and ruined his marriage. The haunting question remains of how truly great Number 7 might have been.

In 1993 Mantle was admitted to the Betty Ford Center for alcohol rehabilitation. Mantle then reconciled with his family, and still a wildly popular sports icon, he spoke out sincerely on the abuses of alcohol. He said he should have taken better care of himself but didn't think he would live that long, based on the premature deaths of his father and uncles.

Alcoholism had destroyed his liver, and in 1995 he received a transplant. Surgery uncovered an inoperable cancer. His life ended two months later at age 63. In Mantle's last at bat, he lent his celebrity name to a foundation to raise awareness for organ donations.

Mickey Mantle had four sons. His third son, Billy, was named after fellow Yankee and good drinking buddy Billy Martin. The fiery Martin went on to make a name for himself as a successful big league manager, yet he died in a fatal alcohol-related auto accident. Billy Mantle, with Hodgkin's cancer, predeceased his father. Mickey Jr. also died from cancer.

When Mantle was in the twilight of his storied career, he still generated the most buzz and fan excitement whenever he came to town to play. One series the Yankees brought their own bat boy on a Chicago road trip, an Italian kid from the Bronx named Tony, whom I befriended.

Nowadays, even washed-up major league baseball players make a tidy income selling their autographs. In the sixties, a signed ball was a prize, but definitely not a precious commodity.

At the end of each game I worked, the Yankees' third base coach handed a brand new baseball to each of the batboys. Never been an autograph hound, I suppose I am sensibly like my dad, who felt the only autograph worth any value was on a check. Nonetheless, I very much desired having the great Mickey Mantle sign his name to my ball. I shared this with my new friend, Tony, who let me in on a secret. It seems the Yankees' clubhouse man frequently forged the in-demand Mantle's signature. I also learned that the bus taking the Yankees from the Chicago hotel to the ballpark that morning was delayed, waiting for none other than Mantle. As a tardy Mickey was about to board, he was intercepted by an aggressive autograph seeker. With one motion, Mantle pushed the man's outstretched arm away and the index cards the man held flew in the air. Mickey got on the bus and the door shut behind him.

Less than an hour later, while his teammates were taking batting and fielding practice, Mantle was found soaking his aching body and probably nursing a hangover in the training room hot tub. Tony persuaded a shy me to follow him into the training room, where we encountered the naked superstar alone with his thoughts. "Hey, Mick, will you sign my buddy's ball?" Mantle willingly obliged, and as I write this I am looking at the genuine autographed baseball relic and recalling the story that goes with it.

LISTEN TO THE KING

Many of us remember actor Yul Brynner of the shaved head and indefinable accent who immortalized the part of the king of Siam in Rodgers' and Hammerstein's classic musical *The King and I.*

Though diverse and fascinating, Yul Brynner's early start in life, similar to Mark Twain's, did not forecast him for stardom. Born in Vladivostok, Russia, the son of Boris, a Swiss-Mongolian inventor, and Marousia, the daughter of a Russian doctor, Yul was named after his paternal grandfather.

Boris soon abandoned the family, and Yul and his sister were sent off to China for schooling. Later, his mother took him to Paris, where Yul found work playing guitar in clubs and befriending Russian gypsies who hung out there. His next pursuit was as a trapeze artist, before a serious accident ended his circus career. At age 21, Yul Brynner moved to the United States to study acting.

I find it ironic that early in his acting career, he failed to land a role because the casting director thought he looked "too oriental." This brings to mind a similar assessment of megastar Clint Eastwood. Early in his career, he was told he would never find widespread acting success because "he talked too slow and his Adam's apple was too big."

The Yul Brynner Head and Neck Cancer Foundation has as its mission providing support, research, and education to eradicate this dreadful, yet low-profile disease.

The Foundation was started as a result of the actor's being treated by Dr. George Sisson. During a 1983 stage run of the *King and I* in Chicago, Brynner, a heavy, lifetime tobacco user, complained about hoarseness and throat discomfort. He formed a close relationship with Dr. Sisson, from whom he learned of the harmful effects of tobacco and its relationship to mouth and throat cancer.

Two years later, Yul Brynner died in a New York City hospital of lung cancer at the age of 65. In the months prior to his certain death, he made a memorable public service antismoking television commercial to be released after his death. "Now that I'm gone, I tell you: Don't smoke. Whatever you do, just don't smoke."

I am very grateful to have Dr. Bruce Campbell as my primary cancer doctor. Knowing him as I do, I have thought it must be very difficult to practice medicine in an area such as cancer, where despite your best efforts, half your patients do not make it.

In discussing that life-and-death issue with this compassionate doctor, I learned he goes on by knowing he is trying his best. Dr. Campbell is buoyed by the medical advances being made and—most importantly—by seeing patients such as me survive and return to health.

Dr. Campbell contributes to *Heads Up*, a quarterly newsletter mailed to patients who have dealt with or are dealing with cancer of the head and neck. I have found his written pieces on the subjects of hope, attitude, happiness, and resolve, from someone on the front line of the fight against the enemy cancer, to be first rate and on target.

The following passage, from the May 2006 issue of *Heads Up*, scores a direct hit on the tragedy of smoking. It is used with permission of the author, Bruce Campbell, MD, FACS, and it appeared under the heading "Life Choices."

The little boy ran circles around his mother as she stood outside of the restaurant smoking a cigarette. The young woman and a friend were engaged in an animated discussion, and the smoke rolled from their mouths and drifted past their faces. Suddenly, the toddler stopped running and squeezed his mother's hand. Once her gaze had focused on him, he smiled broadly. She smiled back at him and he resumed running laps. She took a drag on her cigarette and resumed her conversation. I remember being charmed by the interaction but disturbed by the tobacco.

A few days later, I stood at the bedside with a family of a delightful woman in her mid-fifties. Her smoking-related cancer had re-

quired the removal of her voice box and a course of radiation therapy. Months later, her cancer had recurred and all her treatment options had now been exhausted. She was at peace, slipping in and out of wakefulness, and very near death.

The whole family had tried to prepare for this day and her adult children gathered in a semicircle around the bed. One of her boys sat dejectedly in a chair gripping her hand. As I watched, she slowly opened her eyes. He brightened visibly and wordlessly returned her gaze. She closed her eyes, but they both continued to smile. This, too, was a powerful yet disturbing moment. They knew that her death at such a young age had been preventable.

I was struck that the two scenes were essentially from the same drama, with the second following inexorably from the first. Within a few days, I had witnessed two points along the same arc.

Like me, Dr. Campbell uses quotations to help reinforce his point. This particular piece was headed with the following life philosophy from novelist George Bernard Shaw. "The person I miss most is the one I could have been."

The following note was sent to me by Dr. Campbell as a follow-up to an office visit and test result in the spring of 2001. I can tell you I was so happy and relieved I carried it around with me for weeks and even considered having it framed.

"Your CT Scan was fine. There has been no enlargement of the area where the cancer developed and no evidence whatsoever of any enlarged lymph nodes. I am always happy to give patients good news."

A HEAVY BURDEN

Golf pro John Daly not only smokes heavily but is also overweight. Obesity is the second cause, after smoking, of preventable death in America. It is now at epidemic proportions, with Americans weighing on average about 25 pounds more than in 1960. Carrying excess weight leads to a greatly increased risk of diabetes, heart disease, arthritis, and high blood pressure. Lately, researchers are determining that extra weight also increases the likelihood of breast and colon cancers. Equally troubling is that obesity is now the suspected culprit of a sharp rise of certain once-rare forms of cancer.

I feel fortunate to know Dr. J. Frank Wilson, an internationally respected radiation oncologist at the Medical College of Wisconsin. This good man has dedicated his distinguished career to the fight against cancer. According to Dr. Wilson, "If people didn't use to-bacco, the cancer death rate could probably drop 30 percent. And if they changed other unhealthy behaviors involving diet, alcohol, and exercise, the death rate could drop even more."

There is a quantifiable economic benefit from living healthy. With a pack of smokes costing $4 these days, a pack-a-day puffer could keep $1,460 a year from going up in smoke. According to the Centers for Disease Control and Prevention, smokers' medical costs run about $1,800 a year higher than for nonsmokers. Those who are over-weight have health-related costs that run close to $1,000 higher than average. Understandably, smokers and the obese pay substantially more for life and disability protection, as well.

Dick and Dolores were favorite clients of mine. I was amused whenever we inventoried their investments together and the now-deceased "good guy" Dick would bring up his cigarette account. Wisely, they had given up smoking years before, and now had a couple of thousand dollars to show for it in a fun-money account. Any couple breaking this expensive habit today would breathe easier and expand their budget with thousands of extra dollars a year.

History gives us many lessons. The health saga of one of the nineteenth century's celebrated heroes offers a warning that holds true today. Mark Twain developed a close relationship with Ulysses S. Grant, Civil War hero and later President of the United States. Historians have documented that although Grant was a great general and the indispensable military man President Lincoln counted on to win the war and preserve the Union, Grant as president was a poor civilian administrator, presiding over an administration rocked by widespread corruption. His inattention and misjudgment of charac-ter also hurt Grant in his post-presidential personal finance dealings, when he entrusted his entire fortune to a fast-talking, unscrupulous Wall Street charlatan who swindled him out of his money and left him nearly destitute.

In this era it is difficult for us to imagine a former president and military officer without the income security of a hefty government pension or adequate life insurance. Yet the financial security in retirement of public officials and military officers that now is taken for granted was not available to Grant in 1880.

Twain first suggested and then persuaded his friend and idol to write a personal memoir of his military life as a means of financially supporting his wife, Julia. During the period when he was penning this memoir, Grant complained to her that he was experiencing excruciating pain while eating a peach. Soon after this consumer of thousands of cigars in his lifetime was diagnosed with terminal throat cancer and left his dear Julia a widow.

The former president proved an adept writer. He exemplified courageous tenacity in a race with death to finish a two-volume book that Twain then published. Finished in Grant's last days, his *Personal Memoirs* is widely considered one of the finest works of nineteenth-century nonfiction. Thanks to Twain's foresight and Grant's talent, the royalty payment to Grant's widow was the largest ever up to that time and allowed Julia to live the remaining years of her life in dignity and financial security. She was, however, robbed of the companionship that a healthier lifestyle on Grant's part would have afforded to them both.

LIFE IS GOOD

Let me introduce you to my friend and client John N. When it comes to taking care of himself, he is the polar opposite of the likes of John Daly. John N. is an insulin-dependent diabetic. However, far from limiting him, this very serious chronic and potentially debilitating disease actually makes him more determined to be strong and spurs him on as a husband, father, and volunteer.

John N. is one of the many quiet heroes living strong in our midst.

Although he does not take home a dime in salary or wages, he is nonetheless a valuable producer in immeasurable ways. His best friend and life partner is his wife, Peggy. Together they make a remarkable team, managing to raise and educate their son and daughter, make a living and secure their financial future, and give back to the community—all the while dealing admirably with John's diabetes.

Like more and more couples, theirs is a nontraditional working arrangement. John was one of the early stay-at-home dads. Peggy, an attorney, holds a demanding executive position at a children's hospital. Owing to John's health and Peggy's law degree and earning capacity, this role reversal has worked out well for them.

Stay-at-home is an inaccurate description for John. He has generously volunteered tens of thousands of hours at the parish school their children first attended. Unlike me, John is good at working with his hands. He skillfully restored two of their own older homes, built a science lab for the school, and lent his talent with a hammer to Habitat for Humanity.

George Sheehan, M.D., celebrated marathon-running doctor and author of the bestseller *Running and Being,* along with *This Running Life* and others, had a definite influence on me. Dr. Sheehan was truly a philosopher of life who discovered through the exercise of running, and by accepting the ultimate challenge of the marathon, a way of living.

I have devoured all his books and heard him speak a couple of times at running clinics in the early 1980s. I ran and completed marathons in 1980, 1982, and 1984. When Maggie came into our life in 1985, that was it for this 26.2 mile distance.

Sheehan's books are littered with life planning quotes drawn from such notables as psychologist Abraham Maslow, psychiatrist Viktor Frankl, and especially philosopher William James. "Man must be stretched," James wrote, "if not in one way, then another."

Through his writing, George Sheehan lets us in on his personal life. At the start, we see this New Jersey native as a stressed, out-of-condition, frazzled father of 10 children. He is reborn in midlife through running and gains stature as an enthusiast and guru for the sport. His long-distance uphill journey continues with doubts of faith and periods of separation from his wife and the mother of his children, Mary Jane. The doctor then becomes a patient with prostate cancer, turning to bicycling for his aerobic exercise and reconciling with his family and church. In his last miles, he experiences dying and the ultimate finish line of death from the disease.

Dr. Sheehan felt that the secret to a long and healthy life is to have a chronic disease, then take excellent care of oneself. Returning to the story of my diabetic friend John N., for the last several years, he and Peggy have diligently trained for and completed a 105-mile bicycle ride through Death Valley to raise money for the Juvenile Diabetes Research Foundation (JDRF). According to exercise expert Dr. Sheehan, biking 105 miles is the equivalent of running a marathon. In bike riding circles, the accomplishment of biking 100 miles is called doing a century.

As a result of a lifestyle that includes careful attention to diet and regular exercise, along with complete avoidance of alcohol and tobacco, John is fit as a fiddle. He nevertheless has to be on constant guard to control his diabetes. For example, while he and I were on a training bike ride, he regularly stopped to monitor his blood sugar.

Together, John and Peggy raised over $10,000 for each of the last several years in the JDRF "Ride for a Cure." This cause is definitely close to their hearts, and the money raised makes a real difference. The December 2004 issue of *Forbes* profiled how this charitable organization efficiently puts money to work. JDRF has "a single-minded drive to find a definitive cure for juvenile diabetes." The report states that an effective cure may well be in sight to end this disease. Until that day, I expect John and Peggy N. will continue to saddle up.

When the couple sent a thank you card recognizing our support of diabetes research, they signed it with the affirmation "Life is good." Their lives are good because they have the discipline and commitment to make not just their own lives better but also the lives of others, in spite of the challenges they face.

MY LIFE AND DEATH STORY

My own highly personal life and death story started the third week of March 2000 when I was driving alone to Madison on business. Experiencing no pain or discomfort, I happened to touch my neck and felt a lump on the left side. It seemed strange and definitely different when I compared it to the right side. A flash of panic came over me. Could this newfound lump portend something ominous?

During my latest, now-routine annual follow-up visit with Dr. Campbell, I picked up a brochure in his clinic on warning signs of head and neck cancers, prepared by the American Academy of Otolaryngology, a group that specializes in head and neck diseases. An otolaryngologist is much better-known among us nonmedical types as an ENT, an abbreviation for ear, nose and throat docs.

Since my cancer, I learned that head and neck cancers are fifth on the dark list of cancer killers. I learned that a lump in the neck is at the top of the warning signs for that category of cancer. "Cancers that begin in the head or neck usually spread to lymph nodes in the neck before they spread elsewhere. A lump in the neck that lasts more than two weeks should be seen by a physician as soon as possible."

After finding this mysterious lump, I naturally told Cathy about it, whose training as a nurse makes her more knowledgeable on these matters. She calmed me down and said not to be overly concerned, as it probably was due to swelling and at worst may be infected. She sensibly said if it didn't go away, I should call my doctor.

The next week I attended a quarterly board meeting for the Wisconsin Chapter of the National MS society. After, I was driving John Fleming back to my office to discuss a personal finance matter. Dr. Fleming is a fellow board member and a noted neurologist at the University of Wisconsin Medical School. I was troubled by the suspicious lump on my neck and fortuitously found myself with a trusted and compassionate doctor and personal acquaintance sitting next to me in my car.

Coincidentally, his surname is the same as that of my mother's family. My maternal grandfather, uncle, and a first cousin are each named John Fleming. For all I know, the doctor and I could be distantly related.

So I asked my passenger if I could ask him a personal medical question, and he graciously obliged. Is this, pointing to my neck, something I need to be concerned with and bring to the attention of my doctor? He reached over, felt my neck, and remarked that the lump was in the lymph nodes, and although my wife was likely correct, I would be wise to see my primary doctor. I phoned my doctor the very next day to make an appointment.

Dr. Drayna, my long-time internist, was obviously keen to the warning signs of head and neck cancers. He said something to the effect that I needed to have this sucker cut out, dropped in a bucket, and put on a slide under a scope to find out what we were dealing with. He immediately directed me to an ENT specialist, Dr. Wermuth, who did a thorough examination, ordered the requisite battery of tests, and scheduled me for surgery. I do recall Dr. Wermuth telling me that my one tonsil looked a little funny, but not cancerous, and that while I was under for surgery he would be taking a snip to biopsy.

At my presurgery physical in the office of Dr. Drayna, he tried to relieve my anxiety, noting positively that my chest X-ray was clear and blood tests were normal. He did share with me upfront the possibility they would find I had lymphoma, but not to worry too much, as he felt confident it could be dealt with.

My day surgery ended up far from routine. The lump in my neck was indeed malignant. The surgeon reported the tough news to my wife, who was sitting anxiously in the waiting room. It was not the lymphoma he was expecting, but rather squamous cell carcinoma, a more deadly form of cancer. This was surprising to the medical specialists, as I was up to that point a healthy 49-year-old lifetime non-smoker.

With this particular form of oral cancer, Dr. Wermuth needed Cathy's permission to go back in and surgically remove that funny looking tonsil, as he needed to find the original source. It turned out to be cancerous after all.

Cathy inquired as to the staging of my cancer and was shocked to hear Dr. Wermuth declare it was fourth stage, the absolute worst case. He explained that was due to the size of the intertwined tumors; it had already moved from the tonsil to the lymph nodes. He did offer his belief he had gotten all of it.

Knowing what I was up against, I sought the best local follow-up treatment I could find, which brought me to Froedtert Hospital and the Medical College of Wisconsin. I recall as though it were yesterday sitting beside my wife in the tight-quartered examining room of medical oncologist Dr. Tom Anderson.

Dr. Anderson started by saying mine, unfortunately, was a major league cancer. He, too, was surprised I had squamous cell, as this is most commonly found in older men who are heavy smokers. He would much have preferred to be combating lymphoma, as he had a greater arsenal of treatment options available to successfully defeat that cancer.

Solemnly, Dr. Anderson went on to say that for every other cancer patient he saw with this diagnosis he had to deliver the grim prediction that they were unlikely to make it. In my own case, thank God, he said he had reason to believe I would win out. Because I was 49 and had a whole lot to live for, Dr. Anderson would be throwing everything he had to win this life-and-death struggle.

In the book *No Such Thing As a Bad Day,* three-time cancer survivor Hamilton Jordan speaks for me and for others who face the terror of this disease by writing, "All I ever wanted was a fighting chance."

Dr. Anderson finished our meeting by asking me to confirm the timeline between my initial discovery of the lump on my neck and that day in his office. He asked whether I had actually discovered this lump only seven weeks earlier. After all, he said, it was asymptomatic, meaning without symptoms. I replied that I had never felt better. I had seen my primary physician promptly within two weeks of finding the mass. He had immediately sent me to a specialist, who performed the surgery two weeks later.

As I sat in the medical oncologist's office, less than two months from the start of this odyssey. Dr. Anderson said, "John, if you were a physician, it is likely you would have procrastinated and waited six months, and it would have been too late."

In Dr. Anderson's professional opinion, this cancer would have spread to organs such as the liver, and all hope would be lost. Thank God I followed the course I did. And thanks to Cathy, Dr. Fleming, Dr. Drayna, and Dr. Wermuth for helping to save my life.

AN OUNCE OF PREVENTION IS WORTH A POUND OF CURE

Professional athletes such as Lance Armstrong are told when competing or training to listen to their bodies. That's because we know our own bodies best and should use this familiarity as an early warning system for when something is not right.

Regular monthly self-exams of the breasts for women and testes for men from the age of 20 on is a smart and easy preventive measure. If any changes or abnormalities are noted, a physician should be consulted.

Brian Piccolo was a running back with the Chicago Bears in the late 1960s when he developed a close friendship with teammate and future football legend Gayle Sayers. Like thousands of other young men in their twenties, including Lance Armstrong, Brian was struck with testicular cancer.

The 1971 made-for-television movie *Brian's Song* tells the heartwarming tale of his interracial friendship with Sayers and his courageous fight with the deadly opponent cancer. Sportscaster Bob Costas, who offered the remembrances at his hero Mickey Mantle's funeral service, has said there is not a real guy alive who doesn't cry when viewing *Brian's Song*.

After several years of sitting on the bench, Brian—an undrafted overachiever—finally received some playing time with the Chicago Bears after an injury sidelined his roommate, the gifted Sayers. Determined to make the most of his opportunity, the ultra-competitive

Piccolo vowed to himself to never come off the field, and so played on despite a persistent cough. Late in the season, after scoring a touchdown, he was forced to leave the game due to severe chest pains. Test results revealed cancer, which had spread to his lungs. Seven months later, this athlete died at age 26. Left behind was his grieving wife—they were high school sweethearts—and their three young daughters.

There is a human tendency, probably more pronounced in men, to put out of mind that which you would rather not think about. But procrastination could well prove dangerous. In contrast, I and so many others fighting the odds are living to attest to the reality that early intervention can make all the difference to survival.

As health is indeed more valuable than wealth, each of us needs to find and regularly use a caring, primary doctor—someone you would be inclined to contact immediately when you find a lump, have a persistent cough, discover something out of the ordinary, or anything that just doesn't feel right. It is said that even with the many sophisticated diagnostic tools available in modern medicine today, physicians still base 80 percent of their evaluations on the old-fashioned method of asking patients questions about how they feel and what's bothering them.

HARD TO SWALLOW

Although Ulysses S. Grant suffered from throat cancer, he actually died of starvation, because at the end of his days he could not swallow. In 1885, there were no feeding tubes such as we have today.

To combat my own cancer, I endured seven weeks of intensive radiation treatment targeted to my neck. One of the multiple side effects was that after a while I found it very difficult to swallow. Speaking from personal experience, it is nearly impossible to eat or drink if you can't swallow. To make matters worse, as a result of radiation I developed mouth sores, my tongue swelled, I produced little saliva, and the acidity of liquids I customarily enjoy such as orange or tomato juice burned my throat. On top of all this, I pretty much lost my taste buds, so that everything tasted like metal mush.

As a result I lost close to 40 pounds, averaging a loss of three-quarters to a pound per day over the course of a mere six weeks. Each week the medical and nutrition staff carefully monitored me and weighed me. They came very close to inserting a feeding tube through my nose. To avoid this radical step, I learned to collect a mouthful of ice water to numb my tongue, then work hard to drink and swallow a small volume of nutritional supplement, or what I call liquid fat. An eight-ounce can containing 600 calories sometimes took me 45 minutes of sustained effort to get down. Then I had to rest before trying to consume another can. Swallowing is one of those actions like breathing that we take for granted. Now, I relish the simple act of gulping a cup of water whenever I want.

THE COURT AND CANCER

I find it of interest that of the nine members of the U. S. Supreme Court at the start of 2005, four had been treated for cancer. Former Justice Sandra Day O'Connor, the first woman to sit on the highest court of the land, successfully fought breast cancer in 1988. She is now part of a sorority of over two million American women who survived this insidious disease. Justice John Paul Stevens beat back the prostate cancer he had in 1992. Breast cancer for women and prostate cancer in men are the two most common forms of the disease. The bad news is that the incidence of this gruesome twosome is rising owing to a variety of factors. The good news is that these widespread cancers, as in the cases of Justices O'Connor and Stevens, can be effectively treated and are highly survivable. The key to survival is early discovery and treatment.

Chief Justice William Rehnquist died of thyroid cancer in 2005 at the age of 80. Depending on the type, thyroid cancer is highly survivable, with up to a 90 percent cure rate. As with many cancers, however, certain rare and aggressive forms—which was apparently the case with Justice Rehnquist—can lead to death within a year.

Justice Ruth Bader Ginsburg was treated for colon cancer in 2000. Screening such as a colonoscopy can detect and remove precancerous polyps before they develop into colon cancer. Preventive screening is credited with significantly reducing the incidence of colon cancer deaths.

TV news anchor Katie Couric lost her husband, Jay Monahan, to colon cancer in 1998 at the age of 42. Scarred by her husband's untimely demise, Couric used her high-profile celebrity status to urge colon cancer screening, going as far as enduring an on-air colonoscopy to raise awareness.

In yet another example of health being more important than wealth, Katie Couric recently signed a network TV contract for a reported $20 million annually. Some might look at hers as a fairy tale life; yet, in addition to losing her husband and having to raise her two young daughters as a single mom, in 2001 she also lost her sister, Emily Couric, an attorney, to pancreatic cancer, a particularly lethal disease.

My Aunt Cassie's death from colon cancer and my respect for her memory were my impetus to undergo a routine colonoscopy. The procedure wasn't a big deal, and I felt very good when the doctor told me everything looked normal and I was good for 10 years before needing a follow-up.

Senator John McCain's face shows the visible effects of skin cancer. It is surmised the problem might well have been the result of harsh conditions he spent as a prisoner of war in North Vietnam. Hamilton Jordan also had skin cancer, which he attributes to his youth spent in Georgia as a lifeguard trying to achieve the popular bronzed look.

Skin cancer is prevalent in our nation of sun worshippers, and although it is usually very treatable, no form of cancer should be taken lightly. All can be fatal. Maureen Reagan, daughter of the late president, died at age 55 from skin cancer. Even if a form of cancer carries a 95 percent survival rate, for the 5 percent who don't make it, it is a deadly serious disease.

I must admit when I learn someone has cancer or has died of it, I seek to know the type, their age, and the stage. Then I mentally calculate survival rates and odds as I understand them and compare them to what I personally faced.

THE AMAZING STORY OF MICHAEL MILKEN

In the late 1980s, star financier Michael Milken gained fame and an immense fortune as the "junk bond king." Indicted on securities charges in a case of how the mighty can fall, he was summarily dethroned, ingloriously served 22 months in federal prison, paid a huge chunk of his wealth in fines, and was permanently banned from the investment business.

In 1993 when Milken was released from prison, he faced a graver sentence—that of a deadly cancer. Doctors were certain prostate cancer would take his life before the year was out. Undeterred, Milken sought the best medical treatment he could find.

In a last-ditch effort to save his life, Michael Milken underwent experimental hormone therapy in addition to more conventional radiation. In addition, the former self-professed junk food addict radically changed his diet, avoiding fat completely.

Not only did he survive, but in the same year he started the Prostate Cancer Foundation, kick-starting it with $25 million of his own money. With missionary zeal, Milken now focuses his considerable talents on a revolutionary and effective approach to this particular disease, which strikes 230,000 American men annually.

Amazingly, just as he shook up the staid world of corporate finance in his Wall Street days, he is widely credited with making significant progress against prostate cancer.

According to a feature story in *Fortune* magazine, "Milken has managed to raise the profile of prostate cancer significantly, increasing funding dramatically to fight the disease, spur innovative research, attract new people to the field, get myriad drugs into clinical trials, and, dare we say, speed up science."

In 1993, when Milken himself was in line to be a fatality, 35,000

American men died of prostate cancer. The National Cancer Institute reports that since that time, there has been a 26 percent decline in prostate cancer deaths.

GENETICS AND CANCER

Since prostate cancer is very often a family disease, I believe I carry an inherited gene that will trigger the disease in the coming years. Yet I am not scared, as I am confident it will not take my life.

My father died of prostate cancer at the age of 71. His father had prostate cancer but ended up dying of a cerebral hemorrhage. I know from my father that his grandfather, our namesake, died a painful death from prostate cancer. My dad's only brother, my uncle Bill, had prostate surgery a couple of years back. He is fortunately doing well, owing to early intervention and more advanced treatments. My dad and uncle had one sister, and she had one son, my cousin Michael. Michael recently dealt aggressively and successfully with the appearance of prostate cancer at age 57.

The fact is that prostate cancer, like breast cancer in women, has a definite genetic link. The chances are one of every six men will develop prostate cancer in his lifetime, most often after reaching age 50. The odds go up to one in three for those who have a close relative with the disease. As physicians say on hearing my impressive family history, the risk of my and my two younger brothers facing prostate cancer is high, 80 percent.

Having dodged one cancer bullet, I am vigilant about being blindsided by another. My confidence in surviving a subsequent cancer when it inevitably appears comes from my doctor's and my watching the possibility like hawks. Because prostate cancer is slow-growing, early detection allows for effective treatment and a very high cure rate. However, if it moves beyond the gland it is considered not curable. The outcome is a particularly painful death, such as I witnessed my dad endure.

Two routinely simple screens are used to detect early evidence of prostate cancer while it is confined to the prostate gland and highly curable: the Digital Rectal Exam (or DRE) and the Prostate-Specific Antigen (PSA) test.

The digital rectal exam takes only seconds as part of a routine physical. Your doctor probes the prostate for suspicious lumps. The PSA is a diagnostic blood test to detect abnormally high levels of antigen produced by the body. A normal PSA and DRE are strong indicators that prostate cancer is not present. Each screen is a defensive step to have checked every year. With my family history, I am proud to say I get checked regularly during my annual physical. This preemptive screening is not only smart but also reassuring.

Michael Milken found redemption through his valiant efforts to combat prostate cancer. His epitaph has changed dramatically, from disgraced Wall Street felon to that of savior for millions of men who will face a tamer, survivable diagnosis because of his efforts.

As someone expecting to be victimized by prostate cancer, I derive confidence from knowing that many men such as Michael Milken have come out on top of this potentially fatal disease. In addition to my uncle and cousin, golf legend Arnold Palmer beat back this unwelcome cancer. Senators and presidential candidates Bob Dole and John Kerry are high-profile prostate cancer survivors, as is former New York City Mayor Rudy Giuliani.

Colin Powell is yet another survivor of prostate cancer, a disease especially prevalent among African American men. Gulf War General Norman Schwarzkopf and New York Yankees manager Joe Torre each defeated this male scourge and now lend their celebrity status to the cause of helping other men join their survivors team.

STOCKS FOR THE LONG RUN

Allow me to now make the transition from talk of male prostate health to the world of stock investing.

Success in reaching your own long-term financial planning goal dictates ownership in stocks. As someone wrote in *Kiplinger's Personal Finance* magazine, "The mantra for the long-term investor should be stocks-stocks-stocks."

Wharton School finance professor Jeremy J. Siegel is the author of *Stocks for the Long Run*. As a foremost authority on the value of a patient and disciplined common sense investment approach to stock ownership, he echoes this stance. Siegel states, "I concluded that stocks were clearly the asset of choice for virtually all investors seeking long-term growth. Stocks are the best and, in the long run, the safest way to accumulate wealth."

Over the long term, stocks have clearly proven the best-performing asset class, easily outpacing both bonds and cash. In fact, since 1926 through November 2005, the return of the S&P 500 was 10.4 percent, almost double the return of corporate bonds and triple that of Treasury bills. In the 30-year period from 12/31/75 thru 12/31/05, the return advantage of stocks over bonds and Treasury bills was even better. An initial $10,000 investment made in large-cap U.S. stocks at the start grew in value by the end of that time to $361,929; bonds to $123,700; and Treasury bills or money market cash to $57,065. As an added bonus, stocks have proven the best tonic in the fight against inflation, capable of producing real rates of return (the return after factoring out annual inflation rates).

The good news about stocks is that for investors with a time horizon of five years or more, the odds of stocks outperforming other investment classes are overwhelmingly in their favor. In all five-year periods over the past 50 years, stocks have outperformed other investment classes 83 percent of the time. For those living with stocks for the long run, equities have outperformed other investment classes 100 percent of all 20-year periods.

The downside of these returns is that stock investors must cope with higher levels of risk and volatility. To benefit from these superior investment vehicles, you as an individual must develop the ability to withstand risk.

Stock performance conforms to the classic risk/reward equation. The task at hand is learning how to enjoy the sweetness of bull markets without suffering unduly from the bitterness of bear markets. Although stocks trend up about 85 percent of the time, the pain of down years can outweigh that pleasure. It is a typical pattern for stocks to rise slowly and gradually, but fall quickly and sharply.

Year-to-year volatility in the equity markets tests the mettle of the typical investor. Sensible investors should never lose sight of the dark side (risk and volatility) inherent in stock ownership. But investors with a long-term view have been amply rewarded by the stock market's overall appreciation. Speaking of the risk of stock ownership, I like the message put out by James B. Conant when he said, "Behold the turtle. He makes progress only when he sticks his neck out."

In spite of stocks having the past performance advantage, many an investor remains unconvinced of their future prospects—having been badly burned in the tech wreck of 2000, severely wounded in the brutal three-year bear market of 2000-2002, and painfully aware of the fickle nature of the stock market and fortunes of individual stocks.

Stock market authority Jeremy Siegel confronts this pessimism head on, maintaining that stocks are and will remain an oasis for patient investors. The reward of stocks compared to more stable bonds is known in academic circles as the equity risk premium. Writing in the *Financial Analysis Journal*, Siegel says even the 2 to 3 percent extra annual return (premium) that investors expect with stocks over bonds would provide "ample reward for investors willing to tolerate the short-term risks of stocks."

The most admired stock investor of this era is Warren Buffett. Andrew Kilpatrick is among a handful of authors who have written books attempting to decipher what makes this legendary billionaire tick. In *Permanent Value*, Kilpatrick suggests the answer lies in Buffett's application of common sense. "Common sense may be the most important factor helping Buffett to make more money in the stock market than anyone; he is the only person on the Forbes 400 richest Americans list—and number one at that—who got there by investing."

The longer I am in the investment advisory business, now approaching 25 years, the more convinced I am that a course in market psychology would be a great asset to help investors act in a rational, common sense manner like Warren Buffett. Buffett and other astute investors follow three keys to success in stock investing: faith, patience, and discipline.

Faith often goes out the window in brutal bear markets, such as the one experienced during 2002 when many investors lost patience, panicked, and threw in the towel, exiting the market. In the summer of 2002, in the depth of that market meltdown, Charles Schwab wrote, "In my four decades of working with individual investors, I have never seen such a profound crisis of confidence."

This crisis in confidence also occurred in 1974 when events such as the Arab Oil Embargo triggered a global energy crisis, resulting in a severe recession that played out in the steepest market drop since the 1929 market crash and the Great Depression.

At the low point of this pessimism, the September 14, 1974, issue of *Business Week* ran a cover story titled "The Death of Equities." This respected magazine infamously reported "the flight of individual investors and the breakdown of the markets foreshadow the end of the capitalistic system as we have known it." That pessimism was unfounded.

To be a successful long-term investor, ignore the dips, don't get overly excited about the bursts, and patiently stay the course. High-profile investment advisor columnist Nick Murray amplified this point in the February 2005 issue of the industry magazine *Financial Advisor:* "At the end of the day, what markets do over a given year (or two, or three, or five) doesn't really matter that much." To their detriment, many investors are shortsighted, failing to focus on their long-term financial objectives. It helps to think of investing as more of a marathon than a sprint.

As fund firm T. Rowe Price informs us, a patient, long-term perspective conquers short-term anxieties. "Throughout history, the stock market has witnessed negative events—both at home and abroad—that have impacted its natural ebb and flow. Yet, despite these often catastrophic occurrences, the market has returned to a position of strength and has continued to reward investors over the years."

Forty-year-old Christopher Davis is a rising star in the investment management business. Morningstar named him its 2005 domestic stock manager of the year for ably steering his fund, Davis Selected Advisers.

I believe Davis is a good investment role model based on his common sense, patient, value approach to stock investing. Once he decides to buy a stock for his fund portfolio, he intends to own it for the long term. Referring to his fund portfolio over 2005, "Our turnover last year was around 6–7 percent. That implies a 10- or 15-year holding period." Contrast this patience to that of less successful portfolio managers and most rank amateurs, who trade (churn) stocks or mutual funds much more frequently.

As Nobel prize-winning economist Daniel Kahneman told the Associated Press, "It's clear from the research of individual investors, the main mistake people make is they churn their accounts too much. The advice to be diversified and not do too much is standard advice that people do not spontaneously follow. But not taking that advice is costly."

Vaunted investor Warren Buffett seconds low turnover as a winning investment strategy. "Occasionally, successful investing requires inactivity." Maybe the nontraditional advice, "Don't just do something, stand there," says it best.

Paul Samuelson was a prominent economist as well as author of the popular economics textbook I used in college. His solid advice is along the same line: "You shouldn't spend much time on your investments. That will just tempt you to pull up the plants and see how the roots are doing and that's very bad for the roots."

Christopher Davis was queried in a *Fortune* magazine interview about whether he had any investing resolutions for the new year. "No. But I would say the old lesson that has been reinforced over the past several years is the futility of short-term forecasts. When you look at what's happened in the past five to six years, in terms of stocks both going up and going down, the experts have been consistently and dramatically wrong."

Regarding the future direction of the market, it should be abundantly clear from past predictions that no forecaster possesses a crystal ball. Nevertheless, that fact doesn't slow the steady torrent of conflicting and confusing reads.

All predictions, however seemingly authoritative, should be taken with a big helping of the proverbial grain of salt. Seventy-something-year-old Dick Davis, a retired stockbroker living in Florida, says it like it is: "If indeed the market is unpredictable, then trying to predict the unpredictable has to be the ultimate exercise in futility. Yet, we are inundated by market prognosticators wherever we turn, particularly on television."

Legendary Milton Friedman died in 2006 at the advanced age of 94. He was perhaps the most influential economist of the last half of the twentieth century. This brilliant man and memorable quotesmith said, "The economy and the stock market are two different things."

However, if you listen to the talking heads and prognosticators who fill the airwaves, they would have us believe Friedman's assertion must be absurd. For during the early summer of 2006, it was abundantly clear from their reading of the economic tea leaves that we were headed for stagflation, owing to a fizzled housing bubble and a weak domestic auto industry, coupled with rising energy and commodity prices. Translation: they predicted a slowing economy along with rising inflation. Surely, in such an environment, stocks would not prosper.

Although admittedly counterintuitive, Milton Friedman's observation was astute. In spite of the forecast, the stock market put on an impressive rally that caught skeptics flatfooted, missing out on strong 15 percent returns over the next six months.

It is instructive to learn from the lessons of past bear markets. The worst stock market period occurred in 1931 in the midst of the Great Depression, when the Dow average lost a heart-stopping 43.3

percent. The best year for Dow stocks followed a short two years later when the market rocketed to a 53.9 percent gain.

The S&P 500 dropped 26.5 percent in 1974, which followed on the heels of a steep 14.7 percent decline in 1973 and prompted the-end-of-the-world-as-we-knew-it talk in certain circles. Investors who believed this darkly pessimistic talk missed out on resounding returns for the S&P of 37.2 percent in 1975 and 23.8 in 1976. The S&P lost value in three successive years, off 9.1 percent in 2000, down 11.9 percent in 2001, and recipient of an even bigger hit in 2002 when it coughed up a loss of 22.1 percent.

In the sport of boxing, when a tired, scared, or defeated fighter fails to answer the bell and leave his corner to continue to fight, his manager throws a towel in the middle of the ring. This act signals that the dejected fighter had given up and conceded the match to his opponent.

Investors are prone to give up and throw in the towel during deep bear markets. The cruel irony of investing is that the worse the stock market performs, the higher its future returns will be. It is simple mathematics that proves true time and again, but somehow human nature urges us to bail out before things get better. As the saying goes, the darkest hour is just before the dawn.

In our firm's October 2002 monthly client communication piece, we address the worst period for stocks since 1973-1974 and the Great Depression. In difficult seas I seek out experienced skippers for calm and sound advice. In that issue we quoted veteran mutual fund manager Chuck Royce, founder of the Royce family of funds. According to this long-time portfolio manager:

A bear market is the wrong time to get cautious. It's the right time to increase risk. It's the wrong time to decrease risk. You want to increase risk because there are higher reward possibilities looking out a couple of years. If markets go down, you want to add to your positions, not subtract from them....

Some years back, during a downturn in the stock market, mutual fund firm Twentieth Century Investors (renamed American Century

Investors) ran a series of print ads depicting the bounce-back capability of a tennis ball compared to that of an egg. The point the firm was illustrating was that stock performance is not like an egg that stays permanently splattered but rebounds, similar to a falling tennis ball. Losses in a grounded stock market are not permanent unless the investor sells. Patient and confident stock investors see their portfolio values bounce back, just like they did in 2003. Optimists seeing the glass as half full view the market as a tennis ball, whereas pessimists look at the glass as half empty and think the market acts like an egg.

One former client took strong exception to this optimistic advice, disgruntled over the drop in value of his stock fund portfolio. He barked something to the effect of staying in the stock market was like "throwing money down a rat hole" and instructed us to throw in the towel.

As it worked out, his timing was perfect—that is, perfectly wrong. For the stock market started a strong recovery on October 9, 2002, and the S&P 500 rebounded very strongly in 2003, up 28 percent.

Jeremy Siegel wrote a guest editorial in *The Wall Street Journal* on July 25, 2002, near the very bottom of the doom and gloom of the bear market. Ninety-nine percent of U.S. stock mutual funds lost money in the third quarter of 2002. In a well-reasoned piece titled "Stocks Are Still an Oasis," he correctly called a dramatic market turn. "History is definitive that once investors have suffered this much pain, subsequent stock returns will be very rewarding. Amid all this gloom, the market looks very inviting to me indeed."

Following six straight months of declines in the stock market, stocks moved up across the board during October 2002. The Dow actually recorded its second-best October on record, up a healthy 10.6 percent for the month.

Siegel, in that same guest editorial, chose to quote Frank J. Williams, a renowned early twentieth-century investor. "The market is most dangerous when it looks best; it is most inviting when it looks worst."

Master investor Ralph Wanger, now retired, had a distinguished career as a mutual fund manager, notably with the Acorn funds. According to Wanger, the most important survival skill for stock investors is to stay levelheaded. He warns that deceptions lurk, and that statistics and performance claims can be very misleading.

Wanger says the most important advice he can give stock investors is to "have a strategy, a way of looking at the world of stocks." Most investors do not. Consequently, their portfolios end up as a "haphazard collection of stories," all because they have no plan or discipline, chasing whatever is the latest fad, buying at the top.

Make no mistake about it, investing is a tough, challenging pursuit, made more frustrating and ineffective if not pursued with basic investment sense. Stock ownership should be a patient, eyes-open, long-term proposition. Patience has proven the best response to the risk of volatility.

I wholeheartedly agree with Bill Gross, who uses the following analogy in his book *Everything You've Heard About Investing is Wrong!* "Investing is a long-distance race, and because it is, investors should pattern their behavior after a marathon runner's—not a sprinter's. Marathoners pace themselves, plan ahead, and run within their physical limits. Investors must do the same."

Professor Siegel seconds this timeless wisdom. "The pursuit of hot stocks or the next big thing dooms investors to poor returns."

Following through on Ralph Wanger's call to follow a plan for investing in stocks, and in keeping with my theme of simplicity, I offer T. Rowe Price Spectrum Growth (PRSGX) for consideration as a common sense investment. This broadly diversified fund is made up of 11 actively managed funds from among T. Rowe Price's extensive stock mutual fund menu.

Morningstar gives this all-in-one equity fund its coveted five-star ranking, saying it "provides a terrific alternative to investors who would rather not build their own portfolio of stock funds."

This packaged investment covers the entire stock investment spectrum: hence, the fund's name. With this one fund, the investor gains exposure to both large and small cap stocks, and both value and growth styles, including domestic and international holdings.

A senior T. Rowe Price investment committee regularly meets to review this fund portfolio, with an eye on trimming back on areas they believe overvalued and bulking up where they find good value. In effect, they sensibly practice buying low and selling high and re-balancing.

All in all, a strong case can be made that T. Rowe Price Spectrum Growth is the only stock investment you need to own.

EQUITY INCOME FUNDS: GIVING THE DIVIDEND ITS DUE

An equity income fund is a solid building block in constructing a portfolio that should appeal to conservative investors, such as those in retirement. Two quality income funds worth taking a look at are Vanguard Equity Income (VEIPX) and T. Rowe Price Equity Income (PRFDX).

Funds like these are basically stock (equity) funds whose hold-ings yield above-average returns (income) in the form of dividend payouts. Over the long term (1926–2005), 40 percent of stock re-turns can be traced to dividends, the balance to capital appreciation.

Such a makeup allows conservative investors the ability to play defense and offense simultaneously. In the inevitable down markets, such as we witnessed in 2002, dividends proved themselves by keep-ing a floor under stock prices. In that horrible year for stocks, while nondividend-paying stocks in the S&P 500 were down more than 30 percent, the dividend payers fell by less than half that, at 13.3 per-cent.

Dividend-paying, equity-income type funds are quite capable of outperforming the stock market as measured by the S&P, due in large part to the return the dividend adds to total return. According to Siegel, "You'll find that dividend payers that trade at reasonable valuations are the stocks that did the very best for investors over the long run."

In fact, according to research from Standard & Poors, dividend-paying stocks have historically outperformed nondividend payers by as much as 3 percent annually. Steve Galbraith, Morgan Stanley market strategist, believes, "Dividends, because they soothe shareholders, will continue to drive stock performance." Both the Vanguard and T. Rowe Price Equity Income fund offerings outperformed the S&P 500 in 2000 (big time), 2001, 2002 (by losing less), 2004, and 2005.

Well-managed equity income funds such as these help a retired investor become more defensively positioned and better prepared to cope with the next market decline. By their nature, higher-yielding stocks tend to be low-volatility, value-characterized companies. Yet the managers' focus on yield and dividend income from these stocks need not be at the expense of appreciation potential, which can be significant in bull markets such as occurred in 2003, when the Vanguard Equity Income posted a total return of 25.14 percent. By design, these two profiled funds offer the best of both worlds: upside potential with market appreciation of stocks, coupled with downside protection buoyed by an attractive dividend income.

Brian Rogers is the esteemed long-tenured portfolio manager of T. Rowe Price Equity Income Fund. He shines the light on yet another attractive feature of dividend-paying investments. Most dividend income now qualifies for the tax-favored 15 percent rate, instead of being taxed at the higher ordinary income rate, such as bond or money market income.

For a host of reasons, dividends are now back in style. Shown earlier, the yield from dividends provides an anchor in a volatile market. Many astute investors, including Warren Buffett, John Bogle, and Pimco's Bill Gross believe we are in an environment of single-digit equity returns. Consequently, earning a significant portion of return in the form of a dividend is attractive. For the first time in modern U.S. history, most dividends are taxed at the same rate as capital gains. This means capital gains no longer offer a tax advantage over dividend income. Demographic trends suggest aging babyboomers will shift to more income-oriented investments, continuing to fuel demand for these types of securities in the years ahead.

Investors not in need of current income from their investment in these equity income funds can choose to have that income automatically reinvested. This is a convenient way to accumulate additional shares and substantially grow a portfolio's value over time. Mutual funds are quite flexible, and this election can be easily switched to pay dividends in cash whenever needed. Jeremy Siegel is ebullient, writing in *Money* magazine, "I can't emphasize enough the importance of dividends and reinvesting those dividends."

In November of 2003 I heard Siegel speak at a Financial Planning Association conference in Philadelphia, where he introduced us to ishares Dow Jones Select Dividend Index (DVY) as his favorite investment. This fund is an ETF, or exchange traded fund. It is a hybrid, similar to an index mutual fund, yet trades on an exchange like a stock. Features that include low cost and tax efficiency make these relatively newer investment vehicles popular among investors in the know. At our firm, we put DVY in many of our clients' accounts, believing it makes for a good portfolio ingredient.

Seigel was attracted to DVY as a cheap, pure-play, dividend-paying stock fund. This offering from Barclays Global Investors screens to select 100 dividend-paying stocks, many of which have a history of regularly raising their dividend. The tax-favored dividend yield currently is an appetizing 3.5 percent.

Include fund leader Vanguard as believing in ETFs, as it has notably introduced a lineup of its own offerings. The latest, Vanguard Dividend Appreciation (VIG), is very similar to DVY, as it smartly offers conservative investors a low-cost avenue to a diversified portfolio of dividend-paying stocks.

Diversification as a common sense risk protection technique deserves continual emphasis. What makes DVY and VIG work is not only the juicy, tax-advantaged yield but the wide diversification available from the 100 stock holdings in the portfolio.

John Bogle, writing in the January-February 2006 issue of industry magazine *CFA* to promote his fifth book, *The Battle for the Soul of Capitalism,* says, "For all the inevitable density in the fog of investing there is much that we do know. We know that specific-security risk can be eliminated by diversification; so that only market risk remains (and that risk seems quite large)."

STAY THE COURSE

Recently, an illuminating study crossed my desk from mutual fund group Vanguard. It is directed to investment advisors for use in educating our nervous clients. This piece neatly summarizes the wisdom of maintaining a long-term investment outlook and using common sense to realize the superior performance advantage found in stocks.

To accomplish this, Vanguard effectively uses a line graph that charts annual performance returns for each of the 80 years over the period 1926–2005. This analysis reveals that although stocks averaged a double-digit annual return of 10.4 percent over this long span, this is far from a *normal* or expected return in any given calendar year.

Most investors will be surprised to learn that in only six of those 80 years, or just 7.5 percent of the time, the market performance actually landed within a narrow range of plus or minus 2 percentage points of the historical return average. What we see is that the return pattern for any given year tends to fluctuate widely, both ahead of and below the line, but rarely close to the statistical average. In response to the variable winds of change and in keeping with its nautical theme, Vanguard sensibly urges all of us to "stay the course."

Investors understandably would prefer to have stocks produce a stable, nice fat 10 percent return year in and year out, like a 10 percent CD or bond coupon. Unfortunately, this has not been the nature of stock investing in the past 80 years, nor should it be expected in the future.

To benefit and earn the double-digit, long-term average return of stocks, investors have to exercise patience and discipline. To ignore the short-term movements of the market and focus on prospects for the long term, it helps to put blinders on and tune out all the noise and distractions.

This behavior is admittedly difficult for many fickle investors, as the stock market is like sailing on choppy seas, with wide swings up and down. Panicked investors with weak stomachs bail out in the depths of severe bear markets, such as occurred in 1974, and most recently in the middle of 2002.

Speaking of stocks for the long run, I like this quote from Walter Elliott: "Perseverance is not a long race; it is many short races one after another."

To be a successful long-term investor in stocks takes courage as well as a confident view of the future. Reading the headlines in the paper, watching the TV news reports of escalating war in the Middle East, or just filling up our gas tanks in times of skyrocketing gasoline prices, we admittedly find it difficult to have a positive outlook. There are plenty of clouds on the investment horizon to shake one's confidence, including the ever-present possibilities of higher interest rates, rising inflation, weakening economy, mounting deficits, or a drop in the value of the dollar.

T. Rowe Price prepared a chart to illustrate that the stock market has witnessed disastrous events through the years, both at home and abroad. Yet patient investors with a long-term perspective, capable of overcoming short-term anxieties, have been able to prosper in the market.

We tend to forget that in the decade of the 1950s, despite the Korean War, a prolonged recession, and a major Suez Canal crisis in the always-volatile Middle East, the average annual return of stocks that decade was a robust 19.35 percent.

In the 1960s, the Cuban missile crisis put us on the brink of nuclear war with the former USSR. This tumultuous decade also saw the assassinations of John F. Kennedy, Robert Kennedy, and Martin Luther King Jr. The streets of our major cities erupted in race riots and massive Vietnam anti-war protests. On the global front, the Berlin Wall symbolized the ever-present tensions of the Cold War. Still, stocks in the 1960s posted an average annual return of 7.65 percent.

The global energy crisis and the Arab oil embargo in the 1970s saw us waiting in long lines for gas. The economy experienced a severe recession. President Nixon was forced to resign in the fallout from the Watergate scandal. The stock market had its steepest drop in 40 years since the crash of 1929 and the start of the Great Depression. With all of this, the stock market still turned in a positive average annual return in that decade of 5.85 percent.

The decade of the 1980s was ushered in with the highest interest rates in history. The savings and loan crisis cost us taxpayers billions to clean up. The October 19, 1987, stock market crash was the biggest one-day drop on the New York Stock Exchange. In spite of all this, stocks in the decade of the 1980s averaged an annual return of 17.54 percent.

While it is true that stocks stumbled badly out of the gate the first three years of the new millennium, in retrospect that decline could almost be expected, as the major equity index averaged an annual return of a robust 18.20 percent in the decade of the 1990s.

Such a major advance over this 10-year span was far from steady. Blips occurred along the way, starting with the 1990 Gulf War, including Oklahoma City and domestic terror and the Asian currency crisis in 1997.

My partner, Mike Weil, came across the next quotation from legendary fund manager Peter Lynch, which we find right on:

Your ultimate success or failure will depend on your ability to ignore the worries of the world long enough to allow your investments to succeed. It isn't the head, but the stomach that determines [your] fate.

To summarize, in order to taste success when investing in stocks, it helps to digest the following:

- Invest for the long term. Always remember that investing in stocks is a marathon, not a sprint.
- Buy low and sell high, not the opposite.
- Patiently stay the course.

- Resist the urge to throw in the towel or bail out.
- Market timing does not work; time in the market does.
- Put blinders on and ignore the short-term moves and headline events in order to concentrate on the long-term.
- Be an optimist and view the glass as half full.
- To not diversify is to speculate, so by all means diversify, diversify, diversify.

CHAPTER 5

AROUND THE CORNER

> There is one thing which gives radiance to everything. It
> is the idea of something around the corner.
>
> G.K. Chesterton

Retired TV anchorman Tom Brokaw wrote a best-seller about World War II heroes, *The Greatest Generation*. His inspiration was the life-changing experience of covering the fortieth anniversary of the June 5, 1944, Normandy invasion, the turning point in that epic war.

Spurred emotionally in the process of writing that book, Brokaw coined the definitive description for the World War II generation. In Brokaw's own words, "It is, I believe, the greatest generation any society has ever produced."

Knowing my late mom and dad as I did, along with aunts and uncles, in-laws, neighbors, and now many clients—all of the World War II generation—I completely agree with Brokaw. These extraordinary men and women deserve the title "the greatest generation."

Compare today's climate with what these folks have lived through. Writing in *The Wall Street Journal*, columnist Jonathan Clements puts today's environment into historical prospective:

But let's face it, neither the U.S. economy nor the world affairs are nearly as volatile as they were in earlier decades. Think about it: Today's economic turmoil is nothing compared with the depression of the 1930s or the stagflation of the 1970s. Similarly the current Middle East conflict, terrible as it is, pales next to Vietnam, Korea and World War II.

Adversity, as 92-year-old investing legend John Templeton is fond of saying, is a great teacher, with lessons applicable to both life and finances. The greatest generation was weaned during the Great Depression, came of age in the Second World War, and raised families under the dark cloud of the Cold War. Despite all this, its members went on to build modern America. The World War II generation faced more than its fair share of rough times. Far from being fatalistic, however, it exhibited a sturdy resolve and, as noted in Brokaw's book, is still brimming with a can-do spirit.

Today's younger generations are apt to look at the glass half empty, what with the terror, the aftermath of 9/11, and a changing world economic outlook due to forces of globalism and technology.

American historian Stephen E. Ambrose authored more than a dozen popular history books. His final book, *To America*, subtitled *Personal Reflections of an Historian*, was his farewell. It is touchingly dedicated to his doctor, the nurses, and staff of the Stanley S. Scott Cancer Center at Louisiana State University. Sadly, Stephen Ambrose's life and work was cut short when he succumbed to lung cancer at the age of 69. He was a smoker.

Through his best-selling books about World War II, Ambrose is widely credited with bringing to light the story of "the bravery, steadfastness, and ingenuity of the ordinary young men, the citizen soldiers, who fought the enemy to a standstill—the band of brothers who endured together." In *Citizen Soldiers, D-Day, The Wild Blue,* and *Band of Brothers*, Ambrose often used first-hand accounts of how this greatest generation, despite seemingly insurmountable odds and a late start, united to defeat what Brokaw described as "the two most powerful and ruthless military machines ever assembled."

A native of Whitewater, Wisconsin, Ambrose wrote, "I was 10 years old when the war ended. I thought the returning veterans were giants who had saved the world from barbarism. I still think so. I remain a hero worshipper."

My long-time client Harding Pan is one of those millions of brave young men who dutifully answered the call and served our country in the Army during this terrible war. Harding fought in Europe, where he saw enough action for a lifetime while stationed for 150 successive days. Sixty of those days he was at the front in a foxhole, dirty, exhausted, eating K-rations. He had to be pulled out, too sick with jaundice even to be transported to a hospital.

Harding is the same age as my father, and their war experiences were similar. Each joined up as an 18-year-old. Dad served with the Third Army under General George Patton, while Harding was with the Seventh Army in Southern France. Harding expressed genuine regret at not having met my dad. As Stephen Ambrose observed, these comrades-in-arms and Eisenhower's boys maintained their band as brothers connections.

My father, John McCarthy, was seriously wounded November 19, 1944, when shrapnel tore into his back. He was rushed to a MASH unit, then sent on to a hospital in London where he spent three months recovering. I am proud to have the Purple Heart that Dad was awarded for bravery. My father's younger brother, my uncle Bill, believes this serious injury might well have saved Dad's life. For while he was lying in a hospital bed at Christmastime 1944, his unit suffered heavy casualties at the Battle of the Bulge. The German counterattack was a deadly last-ditch attempt to thwart the Allied momentum building to a march to victory.

The father of my associate Avis, Lloyd Bjelland, jumped behind enemy lines as one of the first World War II trained paratroopers. The boys in his band of brothers referred to Sergeant Bjelland as "Mother BJ," for the 26-year-old Norwegian farm boy from northwest Wisconsin took care of these young fellas in his unit, many of them fresh out of high school. Lloyd was severely wounded when shrapnel almost severed his arm at the Battle of the Bulge. His injuries led to an 18 months' hospital stay in England. When Lloyd's unit was deployed to Europe in the Spring of 1942, he had to leave his bride, Betty, pregnant with their first child. Avis's sister, Barbara, was nearly 3¹/₂ years old before she met her father for the first time.

In the book *Flags of Our Fathers,* James Bradley penned a moving retelling of the six marines who raised the American flag at Iwo Jima in the famous photo. One of the men in that dramatic picture was John "Doc" Bradley, a medic and the author's father. Like most battle-scarred veterans of that Great War, John Bradley sought to shut out his part and put it into the past. According to his son James, who was one of eight children, no copy of that immortal photograph would ever be found or mention of it take place in the Bradley home. When pressed about his heroics and immortality, John Bradley said, "The real heroes of Iwo Jima are the guys who didn't come back."

The father of my good friend Tony, Anthony "Tony" Leszczynski, was awarded two bronze stars for his valiant duty, also in the Third Army. He started out as a lowly private and earned his way up to an officer's rank as a lieutenant. Tony was among the first soldiers to hit Omaha Beach. The movie *Saving Private Ryan* offers a good idea of the carnage and danger Tony and his comrades faced on D-Day. Prior to his passing, Tony was profiled in a feature, "Heroes Among Us," in his small-town newspaper in northern Wisconsin. The story chronicles Sergeant Leszczynski's encounter with the great General George S. Patton himself.

It seems Tony had been involved in a heated disagreement with some local officials, who were protesting his unit's advance through their small French village, fearing a fire fight. At that, General Patton appeared on the scene and asked what was going on. "Son," he said, "the shortest distance between two points is a straight line." With orders direct from the very top, Sergeant Leszczynski and his men proceeded to take the village.

Like Lloyd, Tony also saw action at the Battle of the Bulge. Similar to John "Doc" Bradley, Tony's dad kept tight-lipped when asked what he did in the war to receive his medals. In this, these men were like Gordon Larsen, one of the veterans Brokaw profiles in *The Greatest Generation*. "I didn't talk about the war much. I spent most of my time trying to forget it."

The National World War II Memorial in Washington, D.C., is located between the Washington monument and the Lincoln Memorial. It seems only fitting this honor to the greatest generation sits in the nation's capital between monuments honoring our two greatest presidents.

Dedicated in May 2004, this memorial is a long-overdue tribute to the 16 million who served in uniform in World War II, along with the millions of Americans who supported the massive effort on the home front and, especially, the 400,000 who tragically lost their lives.

While on a family vacation to Washington, D.C., in spring 2005, I made it a point to visit the memorial and pay my respects.

Avis and I had each made a donation and had our fathers' names entered in the registry that is part of the WWII Memorial. When Tony's dad passed away, we also placed his name as a remembrance. His son told me this is what his father would have wanted. Walking among the monuments, I felt weak-kneed and emotional thinking of the extreme sacrifice and courage of brave men like Dad, Lloyd, Harding, and Tony so many years ago.

I am happy that Harding had the opportunity to travel to D.C. with his wife, Dorothy, and their granddaughter to attend the dedication of the National World War II Memorial. From this trip I have a picture of a serious-looking Harding, arm tenderly around his granddaughter, standing in front of the Atlantic monument. Speaking about this event afterward, Harding admitted to being as greatly moved as I expect only a direct participant of that epic drama could be.

THE CLASS OF 1919

I have had the distinct privilege of crossing paths with and getting to know five admirable members of the greatest generation, each of whom was born in 1919. They share much history in common and exhibit many similar traits. It occurred to me that this group of individuals and their personal stories have much to teach us about life and financial life planning.

Possessing 1919 birth certificates means they were born after the conclusion of World War I—the war to end all wars, as it was naïvely dubbed by contemporaries. Psychologists say we are shaped by what happened in our lives at 10 years of age. This group was indelibly marked by the stock market crash of 1929. As a result, their formative years were lived under the severe economic strain caused by the Great Depression.

These five were young adults on December 7, 1941, "a day that will go down in infamy," said President Franklin D. Roosevelt. Japanese forces struck a surprise attack on Pearl Harbor, propelling America's entry into World War II. Each was profoundly touched by this major event of the twentieth century.

President John F. Kennedy, born in 1917, was a contemporary of theirs. In his famous inaugural address, Kennedy observed that his generation was tempered by war. When this young president was assassinated on that dark November day in Dallas in 1963, my five acquaintances were 44. This national loss left a heavy mark on them.

FIVE CLASS MEMBERS

Meet Winifred, a member of the Class of 1919 and a lifelong favorite person of mine and family neighbor while I was growing up in Chicago. Winifred was a war bride during World War II, with two beautiful young children, a dark-haired toddler son Terry and blonde infant daughter Sheila. Her husband, Jimmy, was serving in the army as a pilot stationed at Fort Charles, Louisiana. He would write "My Dearest Wife" every day including Sunday afternoon, September 19, 1944. Tragically, the next day he was killed during a training exercise.

He had been able to see Sheila only once before he perished. Winifred learned of this shocking news via telegram and knew in her unimaginable grief that a last letter would follow in the mail. I am honored to have a copy of this touching, handwritten love letter. Winifred shared the letter with some of the nuns teaching school, who used it to impress upon their students the lesson of how in an instant lives can forever be changed. How different was Winifred's life than the one she had planned.

Another remarkable woman from the Class of 1919 was my Aunt Peggy, who in 1938 left the poverty and isolation of the rocky hills of Connemara in the west of Ireland to attend nursing school in England. Soon, war broke out between England and Nazi Germany, and she was pressed into service caring for the many casualties sent back to England. Nurses were issued gas masks, which they were required to have with them at all times in the event of an attack, although far from fashionable. These young women made do, improvising by using the masks as functional purses to carry their personal belongings. Sadly, Aunt Peggy passed away in 1994, but the surviving foursome class of 1919 is busy carrying on and living strong.

Maynard entered the army in 1941 as a young soldier at the start of World War II. He went on to make the military his career, retiring as an Air Force Colonel in 1974. Maynard now enjoys the financial security that comes from having earned a government pension. During my most recent visit with him, he noted he was approaching the anniversary of his retirement, 33 years, the same length of time he had dutifully served his country, including stints in Korea and Vietnam.

Each member of this hardy band married and raised a family in the shadow of the Great War and under the cloud of the Cold War. Their life spans coincided with an era of massive and rapid change, in which all levels of economic, political and social life were transformed. As a historical guidepost, a birth in 1919 marked the midpoint between two significant periods in American history: 1865 and 1973. In 1865 President Abraham Lincoln was assassinated, the Civil War ended, slavery was abolished, and railroads were crisscrossing the country. By 1973, as middle-aged 54-year-olds, this group witnessed the resignation of President Nixon, the Watergate trials, and daily updates of the Vietnam War and its protests on TV. The Dow Jones Industrial Average climbed to 1000, the Civil Rights movement was making positive inroads, and mankind left its footsteps on the surface of the moon.

This 1919 quintet experienced and saw a lot of life in their years on earth. You can see it reflected in their eyes.

Another woman in this group, Jean, now resides independently at a retirement apartment complex in Phoenix. One spry resident in his nineties regularly flirts with her, calling her kid. I visited her one beautiful Saturday morning in January. As we toured her comfortable first-floor unit, Jean proudly pointed out two framed photos of herself as a vibrant 18-year-old. She is pictured wearing full Native American regalia, complete with a feathered headdress and buckskin. The occasion was a formal ceremony to induct her into the Thunderbird Chief Clan as an honorary member of the Winnebago tribe. A pair of moccasins rests next to the photos, with the whole collection prominently displayed among her personal mementos.

Jean was raised in the central Wisconsin town of Tomah, where her grandfather had pioneered the development of cranberry marshes in the region. After completing high school and before heading off to college, this adventurous teenager opted to postpone her studies to help complete the fall cranberry harvest. Jean toiled in the marshes side by side with members of the Winnebago tribe, working in all phases of the harvest.

It is from this experience the Chief honored her as a member of the tribe. She was given the name Ahoo cho inga, which translated means "blue wings." Jean is proud to be an adopted blue-eyed member of the Winnebago tribe. The first thing I notice whenever I meet Jean is the bright sparkle in her blue eyes. Knowing in greater depth her life story and free spirit, I realize those dancing eyes belong to Ahoo cho inga.

When Evelyn, another member of this same group, relocated to Milwaukee to start a new chapter in her life, I was fortunate to meet her in a client capacity. This energetic and attractive woman looks, acts, and dresses in a much younger manner than her chronological age suggests. Her new neighbors are amazed that she can not only walk at a quick pace, but also jog.

Life is all about dealing with change. For Evelyn, this past year marked a major transition. Widowed for 10 years from handsome George, she felt the time had come to move forward with her life. She sold her large, comfortable home of many years in Michigan and moved west across Lake Michigan to Wisconsin to be close to her daughter, the oldest of her five children. She took up residence in a comfortable retirement community in Milwaukee. Somewhat reluctantly, she gave up driving and sold her car to her granddaughter.

Evelyn expounds on how her life now is different and on a new course. She misses the beautiful sunsets over the lake and walking her dog along the sandy beach, casually tossing pebbles into the water. It has been hard not to have close by what she refers to as the "bosom buddies" she made over the decades. Philosophically, she sees this life passage as outgrowing and moving on.

All in all, the adjustment appears to be going well. In some ways, Evelyn can relate to the situation of a freshman trying to make friends in a college dorm. She posted a notice on her floor inviting interested parties to get together for bridge. Evelyn very quickly noticed the gender imbalance and scarcity of men in the retirement home. She quipped to me that unattached men wouldn't be living there if they had a woman to take care of them, and she chuckled that the few married women can get quite possessive and quickly let one know that Fred or Barney is *their* other half.

Like Evelyn, the others born in 1919 feel fortunate to have loving and caring family members. Unlike Evelyn's situation, distance from relatives is a matter of some concern for the others. Maynard is happy in San Antonio, although his son and only family live in South Carolina. Jean's daughter is in Milwaukee and her son in Alaska. Winifred calls Chicago home, while her daughter, Sheila, and son-in-law, Tim, live in Virginia. Winifred expressed to me on more than one occasion how thankful she is to have Tim in her life, treating her with the same love and support as if she was his own mother.

Like Evelyn, these other super seniors need to be concerned about housing. Maynard resides in the same home he and his late wife built and first called their own, this after a nomadic career spent moving from one military base to another. Maynard says the only way he wants to leave his house is feet first. In this, he is with the vast majority of seniors. According to a survey conducted by the American Association of Retired Persons (AARP), 83 percent of all seniors want to stay put in their own homes. Maynard is happily surrounded by an extended family of close neighbors, many of whom also led lives of military officers.

Winifred has lived in the same three-story apartment building on the north side of Chicago for virtually her entire 88 years. She is a pillar of her neighborhood Catholic Church. Even though the neighborhood has changed dramatically over the years and most of her good friends and close neighbors have moved on or passed away, she feels anchored to familiar surroundings. Winifred, like many, is resistant to change. If and when she does move she wants her housing to have a religious affiliation.

Sisters Kay and Winnie, two sweet ladies in their late eighties, recently moved to my community to share an apartment unit in a retirement housing complex. Both widows had been living independently and alone in their own houses in the Washington D.C. area. Their major life-planning decision to sell their homes of many years and move 800 miles across the country was driven in large part by their advanced age and having loving and caring family members here.

Winnie's married daughter and their family reside in the Milwaukee area and can look after the two elderly sisters. Kay has always been close to her niece, having been widowed for almost 50 years, without children of her own.

I find it fascinating that the last time Kay and Winnie lived together was as girls 70 years earlier. I suspect living arrangements like theirs will become increasingly common in the years ahead.

As a byproduct of their long lives, Jean, Evelyn, Maynard, and Winifred have all lost their spouses and as survivors have pressed on without their mates. Winifred has been twice widowed, but has been blessed to cradle in her arms two great-grandchildren. Evelyn and Jean are great-grandmothers. It is truly special to live to see your children's children. Maynard could join this elite club if he manages to live into his nineties.

None of these individuals can be defined as wealthy in the conventional sense, yet all are financially secure and comfortable. Their life experience has greatly influenced their attitudes toward investment risk, thrift and frugality, debt assumption, and financial security.

They share a decidedly conservative bent and instinctively are risk-adverse, concentrating their investments in the safety and security of federally insured bank products, fixed guaranteed annuities, and U.S. government bonds.

Knowing that they were impressionable 10-year-olds when the great stock market crash occurred in October 1929, we can better understand their skittishness about risking their principal in stocks or stock mutual funds. It should be recalled that the Dow Jones Industrial Average stood at 452 in September 1929, then fell precipitously, with stocks losing almost 90 percent of value before bottoming out at 52 in July 1932.

It is instructive to turn back the clock to the Roaring Twenties, when speculating in stocks was rampant. It was not unlike the late 1990s, when day traders bought and sold Internet stocks with a couple of clicks of a mouse. We now know this was a silly exercise, as so many hot-dot names had no sustainable business or chance of ever developing into profit-making enterprises.

In 1929 at the peak of the stock mania, Bernard Baruch, the famous financier of that era, warned of a bubble bursting. "When beggars and shoeshine boys, barbers and beauticians can tell you how to get rich it is time to remind yourself that there is no more dangerous illusion than the belief that one can get something for nothing."

Warren Buffett is a modern-day equivalent of Bernard Baruch, and in his warnings 70 years later is just as prescient as Baruch concerning the wild speculation surrounding the tech sector. Each spring Buffett stages an annual meeting in his heartland hometown of Omaha, Nebraska, for shareholders of Berkshire Hathaway Inc., the investment holding company he manages that is the source of his vast wealth. This event attracts thousands of faithful followers and hordes of the financial press, who hang on Buffett's every word, anxious to learn what this investment titan with a long-term record of incredible success thinks and foresees.

The 2000 annual meeting took place in April, at the very height of the tech mania. In a case of what have you done for me lately, Buffett had to be defensive in the wake of Berkshire Hathaway's severe underperformance to the tech-laden 1999 Nasdaq. The May 1, 2000, *Wall Street Journal* reported that at this meeting, "Warren Buffett scornfully compared the technology sector's breathtaking runup to a chain letter, in which early participants reap rich rewards at the expense of those who follow."

It was reported that in the question-and-answer period, one brash young investor suggested to Mr. Buffett that Berkshire should now change course and smartly invest in technology, as that sector was clearly in his considered opinion, "the only game in town." According to the *WSJ* reporter, Mr. Buffett bridled when this same investor went on to state that in 1999 he'd been able to "offset my losses in Berkshire" with investments in tech stocks.

Buffett, a stout believer that fundamentals and valuation count, countered that this suggestion would be a mistake. He replied, "We've got an expert here. You can always invest with him." Better to have stayed with the master investor Buffett.

On March 10, 2000, the Nasdaq reached its peak, only to plunge 52 percent by year-end. The same day, Berkshire Hathaway reached a low point for 2000, yet rebounded from there to soar 74 percent by year-end.

Returning to our Class of 1919, when they were in their mid-

fifties—a period in their lives when they might have had discretion-
ary money available to invest—they were appropriately cautious.
They were not adversely affected when the Arab oil embargo caused
stock prices to tank in 1973 and 1974. Each was 68 and comfortably
retired when the stock market lost 22 percent of its value in a single
October trading day in 1987. The roaring bull market of the 1990s
did not tempt any one of them to seek more aggressive investing
styles, and they were able to sidestep the 2000-2002 three-year bear
market.

I notice their affinity toward dealing with financial institutions
that survived the Depression years with which they have a long-term
familiarity. Hence, dominating their holdings, we find names such as
Bank of America, Prudential, a fraternal organization such as Knights
of Columbus, and the strong neighborhood bank. They knew that
banks could fail.

The first question a member of the Class of 1919 is likely to ask
when evaluating an investment opportunity is whether it is insured,
followed by a query about what it is currently paying (yielding).
Preserving principal and realizing income, no matter how minimal,
is foremost on their minds. They care far less about capital gains and
appreciation potential, desiring tangible returns that can benefit them
now.

My Aunt Peggy, and I suspect the others, too, were in the habit
of regularly going to the bank to have their interest earnings posted
to their FDIC (Federal Deposit Insurance Coverage) passbook savings accounts. To this day, Jean wants to have her bond interest distributed to her in a check, comforted by hard evidence of this return
on her investment. Winifred set up two accounts in order to separate
what she considers her money from money that is earmarked for her
grandchildren. Although her account is conservatively invested and
income-oriented, she is psychologically comfortable with variable,
growth-type returns for the younger generation.

As a whole, though, this conservative crowd is not inclined to
buy into potential growth, preferring straight-line, fixed returns over

variability. Dividends and interest earnings hold more allure for them than does appreciation or reinvestment in additional shares of stock. In their minds, it is more important to avoid loss to principal than to put money at risk in pursuit of double-digit returns. They take to heart the wisdom of Benjamin Franklin, who said, "You should be more concerned with the return of your money, than the return on your money."

These folks have a good handle on their personal finances, knowing to the penny their income sources such as pension and Social Security. I would characterize them as good money managers, paying attention to cash flow and able to account for how each penny of their money is expended. They also know the value of a dollar. To them, current prices and costs seem exorbitant, from real estate taxes, utility bills, and other housing expenses, to prescription drugs or even a loaf of bread.

Jean's husband died in 1981. That same year she had open-heart surgery, a necessity that led her to get control of her finances and track almost every penny she spent. Remarkably, she has kept ledgers going back 25 years that record her outgo by category on a monthly and annual basis. Within $100, she is able to account for how much it has cost her to live and what she has spent in the most recent calendar year.

Most people look on budgeting as a nervous breakdown on paper. Not Jean and her 1919 contemporaries, who find it helpful to think in terms of a spending plan instead of a budget. Because no one can hope to enjoy financial security unless expenditures are kept within the limits of income, they are less focused on the net worth statement. There's no debt on the balance sheet. I also see a tendency for them to significantly understate the value of their assets, such as home or investment real estate values.

This group can be described as thrifty and frugal. Some in the younger generation might say they are tight or even cheap. A telling example comes from Jean. She was being charged $9 a month to park her car under a carport designed to provide shelter from the blazing Arizona sun. After just two months, she noticed the charge had risen to $9.20. She decided to drop this parking spot, opting to park in the open for free. Her son was flabbergasted she would let a measly 20 cents influence her, that a couple of dimes tipped the value proposition. Jean had another consideration. She found holes in the overhang and birds would congregate there and leave their droppings on her car.

As another example of the Class of 1919's frugality, the catalyst for my financial advisory firm's involvement with Evelyn centered on her hesitancy to pay the cost to take any of her meals in the residence dining hall. Her daughter sought our services in part as a plan to convince her mother she did not have to live in such a miserly way.

Think about it. These folks know how to go without, having lived with rationing during the war years. As such, it was common practice for this generation to hoard items and not throw away anything that someday might be useful. Both my Uncle John and Winifred told me they always read restaurant menus from the right side, where the prices are listed, before looking at the entrees. Talking of this with our friend Nancy, she noted how it is now fashionable at many upscale restaurants to not even list prices on the menu. Nancy is not at all embarrassed and makes it a point of inquiring of the waiter or waitress the cost of unlisted specials prior to ordering. She also is taken by how many young people are apt to present their credit cards for payment without even viewing their bill.

I observe how these 1919 folks smartly utilize low-tech three-ring binders to organize their finances. Unlike many younger folks, they routinely balance their checkbooks and regularly audit their bank and investment account statements. They scrutinize what they are being charged and pay their bills promptly.

In a meeting with Jean at her kitchen table, we spent time reviewing and interpreting how to read the year-end statement mailed to her for the account under my firm's supervision. She asked intelligent questions and became satisfied that all the information was in order and understandable. She then confided that she had a beef with her bank, having found a discrepancy on the latest monthly statement, since resolved to her satisfaction. In my opinion, her family can rest assured at this stage nothing is getting past Jean.

According to the Securities and Exchange Commission, five million senior citizens are victims of investment scams each year. Regulators are cracking down on abusive sales tactics aimed at the vulnerable elderly. According to Lori Richards of the SEC, "We're taking a hard look at representations made to investors to see if they are overblown and misleading."

Examiners have found that seniors at "free" lunch seminars are often fed a plate full of exaggerated claims. On the menu: "Immediately add $100,000 to your net worth!" "How $100,000 can pay $1 million to your heirs!" "How to maximize your estate up to 10 times for your heirs, based upon current assets."

I see one of these enticing invitations every week. My advice is to ignore the offer, as the free meal is likely to upset your stomach and very possibly crack your nest egg.

All generations need to be on constant guard against the unscrupulous, ill-informed, illegal, unethical, and fraudulent purveyors of financial services and products. According to the Bureau of Consumer Protection, Americans lose a couple of billion dollars each year to so-called investment opportunities that turn out to be scams. Greed too often attracts an unsavory element adept at quickly and painfully separating people from their hard-earned money. The best protection against being victimized by investment or financial services fraud is to practice common sense.

Use all of your senses, including giving recommendations the smell test. If something sounds too good to be true, it is not true. Also, never succumb to pressure to make a hasty decision.

The North American Securities Administrators Association (NASAA) has put out a list of common come-ons used to snare investors. It bears repeating that the risk/reward tradeoff is the cardinal rule of all common sense investing. Put simply, high return and low risk do not go together. Keep this in mind whenever you hear any of the following falsehoods: "Your profit is guaranteed." "There's no risk." "It's an amazingly high rate of return."

According to NASAA, the financial products most often involved in fraud are unregistered securities. Using my KISS method, these landmines can be easily avoided by limiting investing to the large universe of investment securities listed in *The Wall Street Journal*. Following this same line, you are advised to avoid entirely options and commodities.

Our hardy group and their ilk do not procrastinate either, filing their taxes closer to February 15 than to the April 15 deadline. They tend to get anxious about the annual tax preparation chore, fretting their return will not be filed on time or accurately. They should not be the least bit worried, as this age group is by far the most honest among taxpayers.

I have found them, however, to hesitate to discard statements or paperwork out of fear they might be needed at some point in the future. Maynard refers to this as a missing document coming back to bite you. Consequently, each has accumulated a small mountain of old statements, checks, utility bills, and outdated policies. Some even keep the original mailing envelopes and stuffers that accompanied those old statements. They could benefit from a new sense of freedom by opening their mail next to a round-file waste basket and periodically shredding other information, retaining only the most recent statements for their records.

In an era of rampant identity theft, it is a good idea for all of us to routinely shred all confidential printed information, including bank, brokerage, credit, mortgage and tax statements. Anything of personal and sensitive nature should be destroyed. It is smart to also shred all unsolicited credit card applications received. Additionally, anything showing Social Security numbers, date of birth, and so on should be kept from getting into the wrong hands.

Our girl Maggie has a small make-work job, Maggie's Special Shred, which she operates out of the back room of our office. Her fine motor skills are compromised by hand tremors. Consequently, employment possibilities with organizations such as Goodwill Industries are not a good fit for her. Several years ago we purchased a four-horsepower industrial shredder that is safe for her to operate. Unlike her younger brother, Jack, Maggie never gets bored with the repetitive nature of feeding sheets into the shredder for hours at a time.

Her little business of shredding our confidential papers, as well as papers for certain clients and some businesses and organizations, gives Maggie a sense of accomplishment and self-esteem while providing a useful service.

SQUIRREL AWAY FOR A RAINY DAY

Like many financially intelligent individuals of their generation, members of the Class of 1919 have lived well below their means and dutifully managed to save a portion of their income, however modest. Winifred is grateful for what her husband had been able to save working for the railroad to build and leave a secure retirement nest egg for her. These folks are disciplined in their saving and spending, and early in their lives they developed the habit of regularly squirreling away something for the long winter of retirement or that rainy day emergency. This stash might be hidden in a closet or, as Maynard coyly mentioned, buried in a can out back.

As a matter of fact, I recently learned that the father of my close friend Shirley was also born in 1919. Shirley confided to me that despite her late father's having been a small businessman who used bank accounts, he nonetheless hid cash in a metal box under the front porch. That way, should his house burn down or a run on the local bank occur in the manner of a Jimmy Stewart *It's A Wonderful Life*, he would be able to put his hands on some money.

Contrast these 1919 financially successful behaviors to those of people born, for example, in 1949, 1959, 1969, and 1979. Many among these younger generations might very well drive fancy luxury cars and sport the latest in designer fashion. They are likely to also be knee-deep in credit card debt to support lifestyles exceeding their income. No matter how sizeable that income, many individuals today are living paycheck to paycheck. If statistics are to be believed, too many in the younger generation have a negative savings rate. At best, their savings rates pale in comparison to the Class of 1919.

The children of the Depression typically shunned materialism and consumerism, unlike their children and grandchildren. These later generations would be wise to mirror some of their antecedents' personal financial habits. I recall a conversation with a new client regarding his 86-year-old, financially comfortable, widowed mother. No matter how much he and his sister encourage their mother to spend some of her healthy, growing estate, she will not.

Their own children's behavior is 180 degrees removed from that of their grandmother. They are described as world-class competitive shoppers and spenders, and consequently poor or non-existent savers. These descendants would do well to follow the example of their grandmother and never casually take on credit card debt, speculate, market-time the stock market, or purchase anything they do not really need, cannot afford, or can save for and pay for with cash.

I've seen a report commissioned by financial firm Diversified Investment Advisors that surveys the saving and spending habits of generation Y, the grandchildren of the careful spender group, born in the years after 1977. This age group gives lip service to the importance of saving; yet, foolishly, 75 percent would rather take $10,000 today than wait three years for $15,000.

As a whole, the 80-somethings raise their eyebrows and shake their heads at the cavalier attitude younger folks have toward debt assumption, whereas their generation celebrated each fully paid home mortgage and threw parties at which they triumphantly burned the note. Fast forward to today, when many homeowners are encouraged to accept—and willingly do—interest-only mortgages or lower initial rate adjustable-rate mortgages.

Recently, I see banks selling the appeal of lower monthly payments by actively promoting 40-year mortgages. The problem with this length of mortgage is that the principal balance will take forever to be paid off. It is never a financial positive to be heavily burdened with any form of debt, including a home mortgage. A much wiser move would be to take on a shorter fixed-rate mortgage term, such as 20, 15, or even 10 years. One could also accelerate the payoff of a 30-year mortgage principal ahead of schedule.

Just as bad, owing to the widespread use of home-equity loans, many homeowners are carrying two mortgages and have virtually no equity on their balance sheet. In many instances, home-equity lines of credit treat the home like a credit card. In cycles when mortgage rates turn up or home appreciation cools, this risky financial maneuver could cause many mortgage-holders to lose their homes. Indeed, investment pathfinder John Templeton has warned of late, "Perhaps 20 percent of all U.S. home mortgages may be in danger of default." Our seniors well remember the Depression era when millions lost the family farm or were left homeless.

With the advent of the new millennium, each of our 1919 members has faced the inevitable toll that age extracts on health. Though young at heart, they face the hard reality that comes from being a 1919 model. Health issues are always a top-of-mind issue for this age group and, by extension, for their baby-boomer children.

While meeting with Jean at her apartment in Arizona, I inquired about her health. She frankly admitted it could be better. She went on to tell me how her daughter likely saved her life when, during a timely visit, Mary Jo found her mother struggling to breathe. Mary Jo quickly dialed 911, and Jean was rushed to the emergency room of the local hospital. Medical personnel found her heart beating at just 13 beats per minute. Fighter that she is, she surprised everyone and survived this near-death scare. Jean's cardiologist inserted a pacemaker to regulate her heart, and she promised to faithfully take her life-saving medications. As I left, the sun was warming the day, and Jean was eager to take her regular exercise swim in the outdoor pool.

On a beautiful summer Chicago Sunday last year, Winifred's loving family, her many friends and neighbors, and the McCarthy family came together to celebrate her eighty-fifth birthday. More than a few of our old neighbors reminisced about the happy times in the 1960s when a spirited Winifred regularly performed cartwheels to spice up neighborhood backyard parties. The march of time catches up with us all, and Winifred is no exception. Winifred has slowed, but not been stopped, by knee and hip surgeries. After a series of falls she now gets around with the help of a cane. During the time I spent with Winifred recently, she whimsically lamented if only she could do a cartwheel now.

As the only male in this group, Maynard just might be the healthiest. He told me he takes charge of his health, regularly working out. Evelyn describes herself as having no handicaps and enjoys robust health. It is entirely possible that one or more of this 1919 foursome will live to be 100. In fact, centenarians are the fastest-growing demographic age group. The Census Bureau reports there are currently some 71,000 American centenarians, but predicts there will be more than 1 million by 2050. I hope to be one of them.

My maternal grandmother lived to age 100, and her younger sister, Dell, to the ripe old age of 102. This is quite an accomplishment. According to Boston University's Dr. Peris, "About one in 10,000 people in the U.S. lives to 100." Dell's life spanned three centuries (1899–2002). By living to such an advanced age, grandma suffered the heartbreak of outliving a child, my own mother, Peggy.

The terrible reality of outliving your children—even grandchildren—is becoming increasingly common, especially for women living into their eighties and beyond. Winifred lost her beloved son Terry at age 54 when he succumbed to throat cancer. Dell's daughter, Loretta, one of my mom's cousins and a bridesmaid in her wedding, preceded her mother in death from complications of multiple sclerosis. Losing a child at any age is one of life's hardest burdens. From a parent's perspective, the oldest generation is supposed to go first.

Mom died at age 63 from lung cancer, despite having quit the dangerous habit of smoking 20 years earlier. She courageously underwent the radical method of having a lung surgically removed in the hope the cancer could be contained. Tragically, in the cold terminology of this deadly disease, the cancer had metastasized.

I find it disconcerting that 41 percent of people, according to an American Cancer Society survey, believe in the myth that treating cancer with surgery can cause it to spread throughout the body. Then again, a surprising number of misguided people believe it is possible to "catch" cancer from someone else.

AUNT PEGGY

I was blessed to have four strong, intelligent, and independent women as my aunts. I spent quality time with each of them as part of the great gift of being born into a close-knit and nurturing extended family. Sadly, in addition to Aunt Peggy, all have now passed on— Mary Jane, Cassie and JoAnn. I fondly remember each of these fine women, yet in many ways the life story of my Aunt Peggy deserves special mention.

Although she stoically kept quiet about her own travails, I now know from her daughter Mary Joyce that Aunt Peggy contracted tuberculosis during the time in World War II when she lived and worked as a nurse in infected, poorly ventilated, tight quarters in England.

After the war, Peggy followed her sister to the United States, searching once again for greater opportunities than those to be found in war-torn Europe. Eventually, Peggy found her way to Chicago, where she had a cousin and an older sister. This simple beauty met another descendent of west Ireland, my mom's brother Johnny, at an Irish Club in the Windy City. They went on to marry and raise three children who made them very proud.

Aunt Peggy had to be the hardest-working, most disciplined person I have ever had the honor of knowing. On top of being a truly dedicated mother, she worked full-time as a blue-uniformed public health nurse for the City of Chicago. While her children were still in grade school, she looked to once again advance her nursing career at Loyola University. During my frequent visits to her home I saw textbooks piled high on the dining room table next to papers marked with A grades. Aunt Peggy persevered and completed her bachelor of science degree in Nursing (BSN) with highest honors. Her oldest child and my close friend, Dennis, proudly reminded grieving attendees at his mother's funeral that she was the first person in his family to earn a college degree. Although I have no doubt my aunt was highly intelligent, I am equally certain that no student worked harder and more diligently than Peggy.

Aunt Peggy had an extremely close, almost unequaled relationship with her mother-in-law, my maternal grandmother. Both families shared the same large, three-story frame house, a common arrangement at the time, with Grandma's presence in the household enabling Peggy to work outside the home.

My Uncle Johnny worked all hours and all shifts as a Chicago policeman. Theirs was a team approach to family and home that functioned well. Although not blood relatives, Grandma and Aunt Peggy were clearly cut from the same cloth. I suspect this togetherness in purpose could be traced to their shared west Ireland upbringing and their courage to cross an ocean and build a new life.

My aunt's time management skills in balancing work, home, and most importantly family were on display for all to see, and sprang from her indefatigable spirit and iron will. I will never forget that it was my Aunt Peggy at the intensive care bedside of my gravely ill mother—two sisters-in-law, in the final days of Mom's life.

My recollection of that anguished period was of time spent watching the luminous lines of monitoring screens measuring my dying mother's heartbeats, as I desperately hoped to spot a miraculous turn. I was called to the hospital when Mom was at her end and was greatly comforted by my aunt's presence and quiet strength throughout this vigil.

Life—which is often hard—dealt a few blows at times for Aunt Peggy. Because she handled the finances in her household, she was doing business at the neighborhood bank when a freak accident occurred. The elevator door opened and she stepped in, but a malfunction had caused the lift to remain one floor below. She fell down the shaft, landing on top of the elevator, badly tearing up her leg.

Peggy endured a lengthy hospital stay to recover from her painful injuries. When visiting her I was shocked by seeing the many pins grotesquely inserted into her leg. Yet this strong woman never complained about her fate nor felt sorry for herself. Aunt Peggy was truly inspirational.

LIFE IS LIKE A BOX OF CHOCOLATES

My neighbor Winifred has been a significant part of the fabric of my life and the lives of my brothers and sisters for over 50 years . We had the good fortune of growing up across the street from this remarkable woman. To say we think of her as family is to understate her role in our life's journey. She was a constant figure at any life event, be it happy or sad—wedding, funeral, Christening, hospitalization, new house, birthday, anniversary, or summer vacation.

This good woman made it a lifelong practice to send cards to celebrate birthdays and anniversaries. A recipient of these touching remembrances, I recently asked Winifred how many she mailed out.

"About 20 to 25," she guessed.

"Total?" I asked.

Smiling, she replied, "Each month."

Charting the cost of a first-class postage stamp offers one way to measure the steady rise of price increases and inflation over the years. The first stamp Winifred licked and affixed to an envelope cost 3 cents. In November 1979 it was 15 cents, and by the time you read this it will cost 41 cents. "Penny" postcards are now 26 cents.

The generation born in 1919 has seen what inflation can do. Even at a somewhat benign 3 percent annual increase, prices have doubled every 24 years. Today it takes $2.13 to purchase goods and services that cost $1.00 to buy 24 years ago. This amounts to a 113 percent increase in the consumer-price index (CPI), an inflation gauge.

As I mention earlier, the summer of 1967 I spent as a batboy for the Chicago White Sox baseball team. In that year, the average major league baseball player made about $19,000 annually. Today, even a journeyman player can bring home well over two million dollars a year.

In another graphic example of the effects of inflation, many of us can say we paid more for our current car than we did for our first house. In the same vein, some parents these days pay more for a child's pre-school tuition than they did for their own college education. When I worked as a batboy, I recall being paid five dollars a game. Now, five bucks won't get you a beer at a ballpark.

Maynard suggests the secret to a long and happy life is to stay active and busy. As a hobby, he has completely restored two MGs, the English two-seater sports car. He heartily recommends the purchase of a sleek and fast Porsche—as a tonic to keeping young, just like the one he bought as an eightieth birthday present to himself. With so many seniors suffering the terrible effects of Alzheimer's and dementia, all four members of these 1919 contemporaries are still blessed with good mental faculties.

My maternal grandmother was a caretaker rather than a care-receiver up until the advanced age of 95. Grandma kept busy cooking, cleaning, and maintaining a house, but also exercised her mind by solving a daily crossword puzzle. Tellingly, Maynard works out regularly, Evelyn takes brisk walks, Jean swims, and Winifred does swim aerobics. Their generation might be conservative when it comes to personal financial matters, yet they are self-disciplined and possess the capacity to think big and act on their ideas.

I have come to know Jean's daughter, Mary Jo, in a client capacity over the years and have been impressed by and envious of the extensive, worldwide travel adventures of Mary Jo and her husband, Guy. This now-retired couple has ventured to all seven continents and checked out more places listed in the book *The 100 Places You Need to Visit Before You Die* than anyone I know.

Meeting Jean, I discovered that Mary Jo's travel bug and adventurous spirit are inherited. Jean recently visited her son at his home in Seward, Alaska, and just returned from a tour of France with her daughter.

Jean told me "with that twinkle in her blue eyes" that her most exciting travel adventure was snorkeling for the first time in her seventies in the waters of the Great Barrier Reef off the coast of Australia. She has come to believe her family has gypsy blood, because the Bennett family's answer to any crossroad in their lives was to take a trip. Jean vividly remembers her father loading the family of three kids in the Studebaker when she was four, hitching up a trailer, and bravely leaving Wisconsin headed west to Los Angeles. That was in 1923.

To this day, Jean marvels at how her mother managed, since they ate all their meals in the crude trailer they were pulling and slept in it, too. Although their travel was not as arduous as for those who blazed a trail across the continent with horse and wagon, Jean's 1923 mode of travel was much closer in its challenges to those hardy pioneers than today's efforts, which benefit from a modern interstate system, air-conditioned luxury vehicles with onboard entertainment systems, and exits dotted with hotels, fast food, and gas stations complete with clean and comfortable restrooms.

Winifred went off to the beautiful southwest of Ireland to spend time with relatives. She admitted to some trepidation owing to the distance and overseas flight, but called on her ample reserve of courage to say yes to this exciting trip. Back in 1974, she and Gene traveled to Australia to celebrate their twenty-fifth wedding anniversary. Gene had served there as a young man during World War II and had dreamed of some day returning with the love of his life. For their golden fiftieth wedding anniversary, they went on an Alaskan cruise. This inspired Cathy and me to plan something special to mark the approaching silver year of our lives together.

I admire the sturdy resolve the 1919 generation exhibits. Mentally tough, each learned that life is hard and the road at times difficult, but believed it was a good journey. As Forrest Gump famously uttered in the movie of the same name, "Life is like a box of chocolates. You never know what you are going to get."

With her youngest child having reached the age of 50, Evelyn looks back on how each of her five offspring took a different path in life. She is happy each found a measure of success. Once a mother, always a mother. She becomes misty-eyed when sharing the health challenges her son faces living with the devastating effects of the unpredictable neurological disease of multiple sclerosis. I recently asked Evelyn's daughter, Chris, how her mother was doing. Her lofty response: "She's flying high."

Winifred confided to me that since Gene's passing she has found herself thinking back and mourning the loss of her first husband, Jimmy, who died so many years before. She remarked about how different her husbands were from each other, but how each had so enriched her life. She admits to being envious when she sees couples together.

Maynard opined that he has no regrets and would live his life following the same script. He exemplifies how each of the 1919 group developed a healthy philosophy of life, guided by an optimistic, sunny demeanor.

In my latest meeting with Maynard, I found him razor sharp and looking fit, with an upright, military bearing. He dropped me a note as a follow-up to my book project, encouraging me in mission terms to "press on." Maynard signed off as Col. Ham and I noted the return address label showcased the National WWII Memorial.

"Life is like riding a bicycle," said Claude Pepper, the late Florida congressman who achieved fame as a champion of older Americans and who served in office until his death at age 91. "You don't fall off unless you stop pedaling."

Economists and psychologists have quantified that as our society has become measurably wealthier, we as an affluent nation are not necessarily happier. Two researchers at Penn State University have found the best predictor of overall happiness is physical, not material wealth. This generation knows well from life experience that this observation is definitely true, as money has less to do with happiness than is commonly imagined. For, as Ralph Waldo Emerson put it, "The first wealth is health."

Thinking of the group born in 1919, I am not surprised to have read that on average, happy people live nine years longer than their unhappy contemporaries.

Driving home recently, I saw a billboard advertising the giant financial services provider Citibank. It borrowed from the well-known Benjamin Franklin admonition to be healthy, wealthy, and wise, except for the billboard's leaving a space where the goal of being wealthy would have been printed. The accompanying tag line informs us that what is missing is not that important. As Samuel Johnson, the esteemed English literary figure of the eighteenth century gave us: "It is better to live rich, than to die rich." Our 1919 group in their hearts and by their actions lives and understands this truth.

THE PLASTIC PROBLEM

Millions of Americans have a huge problem with plastic, as in credit cards. For far too many, this overspending has reached crisis proportions. The average credit card debt was well above $9,000 in 2004, more than triple the $3,000 balance in 1990. Remember, this figure is just the average. Perhaps the majority of holders use credit cards judiciously and responsibly, sensibly paying off the balance in full each month. As a nation of compulsive borrowers, we have amassed an astounding $1.7 trillion in outstanding credit card debt. It is said this figure is nearly equal to the gross domestic product of Mexico and China *combined.*

A pronounced difference in thinking exists between the children (boomers) and grandchildren (generation X and Y) about the assumption of debt with the World War II (greatest) generation.

According to David Evans, an economist and co-author of *Paying With Plastic*, the year 2003 marked the first year Americans bought more with credit cards than they did with cash. "In 5,000 years there have been only four times that we have changed the way we pay: There was barter to coinage, coins to paper, paper to checks, and then (credit) cards."

Excepting the greatest generation, Americans in general and baby boomers in particular are not at all good at deferring gratification. Jon Hanson points out in his book *Good Debt, Bad Debt,* the "stigma of debt seems nonexistent today. Credit has become abstract and anonymous. The most damaging aspect of today's culture is short-term thinking."

Freda, the mother of my good friend Tony, is a World War II war bride. At the start of this chapter I profiled Tony's dad. The couple met at a USO dance in Freda's hometown in England. After the war ended and Tony's father returned safely from a distinguished battle-field tour, the couple married and went on to build a life together in the States.

Typical of her age group, Freda uses an old-fashioned but effective "Christmas Club" savings account. She has used this separate banking account for many years. These accounts work by automatically transferring a set dollar amount each month, which accumulates and is used to pay for year-end holiday spending. The amount Freda decides to put away becomes her budget for gifts.

Compare this disciplined spending plan to the method used by later generations, which tend to whip out their plastic. Come January, when the credit card bills arrive from holiday purchases, today's spenders find themselves hung over in a deep debt hole. The poet e. e. Cummings, famous for his use of lower case e's for the first part of his name, gave us this humorous but sobering observation: "I'm living so far beyond my income that we may almost be said to be living apart."

Credit cards can be a trap that ensnares unsuspecting users in severe financial difficulties, poor credit ratings, and even personal bankruptcy. Author Hanson encourages readers to gain control over emotional spending. "Avoid the consumer entitlement mentality that can only lead to debt, regret, and broken dreams. No matter the amount of your income, wealth can be obtained, or maintained, only through the amount you don't spend."

The annual Superbowl bombards consumers with ads telling them the only way to watch the big game is on a big screen TV. The 1919 generation has a radically different view of what constitutes a necessity. If after careful consideration they decide to buy an appliance, for example, they save up for it, putting aside a little out of each weekly paycheck until they can pay for it in full and with cash. This method seems a quaint notion to those of us who grew up with easy credit.

Our own household receives in the mail at least two credit card offers a week, easily a hundred over the course of a year. Therefore I was not surprised to learn an astounding $6 billion in pre-approved credit card offers were mailed to American consumers in 2005. Credit card marketers inundate college students and recent graduates with card offers, knowing they have little or no income. For any offer, a smart consumer would always read the fine print.

According to a recent piece in *The Wall Street Journal,* cards are waiving late fees, but with a catch of higher interest rates. "American Express Co.'s Clear card will increase a user's interest rate to 28.74 percent if a consumer pays late twice in a year." At that appalling interest rate, you would be paying twice for that big screen TV over roughly a two-and-a-half-year period. Think if you could find an investment that paid 29 percent every year.

The solution, according to grandma and grandpa, is simple. Destroy the cards and pay by check, cash, or debit card and work to pay down debt. *Money* magazine's Jean Chatzky puts it in simple, understandable terms: "It's just like shopping—backward."

A TRUE COUPLE

Octogenarians Herb and Shirley are long-term clients of our firm and two of my favorite people. As representative members of the Greatest Generation, they possess and exhibit all of the admirable qualities found in their age group.

Happily married for almost 63 years, this loving couple spent the first two years of their married life apart during World War II, while Herb served in the army in faraway India. When I suggested their separation as newlyweds must have been awfully hard, Herb shrugged and said he served with fellas who had several kids back home who were in for five years. Shirley countered that they wrote every day. Besides, many of her girlfriends lived with the same predicament on the home front.

The occasion of my most recent visit was a gracious invitation to see their new retirement residence and join them for lunch in the community dining hall. I found this still-active couple very happy in their comfortable apartment and environment. In his closet you will find a military cap worn proudly by World War II veterans of China, India and Burma. It came as no surprise that they quickly made many new friends among the residents and staff.

They had sold the modest home they built in 1951 where they raised their son and daughter. The couple agreed the time was right to move on and, if anything, should have been done earlier. Shirley marvels at all the "stuff" they accumulated over the past 54 years.

Like many of their contemporaries and as children of the Great Depression, Herb and Shirley are thrifty and frugal. They scrimped and saved and learned how to do without. They lived on an austerity budget all their lives.

Folks like Herb and Shirley are disciplined in their saving and spending. Early in their lives they developed the habit of regularly squirreling away something for the long winter of retirement. As a result, they achieved financial security. Like most seniors, they shake their heads and roll their eyes at the poor savings habits and rich spending of many in the younger generations.

As a nation, we would be wise to mirror the personal finance characteristics of the Greatest Generation. Sadly, as the World War II set passes on, this institutional memory is vanishing.

Mike Arnow is a veteran financial planner and CPA accountant in Milwaukee, having founded his own financial firm, Arnow & Associates. Mike is someone in my industry I look up to and respect. As such, I brought him in to lead a seminar for the benefit of our firm's clients.

Mike led off this educational session using two circle graphs to compare the household cash flow expenditures of the World War II generation in the years 1946-1972 with recent 2005 outgo patterns. This analysis illustrated the extent to which thrift (measured by saving) and frugality (by careful spending) have been replaced by debt and consumption.

Interestingly, in both timeframes, 25 cents of each dollar of income on average is taken up by taxes. The other categories show major differences. Whereas the World War II generation expended another quarter of every dollar on housing, the figure has swelled to 31 percent today.

The Greatest Generation, no matter their income, managed to regularly put away for retirement a dime of every dollar earned. In the study Mike Arnow employed, this retirement savings rate has now dropped to a penny of each dollar – almost nothing.

Saving for retirement is synonymous with *planning* for retirement. Financial planners routinely advise that individuals save 10 percent of their income. I concur, and if this target were met in a disciplined fashion throughout one's working life, most goals—including financial independence and a secure retirement—would be achieved.

James E. Stowers, born in 1924 and served in World War II as an Air Force fighter pilot, went on to great success as founder of Twentieth Century Mutual Funds, now American Century.

Stowers has an unswerving belief that anyone can achieve financial independence. He claims the fruits of financial independence include peace of mind and the freedom to do what one wants to do when one wants to do it. Typical of his generation, Stowers describes family habits of thrift and frugality that include taking a brown-bag lunch of a peanut butter sandwich to work daily and using on-street parking over the convenience of a parking garage. His wife, Virginia, speaks of resisting the temptation to purchase a beautiful fur coat she admired. By similarly postponing high consumption today, we can draw ever closer to the dream of financial independence.

As a consequence of not saving, more than half of American

households today have accumulated little, if anything, in financial assets. According to *U.S. News & World Report*, 41 percent of workers ages 45 to 54 have less than $25,000 saved for retirement.

When I asked Herb what he would advise the younger set to do to help control its spending, he quickly replied, "Stay out of Starbucks."

Before the Revolutionary War, founding father Benjamin Franklin was advising his readers along the same lines when he suggested, "If you are now a drinker of punch, wine, or tea twice a day, for the ensuing year drink them but once a day."

AL HIDA'S STORY

The life story of my client Al Hida is part American dream and part nightmare. The dark chapter started December 7, 1941, when Japanese forces attacked Pearl Harbor, precipitating America's entry into World War II. Until that fateful day, Al was like any other 12-year-old seventh-grade schoolboy living with his brother, mom, and dad in Sacramento, California. Like tens of thousands of peaceful Japanese Americans on the West Coast, the Hida family endured a nightmare when their own American government and their fellow citizens became suspicious of their loyalty.

On May 15, 1942, the Hida family and others of Japanese ancestry living in their community were ordered to leave their homes and possessions behind and relocate to a series of makeshift internment camps. They were herded onto trains under military guard and shipped 300 miles north to a remote camp near the Oregon border.

The living quarters were spartan, at best, with no indoor plumbing and crude facilities located a full block away. They were also inadequately clothed for the cold winter weather. Al and his family, which included his aunt from San Francisco, were soon uprooted and relocated once again to a camp in southeastern Colorado. Al spent two years, two months, and twenty days of his precious youth living under this form of imprisonment.

All told, 110,000 Japanese Americans suffered the indignity of internment spread among 10 relocation camps in remote areas of the western states. This sad saga is one of the worst civil rights violations in our nation's history. It is important to note that thousands of Japanese Americans fought valiantly in the armed forces during the war.

Our government wanted to disperse these Japanese Americans from their concentration on the West Coast, which is how Al's father happened to land a job in Milwaukee. Al and his brother and mother soon followed to Wisconsin. Their struggles continued, however, as housing was tight and difficult to find. They ended up living in a cramped rooming house, and the two boys attended the local high school.

Al went on to college at the University of Wisconsin in Madison, then served his country as a Marine for a three-year stint. He married Vivian, and together they saw that their son and daughter were well educated. Al taught science and biology for 32 years in the Milwaukee public high schools. Rather than forget his painful adolescence, Al went around the state educating students and groups to his personal experience as a Japanese American during World War II.

Perhaps because Al's early life was so disrupted, he and Vivian put down firm roots, living in the same home for 45 years. Only age-related health concerns made them move back to Sacramento to be close to their daughter. After more than 60 years, Al's life journey has come full circle.

BEFORE IT'S TOO LATE

I prefer reading nonfiction to fiction, and I also enjoy the game of golf. Knowing this, Cathy borrowed the book *Final Rounds* from the local library for me to read. I was especially touched by the story's subtitle, "A Father, A Son, The Golf Journey of a Lifetime."

While stationed as an airman in the British Isles during World War II, Brax Dodson was introduced to the game of golf and developed a lifelong love for it. He passed this passion on to his son James, who became a golf writer and the author of *Final Rounds*. This book is a journey of discovery between the two men on life, love, and family.

With Brax nearing 80 and faced with an advanced form of cancer rapidly shortening his days, he and James hurriedly embarked on a trip from the United States to St. Andrews, Scotland, the birthplace of golf, and to other memorable sites he had discovered 50 years before.

A round refers to a game of golf because it is played in a loop around a course. *Final Rounds* recounts a touching love story of the bond between two golf-playing generations, sharing precious time together, reminiscing before the elder Dodson's inevitable death.

Ely Callaway, the founder of golf club maker Callaway Golf, captures the essence of the book in this back-cover endorsement: "A gripping, loving and moving story about a man who does something for himself and his father that all of us should do—before it's too late."

NO REGRETS

> Certainly, travel is more than the seeing of sights;
> it is a change that goes on, deep and permanent,
> in the ideas of living.
>
> Miriam Beard

My father-in-law, Bob, thoroughly enjoyed travel. Thankfully, he was able to exercise this passion, especially in the years following his retirement at 62. He was joined in his adventures by travel mate Kay, his bride of 46 years and mother to their nine children.

Their travels took them to destinations all over the map of North America, including Canada and Mexico, and into Western Europe. Bob was in awe of the natural beauty and majesty of the Rocky Mountains of Colorado, the Banff region in Canada, and the Alps of Switzerland. He loved to seek out restaurants in his favorite cities of New Orleans and San Francisco. Bob and Kay burned off calories, taking brisk walks wherever they visited. Hiking provided them a series of inexpensive, healthful, and rewarding vacations. They discovered that state and national parks all had well-marked hiking trails.

Travel writer Beth Harpaz notes, "Travel can be divided into four basic parts—the planning, the journey, the destination and the memories." Bob found joy in meticulously planning and mapping out each trip. Days were spent charting an itinerary and travel plan. As soon as they returned from one trip, he eagerly turned his attention to their next trip.

The pair kept a journal, recording the sights seen and places stayed so they could rekindle fond memories and recapture favorite experiences on a return engagement.

Once Bob's long career in the foundry business ended, this adventurous couple made a pilgrimage of sorts to Slovenia, the land of Bob's ancestors. Years before, Bob had surprised Kay on their anniversary with plane tickets to Ireland, home of her grandparents.

Over the years my in-laws developed into savvy and seasoned travelers. For instance, they learned that the cleanest bathrooms were to be found in the lobbies of better hotels. They shrewdly discovered that Las Vegas was a smart jumping off point and a base for economy-minded travelers not overly tempted by the lure of gambling. Travelers can readily book low-cost flights to this tourist mecca, locate hotel rooms at reasonable rates, eat responsibly at the many buffet offerings, and find deals on car rentals to explore the vast expanse of the southwest, including high-profile destinations such as Palm Springs, Lake Tahoe, and the Grand Canyon.

It was during a trip to Las Vegas that Bob experienced the fright of an earthquake. As he told it, they were staying high on the twenty-first floor of a hotel on the Strip. He awakened in the middle of the night to the building swaying and the light fixtures swinging. He realized this must be an earthquake. Shaken, he purposely decided not to waken and alarm his sleeping wife, reasoning there was nothing they could do in this predicament. Lovingly, he put his arm around Kay, thinking if this was to be their end, at least they were together and it had been a good ride.

When Kay awoke she felt for herself the aftershocks. Later they learned the center of the earthquake was hundreds of miles to the west in California. Amazingly, there was no damage to their hotel. Their ride together would continue, but they had another escapade to mark the passage.

I was happy to be assigned the regular duty of picking up my in-laws from the airport, be it in Milwaukee or Chicago. I always looked forward to the ride home and hearing Bob recount their most recent journey. So it was on a gray day in spring 1996 that I picked up Bob and Kay at the Milwaukee airport upon their return from Las Vegas, concluding a four-week stint enjoying the sun and sights of the neighboring region. I sensed immediately Bob was not his usual self. Having felt unwell, he had seen a doctor in Las Vegas, who pronounced him fine and sent him on his way. Unfortunately, this would prove to be his final trip, as he was seriously ill with the cancer that would take his life the following January, at age 70.

Multiple myeloma is a somewhat rare blood cancer that painfully erodes the bones. Major League star baseball pitcher and pitching coach Mel Stottlemyre was stricken with this form of cancer and fortunately survived. My father-in-law's cancer was not detected until it was too late, and it proved fatal. These two men not only had multiple myeloma in common; but also lost their youngest sons to the heartbreak of childhood leukemia.

Since the loss of my own dear mother, I fondly call my mother-in-law "Mom." When I speak to Mom about her years of travel, she eloquently expresses how grateful she is to have had a marriage partner who followed through and acted on fulfilling his dreams. She is painfully aware of many others who longed to pursue opportunities in their retirement years, yet put off implementing their longings until it was too late, due to illness or death.

In Mom's words, it would be a shame to not have these cherished remembrances. Consequently, she encourages others who contemplate embarking on an adventure to not put it off, but to emulate the activist bent of her husband and reap the reward of a lifetime of hard work while that is possible. This wisdom from Syndey Harris rings true: "Regret for things we did can be tempered by time; it is regret for things we did not do that is inconsolable."

Cancer patients have been known to harbor an interest in experiencing something larger than life. I, for one, long to see the Grand Canyon in Arizona. My game plan to make this happen involves writing it down on paper, attaching a timeline to it, and envisioning crossing this adventure trip off my list as complete. The following quote from an anonymous source expresses this newfound philosophy of mine. "Life is not measured by the number of breaths we take, but by the moments that take our breath away."

Our firm has as one of its clients a 55-year-old single woman who shared with me her dream, since she was a young girl, of seeing the wonders of Africa, such as Victoria Falls and the Serengeti. She devoted the past four years to helping care for her elderly father. He recently passed away, and I am encouraging this grandmother to take the plunge and book this trip of a lifetime.

For my part, I admit to an interest in climbing Mount Kilimanjaro. Towering 19,340 feet at its peak, it is the tallest mountain in Africa. While this is just a pipe dream for me now, floating the idea of this large-scale conquest may make it seem more plausible. Two things are holding me back. Family responsibility is foremost. But I am also fearful of altitude sickness. I think I am up to the challenge physically but would need to shore up psychologically to carry out this feat.

If I were to get serious, I could do a trial run with some high altitude training in this country. On second thought, perhaps the pipe dream is enough. Zest for renewed life and experience must sometimes be tempered by the limitations of reality. However, moving beyond one's comfort zone can be exhilarating and life-affirming.

AROUND THE WORLD IN 89 DAYS

Leo is one client of our firm who boldly acted on his dream by taking a trip around the world. Years earlier, it was my own mother who encouraged this father of five to take his wife, Mary Ann, on trips—to go places and do things, because life is short. As it turned out, Mary Ann suffered a fatal heart attack at just 57 years of age.

Despite his loneliness, Leo, at the age of 63, boarded the Panamanian-registered ship *Monet* in New York Harbor. He had learned some ocean freighters maintain a couple of private cabins on board to rent out to commercial passengers. This modern vessel was loaded six stories high with 2,000 shipping containers, each the size of a truck trailer.

The voyage lasted 89 days, with two dozen ports of call. The *Monet*'s route took Leo down the Atlantic coast's eastern seaboard, then into the Caribbean and through the Panama Canal. They crossed the Pacific and the international dateline, making regular stops at exotic ports-of-call along the way.

After passing through the Suez Canal, they experienced some unwelcome excitement. In the port of Sayeed in Egypt, passengers were ordered to their rooms when modern-day pirates boarded and raided their ship. Chicago streetwise that he is, Leo felt the raid could have been staged. The passage returned to normal as they entered the Mediterranean and headed to the more secure ports of Europe. They crossed the Atlantic in four-and-a-half days, returning to New York and then home. Leo's daughter Kathleen, one of his five children, shared with me how proud she and the rest of the family were of their father and his spirit in making this trip.

AWESOME CRUISE

My dad's cousin Eleanor McCarthy, mother of 10 and at last count grandmother extraordinaire of 35, arranged, booked, and paid for her entire family of 53 to take a Caribbean cruise in August 2001.

The occasion and inspiration was not a birthday or anniversary, but a celebration of life and the beauty of family on a large scale. In discussing the not insignificant expense, Eleanor felt this was a good investment and rationalized that it was, after all, only money and could not be taken with her to the next life.

When I sought feedback on this trip of a lifetime from a quartet of her grandkids, Matt, Mike, Joe, and John, their eyes lit up and in unison they gave a concise description: "Awesome!"

Eleanor's late husband, John, a doctor, was a wonderful man who cherished his large family. I had the privilege of spending quality time with Doctor John in the last year-and-a-half of his life in my capacity as a financial planner, as he attended to necessary financial, estate, and investment matters prior to his early death from lymphoma cancer. The couple, knowing what he was up against with his health, sold their large home and moved into a nearby condominium.

The good doctor reluctantly gave up his medical practice, mailing a touching goodbye letter to his many caring patients. I know he was grateful for living well and in the embrace of family for a good two years before he died.

After his cancer diagnosis, John and Eleanor embarked on a return trip to Ireland. In *The Fair Hills of Ireland*, Samuel Ferguson's words could have been meant as a summation of Doctor John's love of that beautiful country: "I will make my journey if life and health but stand, Unto that pleasant country, that fresh and fragrant strand, the fair hills of holy Ireland."

I am thankful that my own parents, Jack and Peggy, had the opportunity to journey to the Emerald Isle on a couple of occasions in their later years. My mother was able to get to know her uncles, Pat and John, and spend time with her many first cousins. She saw firsthand the modest thatched roof cottage with a dirt floor in the west of Ireland where her own mother was born and raised.

BIG GRANDMA

The life of her mother, my maternal grandmother, Mary, makes an interesting story. She was the eldest daughter in a brood of 10 children, crowded in poverty on a small plot outside of Galway. Her prospects came down to either marrying the widower down the road with five young children, or crossing the Atlantic to join her cousins in far-off Chicago and work as a domestic.

Like millions of immigrants, she bravely opted for a fresh start in America.

Grandma attempted and failed to book passage on the ill-fated maiden voyage of the *Titanic*. Anyone who has seen the movie *Titanic* is aware of the plight of the Irish, crammed below in third class along with the cargo. Fortunately, my grandmother arrived safely the next year and lived a full life, reaching 100 years of age.

As her eldest grandchild, I recall only once hearing her referred to by her given name of Mary. That was after I graduated from college in 1973 and traveled to the old sod with my cousin Dennis on an adventure to discover our roots. During that memorable visit, Grandma's youngest brother, John, my great uncle, gave me a small gift of a tapestry, asking me to deliver it to Mary. In my family, my siblings and I referred to her descriptively as "Big Grandma" to differentiate her from Dad's mom, who was smaller in stature and hence "Little Grandma." To others, she was respectfully referred to as Mom, Grandma, Grandma Fleming, or Mrs. Fleming, depending on the relationship of the person addressing her.

Big Grandma always seemed to be cooking for and feeding her family, guests, third-floor boarders, even furry strangers. Farm girl that she was, she regularly put out milk for stray cats in the neighborhood. Knowing a good thing, they often became house kits. Grandma had a folksy saying: "Be kind to dumb animals." I came to realize that in her life experience, one wasn't poor if you were well fed. Each and every time I saw her—which, fortunately, was often, because she lived close by—Big Grandma insisted that I have something to eat.

By the time I finished college and joined the working world, Big Grandma was in her eighties and routinely asked me if I worked nights. I recall finding the persistence of this inquiry odd. Only years later did I realize why this question had meaning to her. As the wife and mother of Chicago policemen who drew second and third shifts, she hoped my education had brought me to a station in life that allowed me to work only when the sun was out.

Big Grandma kept her pocketbook closed and I often heard her remark that this or that item was "dear." To an Irishwoman of her generation, this meant expensive. She spent her money on groceries, not on fancy clothes.

WORLD WAR I WAR HERO

Mary Monahan met my grandfather, John Fleming, at a wedding shortly after the conclusion of World War I. To hear her tell it, he was in his soldier's uniform and quite handsome. He also had fled Ireland, arriving at New York's Ellis Island on March 10, 1912, aboard the *Lusitania*. Ironically, this same ship was sunk a few years later by German U-boats patrolling off the coast of Ireland. It marked America's military entry into World War I and sent Grandpa back across the Atlantic as a soldier.

Grandpa was extremely proud of his World War I military service as a member of the 33rd Division, 108th Engineers, Company E. We know this because he had a large picture of his assembled unit prominently displayed in his room.

By Grandpa's own account, Sergeant York received credit as the greatest soldier of the war, when this distinction actually belonged to Sergeant Fleming. Before we dismiss this as an idle boast of a veteran, there is the matter of the "Ripley's Believe It or Not" legend to consider.

My cousin Jack Fleming is my source for the research behind Grandpa's war record and exploits. Like many a member of an Irish Catholic clan, Jack, an elected judge, stands on the shoulders of his parents and grandparents.

Late in September 1918, Private Fleming was serving in the Meuse region of France. He was on a critical mission with his fellow engineers to construct footbridges across a marshy expanse of swamp. They labored hurriedly under the protective cover of darkness to avoid enemy fire and complete their task. Troops were set to march forward at first light and start a major American offensive to dislodge the entrenched German forces and gain momentum to bring an end to this great war. Dawn revealed a heavy fog shrouding the marsh and the discovery that a portion of the just-built bridge had been damaged by shelling during the night.

With no time to repair the damage, six engineers jumped into the swamp, and in waist-high water they improvised by physically holding together the makeshift section. This allowed thousands of infantrymen to advance forward to battle. Legend has it that an officer crossing the bridge, oblivious to the fog-shrouded soldiers supporting him, was startled to hear an admonition from below call out in an Irish brogue, "Go get 'em, sir."

Ripley chronicled this amazing crossing. Although the number of soldiers claimed to have crossed was exaggerated, and the engineers actually took turns shouldering this demanding task, my grandpa was rightly awarded a battlefield commission for his part in the heroics.

After the war, Grandpa wore blue as a Chicago patrolman, an Irish cop. Jack's father, my Uncle Johnny, rose to police lieutenant on the same force. I recall Grandpa Fleming as if it were yesterday, sitting on his enclosed front porch, full head of gray-white hair, wearing a red flannel shirt, with an ever-present pipe, listening to a White Sox baseball game on the radio. To this day I savor the smell of pipe tobacco.

Grandpa told me something that has stayed with me. "Johnny, this has to be the greatest country on earth. I sit here smoking my pipe and the postman delivers me money." And so it was. His well-deserved pension checks arrived regularly in the mail.

My grandparents, like many of their generation, cared very little about material wealth beyond the basic necessities of life. They knew poverty first-hand, experienced life through two world wars, and started and nurtured their family in the throes of the Great Depression. Their wealth was bountifully measured in the richness of family.

INVESTING IN BONDS FOR INCOME AND STABILITY

Pimco's mutual fund founder and chief investment officer, Bill Gross, is universally considered the authority when it comes to bond investing. The standing of this renowned fixed income manager is so great that pronouncements from this brilliant former Las Vegas card shark regularly moves the market.

Gross distilled his common sense wisdom in a book provocatively entitled, *Everything You've Heard About Investing Is Wrong!*

The title's exclamation is a wake-up call, considering that hundreds of billions of dollars continue to flow into bonds and bond funds and play such an integral role in financial and investment planning.

Surveys of potential bond fund investors found the majority believe the best time to buy and own bond funds is when interest rates are rising. This mistake is alarming, but I am sure it represents an accurate reading.

I have no doubt that more confusion and misconceptions surround bond investing than any other investment area. This is why your financial well-being depends on becoming grounded in the basics of bond investing, especially the risk-and-reward parameters.

By design, bonds offer a steady stream of income, potentially greater returns than cash equivalents and traditional savings products, and generally lower risk and volatility than stock investments. They also provide a portfolio with an element of diversification.

Making a case for bonds, Bill Gross reminds us that stocks don't always outperform bonds. According to Gross:

Although stocks are definitely the best bet for the long haul, there have been periods as recently as the early 1970s when bonds and even money market funds did better over a 10- year time frame. It would be a mistake to structure your personal portfolio with 100 percent stocks, especially considering the income advantage offered by bonds.

In 2002, during the deep bear market for stocks, bonds as measured by the Lehman Brothers Aggregate Bond Index were the very top among the eight major asset classes, returning a double-digit return of 10.2 percent. The same story played out in the difficult 1990 market. Bonds also performed well in 2000 and 2001, shoring up portfolios in the process. Bonds provide a counterweight to the variability and risk found with stocks.

Let's revisit an elementary principle of common sense investment advice. Never purchase any investment you don't fully understand. The fundamentals of bond (fixed income) investing are not difficult, if you take time to grasp the basics. A good start is to understand what you actually purchase when you buy a bond.

A bond can be thought of as an IOU. In many cases, a bond is referred to as a *promissory note*. You become a lender to the government, corporations, or municipalities by purchasing the bonds they offer. Each type of bond possesses distinctive characteristics.

Bonds can be purchased individually, in a package, or pooled through a mutual fund. Bonds provide an income stream. Investors in search of current income without capital appreciation should be looking at bonds or bond funds. Fixed income investments get their name because of the stability of return they provide. Contrast this with variable investments, such as stocks, in which the return varies and is inherently uncertain, but which offers potential for capital growth.

You need to be aware of some pitfalls in bonds. In a host of areas, bond principal is subject to fluctuations in market value prior to maturity. Many bonds are also subject to *call* (being paid off prior to scheduled maturity). Also, a wide spectrum of bond offerings exists, each with different risk/reward characteristics. Bonds are interest-rate sensitive. This sensitivity is counterintuitive for all but sophisticated investors, for as interest rates go up, bond prices go down and vice versa. As the general level of interest rate changes, the market value of bonds reacts accordingly. In my opinion, interest rate risk is the most misunderstood risk investors face.

To avoid the subtle risks with your safe, income-producing investments, I advise you to construct a simple and secure bond ladder using U.S. Treasury notes.

To set up a bond ladder, divide the sum you are working with into five equal parts, and invest each part in Treasury securities that will come due (mature) at five different times.

For example, with a $100,000 portfolio, invest $20,000 in each of these T-notes: 1-year, 2-year, 3-year, 4-year, and 5-year. When one of these notes matures, replace it with another that will mature in 5 years.

I especially like the certainty and transparency of Treasuries. Unlike corporate or municipal bonds, Treasuries can't be called. Further, when you hold them to maturity you are guaranteed to realize the full face value of the bond. Bond mutual funds, on the other hand, have no set maturity. Compared to a bank CD, the return on Treasuries is exempt from state income tax and there is no $100,000 insurance limit. Once you own them you incur no carrying costs, and they're still the safest investment in the world. They are also the most liquid and marketable investment to be found.

Treasuries can be bought directly from the U.S. government. Go to www.treasurydirect.gov. You can also readily buy or sell them through a T. Rowe Price or Vanguard brokerage at a very reasonable cost.

Following a KISS investment philosophy when it comes to bonds means addressing the two primary forms of risk, financial (credit) and/or interest rate risk. Basic common sense dictates making sure your safe money is indeed safe.

At our investment advisory firm we employ two simple rules to mitigate against the downside of rising interest rates and defaults or downgrades. You can readily follow the same guidelines.

Rule number one is never invest in individual corporate or municipal bonds. The only individual debt securities we use are U.S. Treasuries, which, as government obligations, are ultra-safe and considered default-free.

A good example of the wisdom of this approach is the financial distress and subsequent credit risk that in 2007 hovers over the once-dominant domestic auto industry. Auto supplier Delphi is mired in bankruptcy, GM is a possibility to follow, and Ford continues to bleed, losing billions.

Bond investors have been enamored with the tempting yields these automakers are paying to attract capital. Yet owing to the deteriorating financial condition of both Ford and GM, the rating agencies have downgraded their corporate bonds to junk status. As a result, bondholders have seen the value of these once-sterling credits drop to just 60 to 70 cents on the dollar.

GMAC (General Motors Acceptance Corp) is the profitable financing arm of GM. Brokers would hawk this corporate bond to conservative investors without any consideration of risk. Yet, owing to troubles at its parent, at this time you can't find a buyer for a GMAC bond on the secondary market for more than 85 cents on the dollar. In other words, at a 15 percent loss of principal value.

Another reason individual investors should avoid purchasing or trading individual bonds is because the bond market is so heavily geared to institutions.

Marilyn Cohen, president of a fixed-income money management firm, refers to "killer spreads," the spread being the difference between bid (buy) and ask (sell) pricing, and she warns that individual investors will be clipped at every turn. Cohen counsels investors to avoid selling before maturity, as it is unlikely they will get a decent price. Thus, the values of bond holdings listed on your brokerage statement are often overstated. The truth is that the retail bond investor (individual) should routinely expect the short end of the stick.

Investors looking for a common sense route to invest in bonds will find that the T. Rowe Price U.S. Bond Index (PBDIX) or Vanguard Intermediate-Term Bond Index (VBIIX) may suit the bill.

Like all mutual funds, these add diversification to effectively reduce risk. The offering from T. Rowe Price has 655 holdings. Both of these recommended funds are concentrated in bonds with intermediate-term maturities averaging about six years, which limits interest rate risk and volatility.

These funds are composed of high-quality bonds, limited to U.S. Treasury, government agencies, and high-grade corporates. The average credit quality is AA. Ford and GM bonds would not currently qualify to be included in a high-quality index fund.

Both of these recommended offerings are pure no-load funds. A noted mutual fund industry figure has stated on numerous occasions: "There are few certainties in mutual fund investing, but 'never pay a sales load on a bond fund' is one of them."

Even the best and most able bond fund managers, including Bill Gross, would be hard-pressed to start out with a 3 percent, 4 percent or 5 percent deficit to overcome. You would be better off with the safety and predictably of CDs instead.

Additionally, these two bond index funds impose very low annual expenses. It should be noted the annual costs incurred by all mutual funds directly influence performance. Informed investors not only limit their bond fund choices to no-load funds but also pay close attention to expense ratios. T. Rowe Price U.S. Bond Index costs .30 percent annually ($30 on a $10,000 investment), and the Vanguard Intermediate-Term Bond Index is just .18 percent. The average bond fund expense is close to 1 percent.

Bill Gross tells us, "In the long run, fees become a heavy load." Over a relatively short time period, lower-expense bond funds inevitably demonstrate superior performance. In the case of our highlighted funds, that performance is anywhere from a .50 percent to 1 percent advantage after the first year.

In addition to having broad diversification on their side, bond funds also provide investors with the valuable ability to reinvest dividends. Often overlooked, individual bonds suffer from a serious problem of liquidity. It is very difficult to sell bonds other than U.S. government securities without a substantial price concession on the secondary market. On the other side, both T. Rowe Price U.S. Bond Index and Vanguard Intermediate-Term Bond Index are listed every day with their prices to buy or sell in the financial section of the newspaper.

Furthermore, the retail customer is unlikely to enjoy the purchasing efficiencies of bond funds. Most often, the individual investor is left with the least desirable securities because the best inventory of bonds has already been snapped up by savvy institutional investors. Bond managers are in agreement that bonds are hard to buy in small quantities for any investor with less than millions in his or her portfolio. Again, the exception is U.S. Treasury bonds.

Investors would be wise to be cautious in the municipal bond market as well. Defaults can and do occur. Poor reporting makes it difficult to assess the credit standing of these issues, liquidity is very poor, and spreads are very wide.

For all these reasons, I recommend in this arena you stick with high-quality, intermediate-term, tax-exempt municipal bond mutual funds. In the next chapter on tax-advantaged investing, I name a suitable fund from both T. Rowe Price and Vanguard.

A legitimate knock against bonds is that they leave bondholders at the mercy of inflation. Bond manager Bill Gross views inflation as a disguised form of tax, devaluing a stream of future interest payments.

In light of this, Gross, along with noted academics, is bullish (favorably inclined) toward the Treasury Department's "inflation indexed" bonds, popularly known as TIPS. Treasury Inflation Protected Securities are U.S. Treasury obligations and thereby considered default-free and ultra-safe. These bonds are designed to be reset in line with increases in the Consumer Price Index (CPI).

This design helps to ensure the protection of investors from the erosion of purchasing power due to inflation.

Although TIPS, like all U.S. Treasury securities, can be purchased directly from the government, I suggest you go the mutual fund route. Vanguard Inflation Protected Securities (VIPSX) and T. Rowe Price Inflation Protected Bond (PRIPX) are choices that take advantage of these unique investment offerings.

Speaking of the Vanguard offering, Morningstar lauds its plain-vanilla approach, saying, "Simple is still beautiful." This is music to my ears. T. Rowe Price's offering also earns high marks.

Owing to a unique tax aspect, TIPS are best held in tax-deferred retirement accounts such as IRAs. At our firm, we were early adapters of TIPs, which now account for our biggest holding inside IRA accounts.

BILL'S STORY

Bill was a sales manager in his late fifties when he suffered a debilitating stroke that left him unable to work. When he came to my office in 1985, he was looking to generate a monthly income from proceeds of a piece of property he had just sold. Assume that the amount he was investing for this purpose was an even $100,000.

Basically, Bill wanted to accomplish two goals with his money. He wanted to generate the highest possible regular monthly income to supplement his pension and disability pay. He also wanted to maintain the $100,000 principal amount relatively intact so his wife and sons would have use of this money should his failing health lead to death.

Since his objectives were clear-cut, it became apparent that high-quality bond funds such as from T. Rowe Price and Vanguard were most appropriate.

The yield on such a portfolio during that time averaged about 8 percent. In effect, the plan called for realizing about $8,000 in annual income with monthly distributions of $667. There was a high expectation the $100,000 principal would fluctuate only mildly. I thought we had agreed on a workable plan.

That weekend Bill saw an advertisement in his local newspaper for a product sporting an outsized 12 percent return. Thrilled, he tore out the ad, believing he had found an incredible opportunity for a yield 50 percent greater than my proposal. Bill's arithmetic was easy: 12 percent on $100,000 is $12,000 a year, or $1,000 a month.

First thing Monday morning Bill called the brokerage firm sponsoring this high-yield debt offering. A broker naturally suggested he would be wise to invest the whole $100,000. Inclined to do just that, Bill agreed to meet with him later that day.

He contacted his wife at work and proudly informed her he had discovered a great deal. His wife, as the voice of reason, suggested that Bill ask my opinion.

Bill did phone me, but the only part of the conversation I could understand was 12 percent. The stroke had affected Bill's speech, making him difficult to understand, especially on the telephone, so I suggested we meet in person. He drove to my office, visions of a 12 percent return dancing in his head.

I informed him this investment vehicle was a high-risk junk bond. Such a speculative investment was unsuitable in his situation. He questioned how I was so certain it was high risk. My reply was simple: the high yield of a 12 percent versus comparative market returns of 8 percent on quality high-grade debt told me so.

Bill and I were on two different wavelengths. He continued to fixate on the potential of a 12 percent return, while I was worried about the substantial risk to his $100,000 principal.

Bill reluctantly followed my advice, prodded by his concerned wife. I did not know that Revco, the holder of this particular debt (borrower), would eventually file for bankruptcy. At the time I was concerned that the financial risk of this single-issue, high-yield junk bond was too great to accept.

Bill passed away about a year later, but at least his widow didn't have to face the loss of income and a principal balance that some five years later paid back only 35 cents on the dollar. J. Kenfield Morley in 1937 had good insight on this topic: "In investing money, the amount of interest you want should depend on whether you want to eat well or sleep well."

A basic tenet of mine is to avoid the big mistake. Academic research has found individuals tend to make, on average, two to three whopper financial mistakes over the course of their working years. The cost of these errors is estimated to add up to a quarter of a million dollars. This not insignificant sum can hurt the goal of feathering a nest egg to secure a long-term retirement.

An example of a huge mistake would be to invest in an individual high-yield (junk) bond, such as Bill was inclined to do. Some statistical studies show that one in 10 junk bonds could default. Bonds can and do default on a regular basis, and the higher yielding bonds carry a proportionately higher risk of financial or credit risk.

To sum up, depending on your age, risk temperament, and income needs, your portfolio should include an appropriate dose of fixed-income bonds. It makes perfect sense to keep your conservative and safe money ultra-safe, such as with U.S. Treasury securities. Work to avoid the big mistake. When investing in bonds, be as concerned with the return *of* your money as the return *on* it.

CHAPTER 6

FOLLOW THE SUN

Do not be too timid and squeamish about your actions.
All life is an experiment. The more experiments
you make the better.

Ralph Waldo Emerson

PREPARING FOR RETIREMENT

When it comes to retirement issues, many Americans are in denial. This is especially true of the 77 million baby boomers, the generation born between 1946 and 1964. Here is a quick reality check. Close your eyes and imagine life without a paycheck. Then, think of retirement as permanent unemployment. Recognize that owing to increased life expectancies, you likely will be retired and without earned income for a quarter to a third of your life. It is a financial necessity to provide for this period of life, which could run from 20 to as many as 40 years—the equivalent of an entire career.

Those planning for retirement must open their eyes and take a good look at the cold, hard truth of financial reality. To get this message means addressing the following: plan now, or you might live to regret it.

Author and futurist Ken Dychtwald is one who believes that age 95 could well become what age 65 is currently, a retirement signpost. Age 65 as the traditional retirement starting line goes back to the late nineteenth century and is credited to Otto von Bismark of Germany. In that era, not many workers actually lived to what was then considered an advanced age. The thinking at the time was that the few who did live that long would be eligible to dip into a social insurance program.

In 1935, with Franklin Roosevelt as president and the country still fighting the grip of the Great Depression, Social Security was initiated, with 65 as the eligible starting age. Back then, the average worker would stay on the job to age 69.

According to the American Society of Actuaries—people whose job it is to know these numbers—a 65-year-old man today has a 50 percent chance of living to 85, and a 25 percent probability of seeing 92. A 65-year-old woman has a 50 percent chance of making 88 and a 25 percent probability of reaching 94. Women, owing to their longer life expectancies and generally lower income at retirement, have an understandably greater sense of vulnerability about their long-term financial security than do men.

A married couple, both age 65 today, have a 50 percent probability of one of them living to 92 and a 25 percent chance of at least one of them making it to age 95. Based on these statistics, having 30-year, two-person retirement spans will become commonplace.

Such longevity, coupled with an expected explosion in medical breakthroughs, is why Ken Dychtwald, president of Age Wave, says by 2046 age 95 will look like 65 today.

An alarm bell should sound just by reading what appears on the 2006 personal benefit statement mailed out by the Social Security Administration (SSA):

It is very important to remember that Social Security was never intended to be your only source of income when you retire. Social Security can't do it all. You also need other savings, investments, pensions or retirement accounts to make sure you have enough money to live comfortably when you retire.

Then there is the following sobering truth, direct from the SSA itself, on the same individualized benefit estimate statement. It reads:

The Social Security system is facing serious future financial problems.... Unless action is taken soon to strengthen Social Security, in just 11 years (2017) we will begin paying more in benefits than we collect in taxes. Without changes, by 2041 the Social Security Trust Fund will be exhausted.

Addressing the issue of the Social Security Trust Fund, former Commerce Secretary Pete Peterson pulled no punches when he said, "In the first place, it's not funded. In the second…you shouldn't trust it."

A gap exists between perception and reality for boomers, who, when surveyed, expressed confidence in their ability to retire in their sixties while maintaining an equivalent or even an enhanced standard of living. A majority claimed they could live comfortably on 80 percent of their current income. Yet, in an answer to a follow-up question, only 27 percent felt they would be able to save 20 percent of their pre-retirement income. This is clear evidence of a credibility gap. When boomers were queried about their actual savings, only 16 percent admitted to putting away 20 percent of their income. I refer to saving a fifth of one's income as a rigorous savings program.

If all this doesn't cause your anxiety and blood pressure to rise, there is the wildcard of retiree health care costs to ponder. Fidelity Investments, in a study put out in 2006, calculates that a 65-year-old couple without employer-provided health care benefits will expend some $200,000 in out-of-pocket health care expenses in their retirement years.

Other studies suggest this number is too low, due to accelerating health costs coupled with increased life expectancy. While annual increases in the Consumer Price Index (CPI) have been relatively modest recently, increases in health care costs have been busting budgets at a double-digit clip. In fact, medical costs have outpaced the CPI for 13 of the past 17 years, and this trend is expected to continue.

The Employee Benefit Research Institute (EBRI) estimates this health cost at $216,000 if a couple lives to 80, $444,000 if they survive to 90, and $778,000 if they live to the ripe old age of 100. All experts agree the majority of affected people badly underestimate this substantial health care cost outlay.

Another sobering study, this one from the Center for Retirement Research at Boston College, confirms that many households are under-saving and unprepared to live comfortably in retirement.

Researchers concluded that without behavioral changes—specifically, substantially increased savings and a willingness to stay on the job to at least age 65, preferably longer—boomers face a drastically reduced standard of living in retirement.

Studies by Merrill Lynch and others find that boomers are saving at only one-third of the rate they need to match the retirement security they imagine. This disconnect is further amplified in the latest annual retirement confidence survey conducted by the Employee Benefit Research Institute, which found that most employees expect to live a long and financially comfortable life. Yet, less than a quarter of those surveyed had accumulated retirement savings of $100,000 or more.

Professor Jack Van Derhei, co-author of the EBRI study, points out that by-and-large, current retirees had traditional defined-benefit pensions and retiree health plans. Today, outside of public employee and government employment circles, these retirement safeguards are increasingly going the way of the buffalo. Boomers should wake up and realize theirs will not be their parents' retirement program.

Part of this misguided perception and overconfidence stems from attitudes shaped by looking at the financial status of current retirees. Their parents' generation, whether or not they acknowledge it, has been fortunate in regard to retirement financial security.

First of all, this World War II demographic group took responsibility and helped themselves by being generally thrifty and frugal. They also had more stable lifetime employment patterns, healthy private pension plans, and retiree health care benefits along with fairly generous Social Security benefits.

In addition, they experienced a big run-up in housing values since the 1970s. The median home price in 1967 was $23,000. The median home price in 2005 was $219,000. Financial assets also appreciated nicely in the 1980s and 1990s. The Dow average was at 880 in the summer of 1982. In the go-go years of the 1990s, average annual returns on investments ranged as high as 18.5 percent. Looking forward, many financial experts expect more pedestrian returns in the market, averaging in the middle to high single digits. Boomers should heed this message and lower their expectations for their return on investments.

Life-planning gurus, including Ken Dychtwald and Mitch Anthony, believe the traditional concept of retirement is a thing of the past. As Dychtwald says, "If retirement isn't dead, it is at least dying."

Mitch Anthony, author of the book *The New Retirementality* and a frequent speaker at financial planning conferences, counsels us to think of retirement differently. He observes, "In the future, retirement will no longer be viewed as an isolated economic event, but instead will be seen as part of ongoing life planning. The new retirementality is the ability to achieve the freedom to pursue our own goals, at our own pace, and find a sense of balance in life, regardless of age." Today, retirement should be thought of more as a journey than a destination.

Owing to insufficient nest eggs, debt burdens, soaring health care costs, increasing longevity, and cracks in the pension and Social Security systems, economic necessity will force many boomers to continue working well past age 65.

Columnist Jonathan Clements points out that just because most folks find it an economic necessity to retire later doesn't mean you have to revise your dream. "Don't like the idea of working past age

65? You could still retire on time. But you will have to invest intelligently and save like crazy." In another column, he calls for the reader to "save like a demon."

Other workers, having reached financial independence and attained security, will still make a conscious decision to postpone retirement past the traditional age of 65. Psychologist and gerontologist Dychtwald conducted a study for financial services firm AIG Sun America in which "we tried to find out what people are really seeking, and the word that kept emerging was 'freedom'—and sometimes that means working."

Robert Carlson, author of *The New Rules of Retirement,* says, "Many won't retire at all, at least not before their health requires it." By continuing to work, you are in effect financing your retirement through employment income. This is a great aid in securing your financial future.

GIB—STILL ON THE JOB

According to the AARP, the new definition of old is 77.5 years. By that measure, one of our clients, Gib, is indeed old at 80, yet he continues to ply his trade as a self-employed heating and air conditioning (HVAC) technician. He works out of an extra garage at his modest home in Oshkosh, Wisconsin, where for almost 60 years he has been keeping his homeowning customers comfortably warm in the frigid winter months and cool in the heat of summer. Despite some age-related health concerns, Gib is reluctant to walk away from his lifetime's work. Financially secure, he is happy to be working and is good at maintaining and servicing furnaces and air conditioning units. He feels his customers need him and rely on him.

The solution to a financially secure retirement could be opting for a simpler and more fulfilling lifestyle. According to Mitch Anthony, "Retirement is a transition where we can re-engage, regenerate, and renew. It's not a time for quitting but for new beginnings."

Another viable option to quitting work cold turkey is downshifting. Many individuals are interested in changing gears, but don't want to or can't afford to stop completely. This transition could also involve downsizing to less expensive housing, perhaps in a new part of the country.

Downshifting could take the form of part-time, or semi-retirement, whereby you cut back on the stress and workload of a demanding position for more flexibility and lighter duty, albeit at reduced pay.

Interestingly, about two-thirds of those who plan to work in retirement want to change their line of work. They seem willing to make the tradeoff between a crummy job with good pay and a good job with crummy pay.

I personally know more than a few engineers and professionals who talk of escaping from what they are doing to become self-employed handymen. They derive satisfaction from working with their hands and seeing the immediate result of a job well done. I am confident a steady income-producing opportunity exists for these individuals because I know there are millions like me who are not handy and need help.

By continuing to earn even a supplemental income during your own retirement years, you take stress off the investment portfolio and are better able to afford the ever-increasing cost of living longer. Also, do not understate the psychic rewards that come from doing meaningful and satisfying work.

MAN OF THE YEAR

A financially secure retirement describes a period of life with new opportunities and freedom from money concerns. A good example of the latter is Andy Grove, who, as former chair of Intel, has no financial security worries. Although now officially retired from the silicon chip company he co-founded in 1968, the now 70-year-old Grove is still very physically active, involved, and busy. He also spends time doting on his two young grandchildren.

What he finds wonderful about this phase in his life is, "I get to pick and choose what I do. The world doesn't get to pick and choose."

For one thing, he relishes being able to exercise every morning, something he always wanted to do, but the pressing demands of running a global high-tech goliath often got in the way.

Harvard Business School professor Richard Tedlow is the author of *Andy Grove*, a biography of the man *Time* named its "Man of the Year" in 1997. Tedlow describes Grove as someone who always seemed happy, balanced, and devoted to his wife, Eve, and family.

From Kevin Maney's book review in *USA Today* we learn, "Grove lost family at Auschwitz. He had scarlet fever as a child, prostate cancer in middle age, and now has Parkinson's disease. He saw Intel nearly fail in 1986, when the Japanese stormed into memory chips, forcing Intel to switch to microprocessors—the guts of PCs."

Tedlow admiringly says of Grove, "The story of the man's life is an inspiration. He doesn't allow himself to be defeated."

Andy Grove, through the Grove Foundation, directs his energy, talent, and financial resources toward those causes and organizations for which he feels a passion. This includes working closely with the University of California San Francisco on prostate cancer research. He also devotes time and money to the City College of New York, the alma mater of this Hungarian-born, Jewish refugee. He still keeps his foot in the door at Intel, but now when he meets in an advisory capacity with current executives it is likely to be for a scheduled two-hour walk and talk.

A FRIEND OF MOM

Like many traditional stay-at-home moms, my mother, Peggy, entered the workforce once my youngest brother and sister were off to school full time. Through a church network connection she found a position and went to work at Mercy Home, west of the downtown loop of Chicago. Mom was an early adoptee of flexible scheduling to balance work and family. She arranged to start her workday after Danny and Sheila left for school and was home before they returned. She did not want latchkey kids. Mom found her skills managing a large family were transferable to an office setting.

Mercy is part of the Catholic Archdiocese of Chicago Charities and does substantial work in educating, housing, counseling, and shaping the lives of young boys and girls. These children are for the most part from broken homes, and they often lead desperate and neglected lives. Mercy Home provides a loving and caring environment and has had much success in rescuing young lives and putting them on a positive track. Working part time for a nonprofit meant my mother's income was meager. Yet Mom found psychological rewards beyond the size of her paycheck, including being a part of something worthwhile.

Mom spent the last 10 years of her life at Mercy, and it was there she made friends with Tom B. With an introduction from my mother, I had the privilege of getting to know this good fellow, and he has since become a favored client of my financial planning and investment advisory firm.

Mom was a good judge of character and took an immediate liking to Tom. As she was older, the relationship could almost be described as that of a big sister. They had in common their Catholic faith, north side Chicago upbringing, and Irish roots, and each was a parent of a large family.

Tom B. and his wife have seven children, the same size brood as my mom and dad. Tom possesses strong organizational skills and capably managed Mission Press, the printing arm connected with Mercy. Mom worked closely with Tom and quickly grew to respect and like him.

To know Tom was to know his wife and best friend, Carol. At the age of 54, Tom's soulmate had a big-time cancer scare that rattled their lives; but, in retrospect, that crisis made their marriage, faith, and family stronger.

Carol was diagnosed with a malignant tumor on her kidney and had it surgically removed. Barely missing a step, Carol soon resumed her busy life, epitomized by serving the less fortunate among us as an active volunteer at Misericordia, which makes a home for developmentally disabled adults.

Cancer brought my mother closer to Tom and Carol. Mom possessed an indomitable spirit, and she was there for them as they dealt with the appearance of this major but not insurmountable health obstacle. Tom and Carol were there for Mom a few years later when she was diagnosed with lung cancer.

WEIGHTY LIFE-AND-DEATH MATTERS

Unlike many people who are uncomfortable around cancer patients, my parents never hesitated to confront cancer head on. I recall my mother helping neighborhood women she barely knew, driving them over the course of their cancer treatments. One can imagine how much support this simple act of kindness provided at a time when it was most needed. After my mother courageously underwent major surgery to remove a cancerous lung in the hope it would save her life, her surgical oncologist asked Mom and Dad to talk to a couple contemplating this same life-or-death health decision.

They willingly met with the frightened couple during their ordeal and counseled them as only those who experienced the same predicament could.

Following in the giant footsteps of my mom and dad, I feel an obligation as a fortunate cancer survivor to help others facing this dastardly disease. As a member of the cancer community and a veteran of the war it wages, I want to be of help wherever I can to those cancer patients in the heat of battle.

My friend and editor Jan waged her own successful battle against breast cancer last year. She now receives the drug Herceptin every three weeks over the course of the first year. This breakthrough drug is supposed to stop cold the reappearance of her particular cancer. It is considered a miracle drug for the impact it offers in the treatment of an aggressive form of breast cancer.

While Jan was at the hospital oncology clinic to receive her drug, a woman newly victimized by cancer sought her out with questions about hair loss and other troubling experiences. Jan held the trembling hands of this scared-of-death woman, answered her questions, addressed her real fears, and offered hope as only someone who has been on the front lines and in the trenches can.

All cancer survivors live with the realization that this ugly disease might return. It is a cruel irony that once struck by cancer, one is statistically more likely to be victimized again, often in a form more difficult to treat. This is not to imply that cancer survivors are doomed. Far from it. The reality is, those who have successfully beaten cancer have reason to believe they will live a normal life span. Sadly, a minority of survivors are pessimists. Having been scarred by cancer, they fail to escape the fearful grip it can hold and do not live life as fully as they can.

The year I struggled with my serious cancer, Martha, our daughter, had been 11. Although Martha did not express her emotions outwardly, Cathy became aware of how scared our daughter was that I would not survive. A year later, the father of a seventh grade classmate of Martha's suddenly lost his life. Cathy wisely suggested I engage in some paternal grief counseling with our daughter. On a nice summer evening, I took Martha on a walk, believing discussion of a serious matter is better addressed while in motion. My health picture and outlook were far better than a year earlier. Just as Martha felt a return to normalcy, her classmate's life was turned upside down by the loss of her father. Martha's anxiety about her own father's survival returned.

I remember informing Martha in our heart-to-heart talk that over half of all cancer victims survive and resume life as usual. Relieved, she admitted she never knew this fact. In her short life experience, she understandably associated cancer with the funerals she had attended for her three deceased grandparents.

Our son, Jack, was in third grade when a classmate of his lost her 30-year-old dad to the ravages of bone cancer. We were alone in the car heading to a soccer game when Jack lowered his voice and asked if I had heard the news about Anna's father, Jared.

The previous summer at a Fourth of July picnic I had met Jared, the father of two young children, who was working to become a physician's assistant. I was aware of the tough challenge he faced. He had already lost one arm to the disease. As Jared and I talked, I learned that although he was holding out hope, his prognosis was poor. I sent him Lance Armstrong's and Hamilton Jordan's inspirational books to encourage him. He expressed his gratitude for my willingness to broach the subject, but six months later, he was gone. I found myself trying to make some sense of Jared's death to my son.

Jack offered that he knew Anna's father had cancer and that I had cancer. I looked at this observation as a teaching moment, but apparently ventured too far with my lecture on weighty life-and-death matters, because nine-year-old Jack soon asked if we could talk about something else.

Hamilton Jordan, himself the father of young children, points out in his book that a child is not able to remember much about a parent who dies before the child reaches the age of seven.

I read this observation during the dark days of my own cancer odyssey. It was the Fourth of July, and I was stretched out on the couch in the family room, too weak and fatigued to go to the park and watch our then five-year-old son compete in that holiday's foot races. Cathy and Jack returned home with smiling faces and a trophy to show me for his having won the race. This definitely picked me up; yet at the same time I prayed I would survive so that our youngest would grow up to know his dad.

REMEMBERING CAROL

Carol, as a long-term cancer survivor, has been a remarkable woman who epitomizes living strong. At the service celebrating her life, her daughter Lucy reminisced that Carol was a superb teacher, a devoted wife, and nurturing mother, and before her death, a proud grandmother. "She volunteered for countless years at Misericordia, played bridge weekly, enjoyed golfing, hosted numerous parties with many good friends, and traveled around the world."

As I sat listening to the service, I mused about how I had visited Carol at her home a few short weeks before her end. As usual, she cared not at all about the business of personal finances, leaving that entirely up to Tom and me. Instead, her genuine warmth was displayed by inquiring about matters of my own health and family. It was Carol I felt comfortable enough with to confide my concerns, one year earlier, on the eve of the surgery that would confirm my own cancer.

Happily, our visit occurred on one of Carol's good days, because during her painful struggle, she experienced good days and bad. I found Carol physically weak, but determined, and she was able to flash her trademark smile. Her spirits were bolstered by having her oldest son, Tom Jr., and her granddaughter spend the day with her. One of their many close neighborhood friends was there, too, visiting in the living room. I recall her introducing me to him not as her and Tom's financial planner but as a friend who had, in her words, triumphed over cancer. These encouraging words have stayed with me.

Carol's daughter Lucy ended the funeral celebration with this parting reflection: "Our mom loved roses. Her beautiful rose garden reminded us all of how precious life is. For in front of her rose bushes reads the sign: Stop and smell the roses."

TOM—A THREE-RING-BINDER PLANNER

Even before Tom became a widower, he always devoted the necessary time and attention to managing the finances and investments. He is what I have observed over the course of my long planning career as a "three-ring-binder" planner.

I find this attribute very much a positive, as Tom and others like him stay on top of their personal finances and monitor them in an organized, well-disciplined fashion.

Thomas Stanley and William Danko, authors of the phenomenal best-seller *The Millionaire Next Door,* found in their academic research that financially successful people have certain traits in common. "Efficiency is one of the most important components of wealth accumulation," they observed. "Simply: People who become wealthy

allocate their time, energy, and money in ways consistent with en-
hancing their net worth."

Impressed with how the use of inexpensive three-ring binders
like Tom's can facilitate the planning process, I and my partners,
Scott Grittinger and Mike Weil, decided to utilize this simple, low-
tech, yet efficient tool for our clients. Its value lies in being visible
and readily located, easily updated by replacing outdated account
statements with the most recent, its contents copied or marked up
when necessary, and brought along as a handy reference when meeting with financial advisors. It also enables a less financially knowledgeable partner or family member to locate vital personal financial
information in a consolidated fashion.

I met with a busy, two-income couple in their late thirties accustomed to using all the latest high-tech gadgets, electronic data re-
trieval systems, and laptops in their positions as professional
engineers. Still, they brought their trusty red binder to their initial
financial planning meeting with me. At the other extreme, a far less
satisfactory meeting occurred with a certain planning client, who while
his wife talked, spent the whole time fumbling unproductively with
his laptop. Low-tech works.

My friend and client Tom B. maintains his three-ring-binder system in his home office, accessible to him on a shelf behind his desk.
I have seen him quickly retrieve any investment statements, tax information, insurance policy, or retirement plan we are discussing.
He keeps eight three-inch binders, each identified by subject on the
spine.

Tom fits to a tee the typical profile of *The Millionaire Next Door*.
After one of our planning and review meetings, he sent a thank you
note for a book I had sent him with an updated net worth statement.
In his own words, "I started doing my net worth on 1/22/83 and have
done it each year since then as a guide." This approach is typical of
those with an activist planning mindset, especially Tom's reference
to using a net worth statement as a guidepost.

To calculate net worth on an annual basis, as Tom does, is a good habit and solid practice. The third week of January is an ideal time, as the 12/31 year-end account values and balances are available then. As a guide, the net worth figure is critical to a personal finance analysis because it provides a clear measurement of financial condition and is a means of keeping score and tracking progress.

The net worth calculation is also a starting point for estate planning. Your net worth represents your living estate. To find your death estate, add life insurance in force. In retirement planning parlance for clients I like to refer to net worth as the nest egg.

In his thank you note to me Tom had also written, "I always did try to save, but I guess with the seven kids and paying for Catholic education for 16 years each and weddings, I'm lucky I have what I have. That sum was $665,000 I didn't invest in stocks and bonds." He was not lamenting this substantial cost outlay, because it was for his family, and would have done it the same way if he had it to do over. He considered it an investment in their future.

An important point is that whatever his expenses, Tom always tried to save. Thomas Edison, a genius, cast light on this subject by saying, "We all make mistakes in life, but saving money is never one of them."

According to the authors of *The Millionaire Next Door,* subtitled *The Surprising Secrets of America's Wealthy*, certain identifiable traits describe those individuals such as Tom B. who, though unassuming, nonetheless demonstrate a degree of financial success. The foremost trait is frugality. Cicero told us, "Frugality includes all the other virtues." For this trait to have an effect, it has to be shared and exercised by both partners in a marriage.

Speaking of her deceased mom, Tom's daughter Lucy said, "If she wore designer labels or lovely clothes, it was only because it fit and she liked the color or because she had received it as a gift. Some people depend on material things to define themselves to the public, but not our mom. If she wanted a five-carat diamond, I have no doubt that my dad would have bought it for her, but it wasn't her style. She was classy and humble, without the show lights."

Unlike Abe Lincoln, with his impoverished log cabin origins, his wife, Mary Todd Lincoln, was accustomed to the finer things money and privilege could buy. She kept Lincoln in the dark about spending considerable sums on refurbishing the White House. When he found out, he was furious, aware of how it would look when soldiers did not have shoes or blankets.

Abe did not need wealth or its trappings to be happy. As he said, "Most people are about as happy as they make up their minds to be."

Tom, with his lifestyle and habit of saving, possesses all the traits of the financially successful. "If you would be wealthy," the financially astute Benjamin Franklin told us, "think of saving as well as getting." Professors Stanley and Danko observe that to slowly and steadily reach the pinnacle of financial independence, a person has to be a compulsive saver and investor. From their book, we learn that millionaires routinely save 15 percent to 20 percent of their current income.

The authors refer to PAWs, or prodigious accumulators of wealth—those with moderate income/high net worth—as those who save a healthy portion of their income. PAWs live very much below their means. This is the polar opposite of UAWs, or under-accumulators of wealth—those with high income/low net worth. No matter how high their income, they spend more than they make and save little, if at all.

Stanley and Danko dwell heavily in their book on the relationship between income and net worth. According to these recognized authorities on building wealth, even if you are not the recipient of ultra-high compensation, the holder of an advanced degree, the beneficiary of a substantial inheritance, or someone who was born clutching a silver spoon, you can be successful financially, as measured by a million-dollar net worth.

Not surprisingly, Abraham Lincoln was a disciplined and diligent saver. As President, he regularly put a large chunk of his $25,000 annual salary into Treasury notes, then reinvested the interest. For help in managing his burgeoning Treasury bond portfolio, he turned to no less an authority than Treasury Secretary Salmon Chase, a member of his cabinet. At that time, Treasuries yielded at least as much, if not more, as they did in 2006.

At the time of Lincoln's tragic death in April 1865 at the age of 56, he and Mary were financially secure, having amassed an estate consisting of $60,000 in government securities, their Springfield home, and land acreage in Iowa and Illinois.

Stanley and Danko observe that most millionaires are first-generation wealthy and currently retired from ordinary jobs or the running of mundane businesses. In research for their book they discovered millionaires among the ranks of dry cleaners, auctioneers, mobile home park operators, rice farmers, and sandblasting contractors. I can add to theirs my own list of landscape contractor, maintenance supervisor, computer programmer, Christmas tree farmer, dairy worker, light bulb distributor, mid-level manager, nurse, cattle broker, mail carrier, and schoolteacher. Tom's small business was printing the tags used by the airlines to identify baggage.

Millionaire-authority Stanley still believes a million dollars represents a hallmark of prosperity, although the effects of inflation mean that today it takes $5 million to equal the $1 million of 30 years ago.

Tom employed another planning tactic the authors would applaud—that of consciously minimizing his income tax burden through the use of tax-advantaged retirement accumulation plans. While employed, he strove to contribute the maximum allowed to such accounts. These tax deductible sums were then able to grow on a tax-deferred basis—in other words, without the bite of current taxation—thereby allowing his account to grow into a sizeable nest egg. Indeed, tax-advantaged accumulation was primarily responsible for putting Tom in a position of financial independence, as he did not have a pension.

To quote from the *Millionaire Next Door*, "Wealth is more often the result of a lifestyle of hard work, perseverance, planning, and most of all, self-discipline."

The book's authors also identified a strong tie between investment planning and wealth accumulation. The PAWs of this world, those who manage to reach financial independence and concurrent retirement security, take financial planning and investment management very seriously. They devote much time and effort to the task and seek objective investment guidance. This diligence pays off.

Tom hired me in 1988, well before his retirement, for independent financial and investment advice. He read my books, attended our informational educational seminars, and generally made himself informed on financial and investment matters. All in all, I categorize Tom as an ideal client. He listened, learned, trusted, and implemented the counsel he received.

I am happy to report that owing to this successful collaboration, things worked out well for him.

Tom is a busy fellow, the epitome of an active retiree. His days are full, and he wonders out loud how he ever managed before retirement. He rises each day at dawn to attend daily morning church services, keeps up his house and property, cooks for his family of 35 at Thanksgiving, travels extensively, hosts his family and assorted close friends at his Florida condominium during the winter months, and is known regularly to assist neighbors in need. Despite a nagging rotator cuff injury, he has eschewed surgery, because it might not help appreciably, but mostly because he is unwilling to slow his pace. He enjoys woodworking and always has projects going, making gifts for his children and toys for his grandchildren. The homes of his family members are chock-full of handcrafted remembrances from their dad and grandpa.

Even though he is now living solo, he has no intention of moving out of his home. He is comfortable where he and Carol lovingly raised their family, and it serves as a familiar gathering place for the now-dispersed family clan.

I find it noteworthy how these now-single men—Tom, Uncle Bob, Uncle Billy, and my dad and Uncle Johnny before they passed on—have always had a strong relationship with their daughters. All of these otherwise independent fellows benefited from having loving young women in their lives, who help when it comes to certain domestic advice and, especially, health matters.

I recall that after my mom died how good my sister Colleen was for my dad, while they shared the home together. My Uncle John and cousin Mary Joyce had the same arrangement when he was not wintering in Florida, as does Uncle Bill and his daughter, Margaret. Dad was very grateful, once referring to Colleen as a good caregiver. My sister Mary Ann took the lead on dad's health care, accompanying him to doctor appointments, asking the hard questions, and communicating the results to the rest of the family.

Unlike women, who statistically see doctors more regularly than men, we as a gender are more hesitant to take a proactive approach to our health care. Tom confided to me that his daughters were insistent he immediately see a doctor to check out a swollen leg. It was good they were persistent, because the examination revealed a life-threatening blood clot, and Tom was quickly hospitalized.

Like any smart financial life planner, Tom has a straightforward vision of what he wants from the balance of his life, and from his finite financial resources in support of that vision. Like most people of his generation, he desires financial independence and the wherewithal to take care of himself without being dependent upon his children or anyone else. He correctly recognizes that as long as he continues to intelligently manage his resources, financial security is a high probability.

According to authors of *The Millionaire Next Door*, the secrets of America's wealthy are that they do not necessarily live in the most upscale neighborhoods, drive luxury vehicles, or display their social status by belonging to exclusive country clubs. Rather, they consciously downscale their lifestyle, believing that attaining financial independence is a higher priority than displaying wealth. A prime example is Warren Buffett, the second-wealthiest person on the planet, who has lived the last 40 years of his life in the same unpretentious, middle-class Omaha neighborhood.

BOB K. AND TOM F., TWO PEAS IN A POD

I consider myself very fortunate to know, work with, and learn important lessons about life and finances from my friends Bob K. and Tom F.

These two gentlemen share a lot in common. First, Bob and Tom F. are devoted family men—loving husbands, cherished fathers, and now proud and very happy grandfathers.

Bob and his wife, Laurel, mother to their five children, recently celebrated 40 years as partners in marriage. Tom F. and Metty have been joined for 37 years and have two daughters.

Both couples find great joy in being grandparents. Bob and Laurel feel blessed to have nine grandchildren, all under the age of nine. Tom and Metty's daughters each gave birth recently to a second child. They now have their hands full with what I have heard referred to as "millionaire's twins," meaning a healthy baby boy and girl.

Meeting for breakfast with Tom F. as I regularly do, our first order of business is always viewing the latest pictures of his offspring and getting an update on them. I asked him what made being a grandparent so special. Tom answered that it makes him feel connected, that a part of him is carrying on in the world. He went on to say that in raising his own children life often seemed hectic and demanding. It is therefore a gift to be a generation removed and be able to step back and observe development and the wonder of life through a young set of eyes. Grandpa Tom's and Grandma Metty's schedules revolve around regular visits to spend quality time with their precious grandkids in the East and in their own home.

It is as a grandfather that Bob K. now chooses to define himself. His license plate reads Bapa, the name by which his grandkids refer to him. Laurel is called Nana, and together they ride the grandparent circuit, visiting their loved ones in a triangle between St. Louis, Indianapolis, and Milwaukee. I have seen Bob positively giddy in anticipation of a weekend stay by the little Indy girls at Bapa and Nana's home.

A telling example of the closeness of Bob's clan is the annual summer gathering for a week at Lake Delton in the Wisconsin Dells. What started 25 years ago with a single cottage is now up to five cottages housing three generations. It's a "can't miss" week that brings everyone together and adds to the memories they are making for each generation's lifetime.

Life for Bob also revolves around his large extended family, including many aunts, uncles, and cousins. He admits he has been blessed in life, first as the second of seven children of his recently departed parents, mate of Laurel, and father to four sons and a daughter. He has a special fondness for all his children's spouses, along with their in-laws.

Though they are blessed in many ways, for Bob and Laurel life has not been all roses. Their biggest heartbreak was the death, a few years ago, of their first grandchild, Spencer, at the tender age of five. Bob had been extremely close to Spencer, who suffered from a congenital heart defect. Despite the child's courageously undergoing multiple surgeries and enduring the valiant efforts of his doctors— culminating in a heart transplant— Spencer's life could not be saved.

Bob wears a multicolored wristband that Spencer lovingly crafted and presented to his Bapa Bob the night before his second major surgery. You won't see Bob without this touching remembrance adorning his left wrist.

Spencer might be gone physically, but he is certainly not forgotten. His parents, Chris and Tina, started Spencer's Fund, a charitable organization affiliated with the Congenital Heart Information Network (CHIN). They raise money at an annual golf outing to assist families in their hometown area of St. Louis who need help with lodging and meals while their children receive medical treatment. Bob proudly points out that his daughter-in-law, Tina, has become an expert on Spencer's condition and now counsels, as only a mother could, distraught families facing this same frightening diagnosis.

Thankfully, the remaining nine grandchildren are all healthy. I suspect the gift of unconditional love Bob and Laurel heap on their grandkids is due in part to having lost Spencer and their realization of how precious are these young lives.

Sometimes in life when it rains, it pours. So it was for Bob and Laurel in mid-2002. Shortly before Spencer's passing, Bob was diagnosed with cancer of the esophagus. The prognosis was grim.

To add to the family's woes, Bob's younger brother Al had been bravely battling brain cancer, which ultimately took his life in September of that same difficult year.

Bob decided against having an extreme surgical procedure for his cancer, opting instead to undergo months of toxic chemotherapy and burning radiation treatments. During this period, I visited with a visibly weakened yet always high-spirited and resolute Bob at his home, and delivered some golf items as a gift for his sixty-second birthday. Bob was determined to play golf with me before the snows closed the course for that season. To a less optimistic man, this would have been wishful thinking, but Bob persevered, and we did indeed play a round at the end of October.

It is said a positive attitude is a beneficial attitude to fight an ugly disease like cancer. Bob surely possessed that quality. He had a lot to live for. The wedding of his youngest child and only daughter, Anne, was held at the height of his cancer ordeal. Bob was determined to dance with her at her reception, and he somehow rallied the strength to do just that. Bapa Bob and Nana have been blessed with grandchild number nine as Anne and her husband Mike recently welcomed their first child into the world.

Tom F. has also been touched by cancer, in his case colorectal. Although brave, Tom wasn't above sharing with me how scared he was this disease could well end his life. During the darkest days of his treatment, Tom expressed the fervent hope he could live long enough to see his grandchildren grow up and graduate from college, and maybe even attend their weddings.

Both Tom and Bob dodged the cancer bullet, admitting they should have listened to their bodies and been more proactive with respect to their health. Bob had persistent heartburn, one of the warning signs for esophageal cancer. He should have brought this to the attention of his doctor much sooner than he did. Tom, who also ignored certain telltale signs and is admittedly stubborn, now counsels everyone he knows to undergo a potentially lifesaving colonoscopy.

Colon cancer is the third leading cause of death from cancer. Consequently, public health organizations and officials urge all individuals over age 50 to have a colonoscopy, a test that allows a thorough exam of the interior of the colon. Speaking of the effectiveness of this screening to detect colon cancer, Patricia A. Ganz, director of cancer prevention at UCLA, says, "We could eliminate this disease if America had the will."

Both Tom and Bob epitomize living strong. Bob triumphantly played 60 holes of golf to punctuate his sixtieth birthday. Having survived a serious brush with cancer at age sixty-two, I like to imagine that Bob will play 75 holes of golf on his seventy-fifth birthday and that his grandchildren will caddy for him.

Tom F. constantly sports a yellow *Livestrong* bracelet I gave him when cancer made an unwelcome appearance in his life. This former marathon runner relishes pushing himself with vigorous outdoor exercise, cross-country skiing in the winter months, and bicycling or roller skating once the snow melts. Recently, Tom was temporarily slowed after undergoing a hip replacement. On top of this, Tom had a cardiac procedure and Metty had open-heart surgery. I am happy to report their hearts are now beating well and they are back to their go-go schedules.

Tom and Bob also have in common being CPAs and graduates of my alma mater, Marquette University. Although enrolled in Medicare and collecting Social Security, these gentlemen are a blur of activity and far from the stereotypical retiree.

Tom continues as a partner in a small CPA firm and is especially busy during annual tax preparation season. A long-time accounting instructor at a local technical college, Tom ably stepped in to take over the class load of his good friend and CPA partner, Dennis. I count Dennis as a friend of mine too, and he is Cathy's and my personal accountant and a valued member of our firm's advisory committee.

In another case of life throwing curve balls, Dennis has dealt courageously with a life-threatening infection caused by his artificial hip. His attitude toward calmly accepting whatever life brings him continually impresses me. When his new condo unit mysteriously burned down, Dennis shook off this major disruption in his life. He exhibited that same quality with this latest health scare. Dennis accepts doing whatever it takes, be it months of antibiotics and/or additional major surgeries to be able to once again play golf, and more importantly enjoy his grandchildren.

Bob has been a highly valuable and respected member of our investment advisory firm over the past seven years as in-house CPA and seasonal tax preparer. Health permitting, Bob plans to continue performing tax preparation services for clients of our firm in the years ahead. He actually professes to enjoy doing taxes and likes the math puzzle each return represents. Most of all, however, Bob is a people person who genuinely enjoys the personal interaction with our clients.

I find myself looking up to Bob more and more for wise counsel. On more than one occasion, Bob pointed out how fortunate we are to have such wonderful individuals as clients and how lucky I am to have assembled the quality group of professionals that comprise our advisory group.

THE HARDEST THING TO UNDERSTAND

In my opinion, CPA Tom F. is the most technically knowledgeable person I know regarding tax preparation and the income tax code. Yet he readily admits that our nation's personal income tax system, as constructed, is way too complex and utterly confusing. In this he would find support from the genius Albert Einstein, who said,

"The hardest thing in the world to understand is the income tax."

Steve Forbes, editor-in-chief of *Forbes* magazine and unsuccessful presidential candidate, has long been an outspoken proponent of not merely reforming the tax code, but of eliminating it completely and replacing it with a simple flat tax. To quote Forbes:

You can take your tax return to a dozen different preparers, and you will get a dozen different returns back because of the complexity and incomprehensibility of the current code. Just to put it into perspective, Abraham Lincoln's Gettysburg Address, which defined the American nation, was just over 200 words in length. America's Declaration of Independence was 1,300 words. The Holy Bible, which took a few years to put together, contains 700,073 words. The federal tax code and its regulations, 9 millions words and rising.

Noted Milwaukee financial planner and tax professional Mike Arnow contends that a simple flat tax, which could be filed on a postcard like Steve Forbes espouses, will never see the light of day. In his realistic view, politicians, being politicians, will continue to use the tax code to influence social policy.

In looking at my most recent personal income tax bill, I am in agreement with H. L. Mencken, who said, "Unquestionably, there is progress. The average American now pays out almost as much in taxes alone as he formerly earned in wages."

A never-ending political debate takes place over tax policy, despite calls from all sides for tax relief and reform. No matter the outcome, my own sentiments are echoed by this question posed by author and humorist Peg Bracken: "Why does a small tax increase cost you two hundred dollars, and a substantial tax cut save you thirty cents?"

As each April 15 filing deadline passes, I am reminded of Ronald Reagan's definition of a taxpayer: "Someone who works for the government, but doesn't have to take a civil service examination."

Financial planning is heavily tax driven. Taxes represent a significant burden, and ignoring their importance jeopardizes your financial objectives. Any dollars saved through tax-minimization strategies can be used to help meet your financial goals.

Unfortunately, according to a Harris Interactive poll, 39 percent of taxpayers admit to doing nothing to try to minimize their 2005 tax return. This is clearly contrary to how financially successful million-aire-next-door types operate.

The tax impact needs to be assessed for every major financial planning decision you make: managing capital gain treatments on an investment portfolio, using tax-exempt or taxable bond income, choosing the best way to build a retirement nest egg, rolling over a retirement distribution, determining which money to spend first at retirement, developing charitable and gifting strategies, formulating an estate plan, or deciding to rent or purchase a home.

FORM 1040 AS A TAX-PLANNING ROAD MAP

Comedian Fred Allen had a humorous take on the income tax form, observing, "An income tax form is like a laundry list—either way you lose your shirt." However, because all financial planning has such a major income tax planning emphasis, the best starting point for you is to gather your most recent 1040 tax return and take a couple of minutes to study it. Involve your spouse, if it is a joint return.

Even the most basic financial planning demands an analysis of the income tax return. Whether or not you have your taxes profes-sionally prepared—or, perhaps, especially if you do—you will ben-efit by having a basic understanding of the federal tax structure. As an advisor, I always carry 1040 tax forms with me so I can illustrate tax-planning implications to clients. The first thing I do when ana-lyzing a tax return is to isolate the taxable income line.

This important line item is emphasized in bold print on the form as *taxable income*. That figure is the result of all preceding computa-tions. As the name implies, it refers to the actual amount of your income that is taxable. From a tax standpoint, the taxable income figure represents the bottom line, the dollar amount of your income subject to federal income tax.

Knowing both your filing status and taxable income means you can quickly identify your marginal tax bracket simply by referring to the IRS tax tables.

The terms *tax bracket, bracket*, and *marginal tax bracket* are synonymous. Most taxpayers have heard these terms, yet few can quote me their personal tax bracket. Fewer still are able to express the importance of this percentage to their own financial planning.

Knowing your marginal tax bracket and comprehending its implications are at the heart of tax planning. For example, Nancy falls into the 25 percent bracket. This means, if she receives a $1 raise, 25 percent or a quarter of this raise is eaten up by federal taxes. If Nancy is able to reduce her taxable income by $1, perhaps by making a deductible charitable contribution, she lightens her tax load by 25 percent or 25 cents for that $1.

It helps to visualize the concept of marginal taxes by thinking of a stairway, with each step representing one of the five steps, or brackets, in our progressive tax system.

Don't confuse marginal with average. Marginalism is an economic term used to define the impact on the next dollar. Note that as your taxable income increases, the tax bite on those dollars gets progressively higher. I like to refer to this phenomenon as "The more you make, the more they take."

As you progress up the taxable income stairway, the air becomes heavier, with taxes choking a greater share of your income. Higher tax-bracket payers are naturally more inclined to seek relief from the voracious appetite of the tax collectors. But I emphasize that the edge of a tax rate increase is a step, not a cliff.

PLANNING POINTER

I hope everyone appreciates the stark contrast between tax avoidance and tax evasion. Tax evasion is illegal. Avoid tax evasion at all costs. Tax avoidance is perfectly legal and is an important aspect of tax planning. According to one of the most influential twentieth century economists, John Maynard Keynes, "The avoidance of taxes is the only intellectual pursuit that carries any reward."

Tax planning is a search for ways to minimize taxable income. Financial and retirement planning go hand-in-hand with effective tax planning. High-bracket taxpayers are often frustrated to see a third or more of their investment income go down the federal tax drain, particularly true with the top 31 percent, 36 percent, and 39.6 percent tax rates. Tax-exempt income is an option for them to consider.

Municipalities are allowed to attract investors with bond income exempt (free) by law from federal taxation. This tax advantage helps municipalities secure financing at a favorable cost, because high-income investors find these lower tax-exempt returns attractive.

Individuals, however, sometimes let the reduction of taxes override other financial considerations. I have witnessed individuals so intent on avoiding taxes they willingly accept a lower after-tax investment return. Taxpayers in the 15 percent tax bracket, for instance, are left with more after paying taxes than if they had opted for a tax-free return.

In my considered opinion, the only route to take to invest in municipal bonds is through a tax-exempt bond mutual fund. I strongly advise against purchasing individual municipal bonds.

Two excellent fund choices are the Vanguard Intermediate Term Tax Exempt (VWITX) or the T. Rowe Price Tax-Free Intermediate Bond (PTIBX). Either of these quality no-load, low-cost municipal bond funds would serve as a core tax-free fund.

These funds offer broad diversification, professional credit surveillance and selection, controlled volatility, ready marketability and liquidity, and the ability to receive dividends as current income or reinvestment.

TAX-SAVING STRATEGIES

It is important to know and track the tax (cost) basis of all your holdings in a taxable account. Tax-planning opportunities exist to make lemonade out of lemons by selling at a loss. Taking losses is known as harvesting. Capital losses can offset capital gains dollar for dollar, and a net loss of up to $3,000 per year can be used against income on federal returns, with any excess carried forward.

A tax is applied on the appreciation (profit) realized upon the sale of a capital asset. Capital assets include stocks, bonds, mutual funds, and real estate. A capital gain is the difference between the purchase price (cost) and the sales price. Prior to sale, your gain/loss is just on paper and hence unrealized. A sale transforms a paper profit into a realized capital gain in the year of sale.

One of the major changes in the most recent tax law is the reduction in the long-term capital gains rate from 20 percent to 15 percent. This may change, and it is important to be aware of current law at the time you are making tax-based decisions.

Income shifting (transferring the tax bite) could allow grandparents to gift highly appreciated stock to their grandchildren, perhaps for education expenses. Upon the sale of the transferred asset, a lower capital gains tax is potentially owed by the younger owner. Other points to consider include:

- Investments generating tax-favored capital gain or dividends are preferred over those that produce ordinary income.
- Attention should be given to the type of investments you hold in taxable accounts and place inside tax-deferred accounts. Investments that pay you ordinary income, such as bonds and bond funds, might better be held inside a tax-deferred account. Also, remember that capital losses cannot be taken in retirement accounts such as IRAs.
- The attractiveness of dividend-paying stock funds has been enhanced under current tax law.
- The appeal of variable annuities has been lessened, because once withdrawn, these tax-deferred accounts are taxed as ordinary income, no matter how earned.

In a revolutionary change, qualifying dividend income (such as from stocks or stock mutual funds) is also tax favored at the same maximum 15 percent rate as long-term capital gains. Previously, dividend income constituted ordinary income. As the name indicates, ordinary income receives no special treatment and thus is subject to the full brunt of taxation.

Interest income from bank money market accounts, bank CDs, and bonds is taxed at ordinary income rates, as are non-qualifying dividends derived from mutual fund money market and bond funds.

In investing, you should contrast capital gain, tax-favored dividend, and ordinary income for tax planning purposes.

Working alongside CPAs such as Mike Arnow, Bob K., Tom F., and Dennis, I see their uncompromising integrity and basic honesty on display. These qualities are comforting in an era where too many accountants have been hauled off to jail and the profession sullied by high-profile accounting scandals. As old-time comedian Milton Berle quipped, "My accountant just went into business with General Motors. They make the cars, he's making the license plates."

We must learn to operate our personal financial affairs in a constantly changing tax environment. It's a difficult task because we are dealing with a moving target. Tax legislation is a product of partisan gamesmanship, political compromise, and lobbyists' pressures. As Mike Arnow reminds us, there is an old saying that you really wouldn't want to see either sausage or tax legislation being made.

A prime reason individuals fall short in pursuit of financial independence is a failure to understand and apply the tax laws. The challenge is to uncover planning opportunities built into the tax laws.

TARGET RETIREMENT FUNDS—A SIMPLE PATH

Knowledgeable observers agree that a key reason for Americans' dismal savings rate is that too much complexity exists in tax-advantaged saving plans. According to *Forbes* magazine, "There are at least 11 kinds of retirement accounts, with different rules for who's eligible, when you get phased out, when you can, can't or must roll something over, when you get docked for taking out too little, and when you get smacked for taking out too much." They make light of the ever-growing array of tax-deferred savings vehicles and the idea they are anything but simple.

According to the U.S. Department of Commerce, the personal savings rate has declined precipitously since 1990, when it was 7.8 percent, compared with less than 1 percent in 2005. It is estimated that less than half of all households in the age bracket of 45 to 54 have adequate retirement savings put away.

For the vast majority of individuals, the perplexing choices and bewildering maze of how to invest their 401(k), IRA, and other retirement accounts presents an overwhelming and frustrating puzzle. The fact is, most plan participants are rank amateurs when it comes to investing, consequently doing a lousy job at solving this vitally important retirement security task.

This job of managing your own retirement nest egg is too often one for which you are not well-suited. For starters, you face the daunting task of choosing among dozens of different fund options. The most recent 401(k) menu I reviewed for a client had over 100 funds listed. The only information you might have is past performance, which is a dangerous criterion to use by itself.

Plan participants routinely tend to make the common errors of chasing performance, attempting to time the market, and failing to adequately construct a diversified portfolio. Sadly, the result can be a dismal performance at a time when nest eggs must be intelligently managed if individuals are to reach financial independence in retirement.

The solution, using my KISS method, is to make one clear decision to pick a target retirement fund that neatly corresponds to your age and planning horizon. Fortunately, Vanguard and T. Rowe Price, as progressive mutual fund complexes, recognized the value of so-called target funds for retirement accounts and were among the first to make them available.

Specifically, the Vanguard Target Retirement 2025 (VTTVX) and T. Rowe Price Retirement 2025 (TRRHX) offerings have been professionally designed to work well for an investor planning on retiring at or near 2025. For example, if you were born in 1960 you will turn 65 in the year 2025. Either age-appropriate fund would be an ideal choice. There are fund choices for those targeting the years 2015, 2020, 2030, 2035, 2040, and 2045, as well.

The beauty of this type of fund is you can make just one logical decision, then sit back and relax in confidence, knowing your retirement investing is on track as well as on target.

In this one investment package you receive effective diversification. The T. Rowe Price fund is composed of 11 of the company's actively managed mutual funds, covering the full spectrum of asset classes. The Vanguard fund is equally diversified, with four of its broad-based index funds.

In addition, each of these target funds has been professionally designed expressly for retirement accounts. Portfolios are continually being supervised and actively managed. These funds are unique in that the asset allocation mix is adjusted over time to a more conservative composition, one that favors more bonds, fewer stocks. Such investments function on automatic pilot.

The accepted wisdom in investment management is that as one becomes older the portfolio should shift to less volatile and more preservation conscious. The investment management team maintains some flexibility in adapting to market conditions and regularly rebalances the portfolio.

Rebalancing is a proven investment management technique that professionals, such as pension funds, use to help keep a portfolio in balance, keep the risk profile in check, and boost performance. Individuals, at the other extreme, recoil from rebalancing as if it was the plague, for it takes courage to buy low and sell high.

Although Vanguard and T. Rowe Price take slightly different approaches, I believe you can't go wrong with either of these no-load, low-cost, common sense investment vehicles. I have only one caveat, and that is to use only one target fund for a given retirement account, as these one-stop shopping vehicles are not meant to be mixed and matched.

To execute this KISS plan, simply invest 100 percent of all new contributions and current balances to your selected target fund offering. Then resist the urge to monitor too closely or switch. As the Vanguard Group says in a print ad targeted to retirement plan savers, "Sometimes, the best way to manage your retirement fund is to ignore it."

Listen also to the down-home wisdom of Darcia from Detroit, a student in a retirement investment class I led: "Invest much and don't touch."

In an opinion piece in *The Wall Street Journal*, Robert L. Reynolds, vice chairman of Fidelity Investments, builds a strong case for what he refers to as "lifecycle" investment strategies, which "offer the greatest chance for retirement savers to accumulate the largest possible nest eggs, while reducing risk and volatility as retirement age approaches."

Reynolds goes on to say, "Fidelity research shows that lifecycle funds deliver higher returns, at less risk, than a solid majority of participants actually achieve on their own."

Data from benefits firm Hewitt supports this research. Hewitt found that people who used lifecycle funds in 2005 made 50 percent more than those who overconfidently managed their 401(k) dollars themselves. I wholeheartedly agree with Reynolds' assertion that lifecycle, along with target funds, "represents today's best practical standard for retirement savings."

LINDA—GIVING THE BEST SHE HAS TO GIVE

Cathy and I, at the invitation of Linda, attended a fundraiser for Kyle's Korner, a Milwaukee-area non-profit that serves the emotional needs of children who suffered the death of a parent. Linda and her teenaged daughter, Megan, were on the program that night, telling their very personal story of how this support group helped them survive a terrible time. Three years earlier, Megan's father took his own life. Pat had been under a doctor's care to treat depression when, at his family's cottage in northern Wisconsin, he hung himself. This tragic loss brought unimaginable grief to this family. It took much courage to share their tearful story, while a picture of their departed loved one was projected on the screen behind them.

Linda told of how in the numbing days following their profound loss, her children would constantly cling to her, sharing the same bed, afraid she too would leave them.

In my view, Linda is truly living strong. If she can persevere and carry on, anyone can. Her life is totally dedicated to her four children. In addition to lending her support to worthwhile causes such as Kyle's Korner, Linda has gone back to school and is now diligently working toward a graduate degree in grief counseling.

I feel truly privileged to have crossed paths with this special woman. Her inspirational story has much to teach us about life, about what is important and what is not, and how to handle the cards you are dealt. In this, Linda is following in the footsteps of a remarkably strong woman, Eleanor Roosevelt, who said, "You have to accept whatever comes, and the only important thing is that you meet it with the best you have to give."

FINANCIAL PLANNING PIONEER

I knew Lynn Hopewell only from afar, but was touched by learning of his death at age 69. H. Lynn Hopewell was one of the giants in the financial planning profession and someone I looked up to and learned from.

My first exposure to this brilliant man, a Harvard MBA, was at a 1986 financial planning conference in Chicago. He led a breakout session I attended about retirement planning.

I came away highly impressed by his intellect and practical, real-life approach to pure planning. I was excited to have found in Lynn Hopewell a visionary, a leader, and someone in whose footsteps I could follow in the then-infant field of financial planning.

In 1986, the financial planning community was dominated by high-commission product providers. That year's exhibit hall was loaded with vendors of oil and gas and real estate limited partnerships, who aggressively hawked them as tax shelters.

In a wave of change, tax reform legislation later that same year effectively killed limited partnerships. They had enriched the general partners and sales forces, leaving the lowly limited partners holding the bag with a lousy investment for which there was no secondary market. To add insult to injury, an investor needed a professional preparer to file an otherwise simple tax return.

As someone relatively new to financial planning, I felt uncomfortable about this high-pressure sales environment and made a decision to not use its products. In the early years, many advisors in the nascent financial planning field had migrated from life insurance sales, drawn by plentiful prospects and high commissions. I am proud to say I resisted the lucrative commission route.

It was therefore reassuring when someone of Lynn Hopewell's professional stature publicly disdained commissions and embraced the fee-only method of doing business. He had come quickly to the conclusion that a fee-only approach better aligned the interests of client and investment advisor. By the time of his death in 2006, this method of compensation had grown to be the accepted industry norm.

Financial planning software in the early years was an overly simplistic and not very useful tool. Hopewell almost single-handedly changed that in 1987 when he published "Making Decisions Under Conditions of Uncertainty." This pioneering paper brought him national recognition for his work on retirement planning and served as a wake-up call to financial planners.

The essence of financial and retirement planning is about adapting to an ever-changing scene. Far from being static, variables that include investment returns, inflation levels, tax rates, income streams, and expense outflows all factor in to make a constantly changing picture over time.

Planners now have sophisticated tools to simulate these changes, play what-ifs, stress-test worst-case scenarios, assign probabilities of success, and make more intelligent financial and investment decisions for clients.

Both T. Rowe Price and Vanguard developed and make available quality online planning tools you can use to get a clearer picture of your probable financial future. Lynn Hopewell, in fact, helped develop the retirement planning software for T. Rowe Price.

If you want formulas, I'll give you formulas. If you want rules of thumb, I'll give you rules of thumb. But as much as you resist it, the correct answer to your question is "it depends."

This advice comes from financial columnist Humberto Cruz, responding to a reader's request for a rule of thumb about how much retirement savings is enough.

I'll give you an eye-opening rule of thumb. Your nest egg needs to be 25 times what you anticipate your required initial retirement investment income draw to be. For example, if you will need to take $1 of investment income at the start of your retirement, you better have $25 in your investment portfolio pot to do it.

Put another way, assume you estimate the need to pull out $40,000 in income the first year of retirement. You should accumulate 25 times that amount, or a cool one-million-dollar nest egg to feel secure about not running out of money before you run out of breath.

This is based on a widely accepted safe withdrawal rate of 4 percent from T. Rowe Price and others ($1,000,000 @ 4 percent = $40,000).

Keep in mind this $40,000 annual sum will eventually need to be $75,000 a year, assuming even tame inflation of 3 percent a short 20 years down the line. Inflation's ravages are cumulative, and over time will erode the purchasing power of an income stream, shrinking the value of today's dollar to just 25 cents.

If your initial draw-down requirement is $100,000 in year one, you would need a nest egg of $2.5 million to sustain a 4 percent withdrawal rate (4 percent of $2,500,000 = $100,000).

Steven Silbiger, the author of *Retire Early? Make the Smart Choices*, offers this good advice: "creating an investment withdrawal plan that minimizes your chance to run out of money is the key to your successful retirement and peace of mind."

The author also correctly reminds us that investing for retirement is quite different from investing during retirement. Consequently,

"You (or your advisor) must be willing to do the midcourse corrections if returns or spending projections change."

Harry Lynn Hopewell led a fascinating life, and I suspect felt man enough to use his unisex middle name. He was a star high school football player, garnering all-state and all-South honors his senior year. His team went on to win the 1954 Virginia Group 1 State title.

His athletic prowess brought him offers of football scholarships; but, characteristically, this Eagle Boy Scout opted instead to dedicate his college years to academics and engineering studies. Once retired, he did reminisce about his high school gridiron exploits, penning the book *Sprinting Past Our Lives as Boys*.

After college, Lynn went to work as a communications engineer with the Central Intelligence Agency (CIA), traveling all over the world and spending time in 40 countries before he reached age 27.

Like many of us in the financial planning field, Lynn Hopewell gravitated from another career. At age 41, after 20 years in government, telecom, and computer systems, he made a mid-career move to financial planning, having discovered a way to make a living by using his talents to actually help people.

Hopewell spent the next 20 years of his life as a CFP doing just that. He quickly rose to prominence within the profession, tirelessly helping to advance the field as editor of the *Journal of Financial Planning* and as a member of the CFP Board of Governors.

It helps in life and in a career to follow someone who has cleared a path. Lynn Hopewell was 15 years my senior, and I made a point to follow his precepts since our first encounter in Chicago in 1986.

After 20 years as a practitioner, having built a rewarding financial planning and investment advisory practice, Lynn Hopewell successfully transitioned in 1999 to what would prove to be the final chapter of his life.

His was another example of someone having reached the financial independence that allowed him the freedom to pursue whatever he wanted to do over the balance of his life. Never one to sit still and always a prolific writer, Hopewell poured himself into writing five books and a weekly opinion column for his local newspaper. He continued his active involvement with his Episcopal Church and his education initiatives.

As a local historian, he explored his family's extensive genealogy, whose roots in Virginia went back 300 years. His great-great grandfather, Strother Seth Jones, was a Civil War Confederate officer in the acclaimed Black Horse Calvary. Hopewell's fascination with the history of his family, the State of Virginia, and the epic Civil War culminated in a labor of love and two more books, *The Bravest of the Brave* and *The Bravest Man in Lee's Army.*

LIFETIME ACHIEVEMENT

Whenever someone is honored with a Lifetime Achievement Award, I am conditioned to assume they must be sick and that death will soon follow. Such was the case with Michele Cody, a founder, leader, and the face I associated with our local Milwaukee financial planning chapter. Michele was the very deserving recipient of the 2004 FPA (Financial Planning Association) Lifetime Achievement Award.

I reached out to Michele during 2003 as she battled the cancer that soon took her life. Up to that point I knew her only as a professional associate. But through a series of phone calls, personal notes, and the act of trading books, we became closer. When it looked like a bad ending, Michele told me she went back to her home in Tacoma, Washington, where her three sisters and mother lived, to "bask in the warmth and love of family."

Michele's signature was her smile, and she followed a life philosophy to "find goodness in everyone you meet." Michele Ann Cody died in April 2004 at age 61 from mesothelioma, a rare form of lung cancer.

It is common for cancer victims to want to determine a cause for the appearance of this unwelcome and deadly disease in their lives. Michele had done microbiology research on monkeys in graduate school at the University of Wisconsin some 40 years earlier, and it was surmised this might have had something to do with her cancer.

In January 2006, I read with interest and some trepidation that Lynn Hopewell received a Lifetime Achievement Award from the FPA for his significant contributions to the profession. His remarks at the award ceremony say a lot about him as a man, the value of financial planning, and the profession he found and furthered.

Nick Murray said it best…financial planning is all about love. It is love for a spouse that makes you want to be sure you have enough money to last for both your lifetimes. It is love of your children that drives you to launch them into a life with a good education, make sure you do not become a financial burden for them, and enter the no-fun world of estate planning. Love is what drives people to your office. The financial and investing world is a jungle full of danger, and they need a competent guide. How fortunate I was to have found a way to earn a living that was so rewarding—helping people to love.

Consequently, when word of Lynn's death came just three months later, I suspected he too, might have faced a terminal illness. I sent an e-mail to Glenn Kautt, his friend, mentor, and the planner who had succeeded him in his practice, expressing my sympathy and inquiring of the cause of death.

According to Glenn, "Lynn died from a cerebral hemorrhage, due to a fall where the bleeding went undetected for a day or more. He went to sleep, and by the time attempts were made to revive him, he was already gone."

This tragic ending reminds us of how short, precious, and unpredictable life is. Here, I had been mildly envious of Lynn Hopewell's comfortable post-planner phase of life, only to discover it had been abruptly cut short.

LINKS ON A CHAIN

Similar to Lynn Hopewell's interest, I enjoy tracing my ancestral roots, believing it is life-affirming to know your place in the chain.

My dad's younger brother, my Uncle Bill, is the sole surviving relative from that generation. He recently shared with me some exciting information he had uncovered on the family tree of my greatgrandfather and namesake, John T. McCarthy.

As a first-born son, I am proud to carry the name of John Thomas McCarthy. Like my father and grandfather before me, that puts me as the numeral IV in a line.

My own father, John T. III, was very close to his grandfather, for they lived together in the same house until great-grandfather died in 1939 at age 81, when my dad was 14. Dad kept a photo of his grandfather on his bedroom dresser all his life.

Since the passing of my Aunt Mary Jane, I—as a John Thomas—inherited a large oil portrait of her grandfather. My father cherished owning his grandfather's exquisite gold pocket watch inscribed with his name. Sadly, my parents suffered the indignity of a series of burglaries at their Chicago home. This irreplaceable keepsake, despite being well hidden in a bedroom closet, was discovered and stolen. My father had shown me my great-grandfather's watch on occasion and told me it would be handed down to me some day. Its senseless theft was a priceless loss of a possession of the patriarch of the McCarthy family.

My Uncle Bill's great-grandfather, and his own namesake, William McCarthy, was born in Ireland. There he married Mary Collison, we believe in Dublin. They suffered the grievous loss of their five young children during a plague that swept their troubled native land. This tragedy was undoubtedly the impetus for the couple to bravely cross the stormy ocean and seek out a new life. William and Mary eventually settled in the small Canadian farming town of Lucan, outside London, Ontario.

Mary had Collison relatives in this rural community, and we think so did William. It is there they started their family anew. They had five children in Canada, including my great-grandfather, John Thomas, and his twin sister, born in 1858. Family legend has it these newborn infants were so tiny, each slept in a cigar box on the fireplace mantle—their first bed.

My family and I like to get a jump on summer vacation, so this year we traveled to Toronto in early June as soon as school let out. I had last visited Toronto 30 years before. My brother Larry and I spent some time there on our way to the 1976 Summer Olympics held in Montreal. I have wanted to return with my family to this world-class city ever since.

Locating Lucan on a map, I made plans to stay a day in London, Ontario, having felt a strong tug to spend time near the birthplace of my great-grandfather. After checking into the hotel in the afternoon, Martha, Jack, and I set out to see if we could find Lucan and maybe learn something about our roots.

Lucan is about 20 kilometers or 12.5 miles outside the city limits of London, with a population of some 300,000, home to Western Ontario University and a regional medical center. We found Lucan to be a bucolic community, dotted with family farms and a sleepy, three-block-long Main Street. The town sign welcoming us to Lucan was adorned with shamrocks, a hint to its Irish heritage, and listed a population of 900. We were about to discover much more than we had anticipated.

As we were to learn, Lucan had quite a rich and colorful—some would say infamous—past. The first settlers of this heavily wooded and wild tract were free blacks who, starting in 1829, were fleeing Ohio and the economic desperation and discrimination they knew there. Before that, many had slipped the yoke of slavery, escaping north on the Underground Railroad.

The Lucan settlement began to decline some short years later, however, as they found the conditions and elements too harsh. For the most part they moved on.

In the 1840s, the Negro population began being replaced largely by Irish, who came primarily from Borrisokane, Tipperary, also fleeing persecution and seeking opportunity and a better life in the frontier of the New World.

The Irish settled and farmed small plots hacked out of the forests clustered along what became known as the Roman Line—thereby distinguishing it from the Protestant Lines, as all of them were Roman Catholics.

While walking the streets of Lucan, we stopped to tour a primitive log cabin (shanty), which now houses the local heritage museum. Being a history buff and having a personal interest in the subject, I picked up the book *The Donnelly Album* by Ray Fazakas, a well-known Hamilton, Ontario, lawyer.

In this book, which I eagerly read, Fazakas chronicles the story of the boisterous pioneer community of Lucan, one that earned the reputation as "the wildest town in Canada." This well-written and researched tome tells the violent saga surrounding the Donnelly family, of whom five members were brutally murdered the night of February 3, 1880, by a revenge-seeking mob of neighbors from their own St. Patrick's parish church. No one was ever convicted of these grisly murders, which climaxed a famous feud.

The first John Thomas McCarthy, my great-grandfather, was born into this wild west Irish-Canadian outpost, shortly before the outbreak of the Great Civil War in the United States.

He was baptized along with his twin sister, Madelyn, at the church named for St. Patrick, who, as you may know, is the patron saint of Ireland. This sturdy brick church was built in 1855 and still functions today on the Roman Line, in Biddulph Township, Lucan, Ontario. Next to it stands the stately pastor's residence and the original one-room schoolhouse. We learned these three structures—church, house, and school—are the oldest surviving such trio in the province of Ontario.

Next to the church is an idyllic cemetery, where we discovered to our excitement the gravestones marking dozens of blood relative McCarthys, including John's older brother Joseph (1856–1941), his wife, Elizabeth, and their three sons. I have reason to believe there are McCarthy descendants living today in Lucan. My intent is to see if I can make contact with them.

Interestingly, Joseph McCarthy is found in the book *The Donnelly Album,* where he is listed as a member of the Biddulph Peace Society and a signer of a petition against the notorious Donnelly family.

As we understand it, John McCarthy was college educated and a seminarian studying for the priesthood. Family folklore has it that the rector came to the conclusion John did not have a priestly vocation, as he was seen on occasion in the company of young women.

Perhaps understandably, a 22-year-old John McCarthy opted to leave Lucan and Canada and emigrate to Chicago at about the same time as the Donnelly massacre. It is in this bustling city in the USA he launched his adult life and found a bride.

Chicago at the turn of the century was one of the fastest-growing cities in the world. Much of its growth can be attributed to its role as "Player with railroads and the Nation's Freight Handler," as described by Carl Sandburg in his classic poem "Chicago."

Chicago would prove ripe for an ambitious, industrious, and intelligent young man anxious to make his mark in the world, to raise a family, and to escape the problems and limits of his Canadian hometown of Lucan.

In Chicago, John met and married Mary Hennessey in 1888. Mary was born in County Cork, Ireland, and herself had followed a wave of immigrants to Chicago, landing in this country in 1886 at the age of 22. John and Mary had five children, including my grandfather, John Thomas II.

We do not know much of my great-grandmother, as she died at age 45 in 1909. Their youngest child and only daughter, Madeline, was just seven years old at the time, and my grandfather a teenager of 16.

The immigrant experience at the time was not one of streets paved with gold, but rather mud and ruts. Again, from the Sandburg poem of the same name, Chicago was "Stormy, husky, brawling. City of the Big Shoulders." With all this energy, plenty of entrepreneurial opportunity presented itself.

Seeing such an opportunity, John started out using horses to bring firewood from outlying areas into the city. He contracted to haul hay, feed, and whatever was needed along the North Shore of Chicago.

Like all of us, John experienced challenges over the course of his long life. Because multiple births were a rarity in 1858, from the very start he proved a survivor. After the premature death of his bride, he carried on and raised his brood of five school-aged children alone. It was common in that era for children to be orphaned, and we believe he took in and cared for a couple of young boys his sons' ages, as well as two nephews.

Chicago in the Roaring Twenties and during Prohibition was famous worldwide for the notorious mobster Al Capone, widespread bootleg liquor, and speakeasies. We know for a fact many trucking and warehouse firms during Prohibition made illicit fortunes in this activity. There is no hint that my great-grandfather did anything illegal. Looking back, I believe it must have been tempting.

Reminiscent of the Donnelly family massacre of February 3, 1880, in Lucan, Chicago's St. Valentine's Day massacre February 14, 1928, took place on North Clark Street less than a mile from my great-grandfather's family trucking operation. On that infamous day in Chicago's history, seven members of a rival bootlegging operation were gunned down by Capone gangsters. Posing as uniformed policemen conducting a raid, they ordered the unsuspecting men to line up with their hands against the wall. They were cold-bloodedly murdered in a hail of machine gun fire.

Early in the twentieth century, at about the time of World War I, motorized trucks replaced horses for horsepower. Modern businessman that he was, and with his four sons coming of age, John McCarthy shrewdly adapted by establishing a trucking and warehousing operation, transporting among other products cheese for Kraft.

Chicago experienced a massive building boom in the 1920s, with new single-family homes and apartment buildings rapidly sprouting throughout the city. This provided a golden opportunity, and the family smartly capitalized by expanding into residential moving and storage of furniture and household goods, starting the McCarthy Moving and Storage Company.

In the late 1920s, despite having reached the then-advanced age of 70, my great-grandfather took the leap of faith that is the hall-mark of all entrepreneurs. He invested in building a four-story ware-house to serve this growing market. It was state-of-the-art for its day, designed to be fireproof, with a large freight elevator and truck-ing docks.

Fireproof was very top-of-mind for risk-conscious business-men of that era. To place this concern in context, it helps to remem-ber my great-grandfather arrived in Chicago not long after the great Chicago fire of 1871. In fact, he claimed he could see the black smoke from that fire hundreds of miles to the east in his home in Canada.

It also helps to know that much of the feuding surrounding the Donnelly family centered on allegations of arson. In the impres-sionable days of my great-grandfather's boyhood in Lucan, a com-mon occurrence was for barns and wooden storage sheds to burn to the ground. Thus, his brick warehouse had thick concrete floors and steel doors. Today, the McCarthy Storage building, though no longer owned by the family, still stands, in use as a self-storage facility.

Uncle Bill informs me the family almost lost the property dur-ing the Depression. Seems a shady financier stole some funds, caus-ing the family to pay for the warehouse twice. Through all this, they managed to survive, persevere and thrive.

My grandfather, his three brothers, and his brother-in-law all became actively involved in the family business. Family folklore has it that as a young man my grandpa once knocked out a recalci-trant horse by punching it with his fist. We don't know if this is true or not, but I do know my grandfather was one tough guy.

It is instructive to reflect on the magnitude of the economic changes and massive transformations my grandfather witnessed over the course of his life (1894–1970). As a teenaged boy, he worked with horses, though apparently not always civilly. In his twenties, newly married, his job and the entire economy were revolutionized by motorized trucks replacing horsepower. A year before his death, he watched a television screen showing man walking on the surface of the moon. It is hard to imagine the changes that will surely occur over the lifetime of his great-grandson, Jack.

Living as we did a short quarter of a block away from my McCarthy grandparents, I was fortunate to see them often while growing up. One early spring night when I was a senior in high school, we got an urgent phone call from my grandfather telling us something was wrong with Grandma. Fortunately, most of my family happened to be home that particular weeknight. Mom, Dad and I rushed over, while my oldest sister, Mary Ann, held the fort at our house with the younger children. An ambulance was summoned, and Mom and Dad followed it to St. Francis Hospital.

I stayed behind with Grandpa, and in some respects drew the toughest assignment. Grandpa was understandably anxious about his ailing wife. He told me it should be him to go first, and he desperately wanted to trade places with his bride.

I have reason to believe Grandpa had been living with prostate cancer for many years. He had witnessed his father die a painful death from prostate cancer 30 years before, so he knew his fate. Yet most men with prostate cancer end up dying from some other cause. My dad and aunt knew of his cancer cloud, but if my memory is correct, they consciously decided to keep it from my grandmother, not wanting to worry her.

I sat with him that evening, with all that was going through his mind, and had a heart-to-heart discussion on life and finances. As I was soon to head off to college, Grandpa inquired about my career plans. I said I really didn't know, but thought business of some kind. I had been accepted in the business school at Marquette University. Grandpa suggested I might want to consider law, pointing out that my two uncles who drove Cadillacs were attorneys.

Grandpa proceeded to produce a bottle of whiskey. We shared a couple of shots to settle our nerves. I think he honestly considered liquor medicine, and this whiskey was offered for medicinal purposes.

As it turned out, Grandma was all right but would remain in the hospital, having suffered a stroke. When my Mom and Dad, as well as Aunt Mary Jane, returned from the hospital, they found Grandpa and me side-by-side, asleep on the sofa, with a couple of empty glasses and an open whiskey bottle on the coffee table.

Six months later, Grandma and Grandpa celebrated their fiftieth wedding anniversary. I returned home from college to attend this happy occasion.

LITTLE GRANDMA

Grandma Maggie, a/k/a Little Grandma, is our dear Maggie's namesake. She too had quite a life story to tell. Margaret O'Connor was raised in a tough area on the near north side of Chicago under trying circumstances. At the young age of 12, she was orphaned by the premature death of both parents.

She married at age 21 and had three children, each of whom produced seven of their own, giving her 21 grandchildren. On all occasions Grandma wore a bracelet with a charm and the name and date of birth for each of these beloved grandchildren. A diabetic, Grandma used a cane to help her get around after suffering a broken hip some 20 years before.

Grandpa got his wish of preceding his mate. Like Lynn Hopewell, he died suddenly of a cerebral hemorrhage, only five months after their golden wedding anniversary celebration. Grandma Maggie left this world about a year later, probably from complications due to her diabetes. I was enriched by having them in my life, teaching me valuable life lessons as only grandparents can.

My father was the only one in the third generation who chose to enter the family business. As it came to pass, Dad's father and three uncles all reached retirement age at about the same time, and each faced some health issues. All of their assets were tied up in the value of the business, trucks, and buildings. They had not planned for retirement. In those days there were no pensions, or life insurance in force, or business succession plans. To finance retirement security for themselves and their wives, they felt compelled to put the business up for sale.

The buyers smartly purchased the good name of McCarthy as part of the deal. Dad stayed on for a few years before going to work for another moving and storage company. Despite the ups and downs of the moving business, Dad told me it provided him with a livelihood and the ability to take care of his family for 50 years.

My father witnessed the painful death of his grandfather from prostate cancer. Years later, I saw my father's life end in the same way. A week before my dad's death, I brought to his bedside our son, his nine-month-old grandson. I have never forgotten how I felt watching my father tenderly kiss Jack's forehead.

At the cemetery following Dad's funeral service, I was cradling our son, Jack, when I was approached by my dad's cousin Billy McCarthy. I introduced him to the baby as John T. McCarthy the fifth. Billy, having known well John T. the first, second and third, touched the baby and told him, through me, that young Jack had quite a legacy to live up to.

The baton had been passed to me, as it someday will be to Jack. I have much to teach him about life planning and the family legacy he inherited.

CHAPTER 7

WINDS OF CHANGE

The four most dangerous words in investing:
This time it's different.

Louis Rukeyser

I was saddened to hear of the passing of Louis Rukeyser, who died in May 2006 at the age of 73 from bone cancer. He was truly a legend in the field of financial journalism, having hosted the nationally acclaimed public television program, *Wall $treet Week*, from 1970 through 2002.

As America's most trusted financial and economic commentator, Rukeyser had a talented combination of wit and wisdom, which he delivered in a unique style to help the masses make sense out of the often arcane workings of the stock market and the economy. His Friday evening show was a staple for me and millions of other devoted viewers.

If you ask our dear daughter Maggie about Lou or Louis, she will quickly associate the name with Rukeyser. Maggie, now a grown-up 21, was exposed to the program through my many hours of viewing it over the years.

I am grateful to this departed gentleman, for his television program helped instill in me a positive, common sense approach to the topsy-turvy world of investing and personal finance.

I had the opportunity to hear Lou Rukeyser speak on a couple of occasions and distinctly remember his appearance at a financial planning conference I attended in San Francisco in September 1989. He foresaw the emergence of a business model in which objective, independent investment advisors, such as our firm, would be compensated from ongoing fees, rather than broker transactions and product sales commissions, the prevalent model at that time.

As he saw it, the planning engagement should be more holistic in scope, and advisors should be paid for portfolio surveillance. In his view, many times the best investment strategy is to eschew activity and patiently hold. Over the ensuing years, this has become a widely accepted method of doing business in our industry. The pull-no-punches Rukeyser was way ahead of the curve.

Louis Rukeyser is credited with inventing the job of financial journalism broadcaster, having been the first in a field of one. Prior to the start of his television program in 1970, conventional wisdom held that investing and economics were subjects too dry and complex to appeal to a wide audience. The immense popularity and longevity of his hit television show proved consumers were indeed hungry for sound advice and solid information, provided it was delivered in an understandable and entertaining fashion.

Rukeyser was perhaps best known for his humor. A prime example was his response when it was said that he had given birth to the entire industry of financial journalism. Lou quipped, "and I don't even have stretch marks."

Lou Rukeyser attracted a horde of esteemed experts who appeared as guests and complemented an assembly of semi-regular panelists. A roster of a half-dozen of his most popular guests over the years included Vanguard founder John Bogle, a trio of superstar investors in John Templeton, Peter Lynch, and bond guru Bill Gross, as well as Harvard economist John Kenneth Galbraith and *Forbes* magazine publisher Steve Forbes.

Reminiscing on the passing of this legendary figure, John Bogle paid Rukeyser the highest compliment by referring to him as a simplifier and lauding him as someone who communicated in non-intimidating, plain-speak English. Steve Forbes remembered Louis Rukeyser in his magazine, contending the secret of the man's extraordinary, long-run success was due to his unbridled optimism and a true belief in U.S.-style entrepreneurial capitalism. According to Forbes, Rukeyser fervently believed the individual investor could profit in the market by "getting good advice and sticking to basic common sense rules." Forbes went on to remind us, "While respectful and gracious, Lou never took experts *too* seriously. He also avoided getting caught up in fads and emotions."

The month of May 2006 also saw the passing of celebrated Harvard economist John Kenneth Galbraith, a giant in his field, literally and figuratively, at a gawky 6 feet, 8 inches tall. The author of such mainstream, best-selling books as *The Affluent Society* and *The Age of Uncertainty* died at age 97.

USA Today ran a dual piece on the passing of these two giants, claiming favorably that each possessed the common touch. "Like Rukeyser, John Kenneth Galbraith was a popularizer who used public television to reach the masses. His subject, economics, is so dreary that it is often called the dismal science. Even if Galbraith never won the Nobel Prize, he was, like Rukeyser, a kind of economic and financial evangelist."

From his vaunted standpoint, John Kenneth Galbraith greatly respected the unique expertise and credibility of Louis Rukeyser. He commented publicly in 1989 that in his opinion, "there is only one television program on business and economics (that) is worth watching."

One of the most popular cable TV shows on the stock market today is *Mad Money* with Jim Cramer. Cramer is a former hedge fund manager, the antithesis of Lou, lacking the master's dignity, style, and class. In this regrettably successful show, Cramer rants and raves, accompanied by campy sound effects. In contrast to *Wall Street Week, Mad Money* seems a poor excuse for a financial program.

Rukeyser's unparalleled success story was not without bumps in the road toward the end. After superbly hosting his mega-hit show for 32 years on Maryland Public Television, the 69-year-old was summarily pushed out by the show's young and brash producers, who foolishly thought the program needed to be revamped with a more youthful look.

A disgruntled Rukeyser took his program and format to CNBC, and his faithful audience followed. The show thrived in its new spot for six months, until Lou underwent back surgery, which revealed the malignant cancer that would take his life.

Rukeyser's constant enjoyment of life was evident. Had illness not interfered, undoubtedly he would still be on the air, spreading the good news of the market. I miss seeing Lou Rukeyser, sitting in his leather chair on the set of his show, and signing off with his trademark wink that signaled to investors, "Keep the faith."

In volatile times, we could all use some of Rukeyser's steadfast optimism and remember his core belief—that stocks will continue to grow in value over the long term, and the promise of America and the U.S. economic system will continue to compete and prevail. Over the many years of his program, Lou always dismissed rampant pessimism and derided overly bearish sentiment by adopting a glass-half-full optimism.

BEAR TRAP

One such discredited bear was Howard Ruff, whose best-selling *How to Prosper During the Coming Bad Years* appeared in 1979 and convinced a lot of supposedly sophisticated investors of an imminent collapse. He drew a lot of attention for his prediction of a coming major depression that would rock the country over the balance of the century.

His advice was to shun financial assets, especially stocks, and instead, "Buy gold, silver, and diamonds before it's too late!" Howard Ruff prospered, selling his "Ruff Times" scare tactics. But as we now know, this was terrible advice, and anyone who mistakenly followed it missed out on the greatest bull market ever.

The American economic system is resilient and dynamic, and it continues to be the envy of the world. One thing foreign managers would like to emulate about the United States is our optimism about the future.

Despite economic advances by the likes of China and India, foreign managers admit to not being able to replicate the innovative, risk-taking entrepreneurial drive that is a hallmark of the American economy. It is good to remember that back in the 1980s the Japanese were supposed to wrest the mantle of economic superpower from the United States. History has shown how far off the mark that prediction was.

Count a Britisher, Sir Harold Evans, as one who believes in our future. "The U.S. has been—and remains—the source of most of the innovations (from steam engine to search engine) that created our modern world." He goes on, saying "innovation will continue in America. It is in the nation's DNA."

It is helpful to take a more optimistic view of what the future holds. Futurist Peter Schwartz, the author of *Inevitable Surprises*, sees a "long boom" that will take the Dow stock average on a long upward ride all the way to the year 2030. I feel confident forecasting that the Dow, perched at a record peak of 12,000 late in 2006, will soar to 35,000. The big question, and one I am not prepared to answer, is in what year or even what decade this summit will be reached.

I fully agree with Schwartz's contention that globalization is an unstoppable force. Rather than this phenomenon's being a negative, productivity and living standards will grow worldwide, driven by advances in information technology and breakthroughs in life sciences. Encouragingly, inflation should remain in check due to productivity increases brought on by new technological advances.

Economist Barry Asmus is the author of *The Best Is Yet To Come.*

As the title suggests, he, too, is optimistic about the future. According to Asmus, the 1970's double-digit inflation won't happen in the twenty-first century. A stable price system has been created over the last 20 years in the United States that will persist and form the basis for continued economic growth.

Asmus points to the cell phone as an example of what he terms "digital deflation." Since its introduction, this product's price has been reduced significantly, yet is far more technically advanced. Young people now use the cell phone instead of a land phone and as a watch and a camera. "In every other expansion, things got better, but not necessarily cheaper. Now, they are better, cheaper, and faster. Now we have digital deflation." Speaking in 2004, Asmus foresaw a "long boom" for the economy and stock market. "It looks very good for the next couple of decades."

New York Times columnist Thomas Friedman has written *The World Is Flat: A Brief History of the Twenty-First Century*. He sees a dramatic era of innovation, observing "the flattening of the world means we are now connecting all the knowledge centers on the planet together into a single global network, which could usher in an amazing era of prosperity and innovation."

Forbes columnist Paul Johnson is an eminent historian and author. Echoing Friedman, he thinks we should be prepared for rapid advances in technology. This is from his column:

The industrial revolution occurred less than 250 years ago. We've harnessed electricity for only 150 years, atomic power for scarcely half a century. The rate of advance is accelerating very fast indeed, yet the pace is going to quicken at a speed we cannot now imagine. Regarding technology, humanity is still in the lowest steps of a gigantic staircase reaching into the sky.

I am fueled by the realistic hope that a safe, economical, and environmentally clean alternative to fossil fuels and the internal combustion engine is not too far away. Friedman issued a clarion call in his book for this generation's moon shot: undertake a crash program on a massive scale to develop alternative energy to fossil fuels, coupled with conservation, with the audacious goal of America's becoming energy-independent within a decade. As Paul Johnson points out, wind farm technology today is scarcely more advanced than the windmills of an earlier time. He suggests we can do better and we will.

Chalk up Jeremy Rifkin as someone who sees an energy revolution around hydrogen that would free the world from a reliance on oil. The author of *The Hydrogen Economy* and the president of the Foundation on Economic Trends believes historic change is shaping up. "The harnessing of hydrogen will alter our way of life as fundamentally as the introduction of coal and steam power in the nineteenth century and the shift to oil and the internal combustion engine in the twentieth century. Making the transition to a hydrogen economy represents the single most important challenge and greatest opportunity of our time."

Is this blue-sky wishful thinking? Maybe. But dozens of hydrogen-powered cars are being tested on American roads today. While these experimental vehicles cost a million dollars apiece and have an effective range of only 100 miles or so, with virtually no refueling stations in existence, every significant advance has modest beginnings.

In this vein, Harold Evans, author of *They Made America*, reminds us of what resulted from Thomas Edison's 1879 invention of the light bulb. "But the bulb was only the beginning, for this enterprising American genius went on courageously to develop power systems, design networks, mass production techniques, metering and marketing, all against monumental challenges."

Evans wants us to know of another innovative inventor who made America. "Edison lit the world expensively at first. But it was his assistant, Samuel Insull, a naturalized American and business genius in his own right, who some years later in Chicago found the way to make electricity prices fall over six decades, an incalculable boon to life and work."

The pessimists among us cry that today is different and the promise of tomorrow is bleak. They point out we are in a war on terror, our young people are not what they used to be, there are no longer the opportunities and good-paying jobs, and it costs a small fortune just to fill up a gas tank.

After the horror of 9/11, political science professor Ray Licklider of Rutgers University, as quoted in *USA Today*, put the terror threat in perspective: "We survived years of knowing we were on the edge of thermonuclear war. I spent much of my career working under the assumption that the world was going to be incinerated in the Cold War. That makes terrorism look like small beans. Much of our problem with the fear of terrorism is that it is so new and strange to us. It is a matter of getting used to it."

Undoubtedly there will be dark days ahead. We should be psychologically prepared for the inevitability of future terrorist attacks and geopolitical challenges that will affect both our own and the world's economics. These are the realities of life in the twenty-first century. In order to lead a life of emotional and financial well-being, however, I believe it is necessary to adopt a "glass-half-full optimism."

There is always enough worry to keep one up at night. Today we are burdened with a difficult war in the Mideast, the specter of terrorist acts, an economy that sometimes misfires, a volatile stock market, mounting budget deficits, political divisiveness, and geopolitical hot spots throughout the world.

Yet these very real challenges pale in comparison to the seemingly insurmountable crises President Franklin Roosevelt and the American people faced in the 1930s with the Great Depression, and in the 1940s with a world war on two fronts against powerful adversaries in Japan and Germany. Investment advisor William Bernstein looks at it this way: *Better a hundred Bin Ladens than one Adolf Hitler. When you look at things from the long term, life looks good.*

FALLEN HEROES

In our modern society, many question whether we still produce heroes in America. Peggy Noonan is confident we do and firmly reminds us never to forget the 343 fallen New York firefighters who valiantly sacrificed their lives to save thousands fleeing from the two World Trade Center towers on that fateful day of 9/11.

Writing in her book *A Heart, a Cross, and a Flag,* in a piece titled, "Courage Under Fire," Noonan speaks loudly for the heroes who entered American history that day:

But the 300 didn't happen to be there, they went *there. In the now famous phrase, they ran into the burning building and not out of the burning building. They ran up the stairs, not down, they went into it and not out of it. They didn't flee, they charged.*

Peggy Noonan tells us many of the fallen firefighters were Irish Catholic. She relates the story of one such hero, Patrick Byrne. Now we learn Patrick Byrne was her grandfather's name, as well as her cousin's name. Her brother helped track down who this missing 9/11 firefighter was, putting a face with the name. Noonan tells of showing the picture to her own young son, imploring him emotionally, "Never forget this—ever."

I have in my home office an inspirational picture with accompanying quotation. It shows a firefighter's jacket and helmet hung between the American stars and stripes and the green, white, and orange flag of Ireland. The ancient Greek Thucydides could have been speaking of "Courage Under Fire" and Patrick Byrne when he wrote, "The bravest are surely those who have the clearest vision of what is before them and yet go out to meet it."

In the wake of the horror of 9/11, I found comfort in the words of the great American poet and biographer Carl Sandburg, who is renowned in my birthplace of Chicago. This fabled Lincoln historian wrote:

Always the path of American destiny has been into the unknown. Always there arose enough reserves of strength, balances of sanity, portions of wisdom to carry the nation through to a fresh start with ever-renewing vitality.

Colin Powell's life is another inspirational, ongoing American success story; one he says could have happened only in America:

Mine is the story of a black kid of no early promise from an immigrant family of limited means who was raised in the South Bronx and somehow rose to become the National Security Advisor to the President of the United States and then chairman of the Joint Chiefs of Staff.

Powell's remarkable journey continued to propel him higher as Secretary of State. This distinguished American continues to be a beacon of hope working with the Boys and Girls Clubs and as chairman of America's Promise, an organization dedicated to building character and competence in young people by promoting mentoring relationships with adults.

In life and finances, it all comes down to a reason to believe. Benjamin Burt gave us the thought, "True prosperity is the result of well-placed confidence in ourselves and our fellow man."

TWENTY-FIRST CENTURY NEW ERA GROWTH

Long-term investors wanting to put some excitement in their portfolios and also to fuel growth should consider adopting an approach used by institutional investors, such as large pension plans.

In a "core and satellite" tactic, the majority of a stock portfolio would comprise plain-vanilla investments, such as those I profile in my earlier chapters. Outside of this center core, smaller investment allocations would be made among specialized and sector mutual funds. Charles Schwab, founder of the financial services firm that bears his name, speaks of employing a similar strategy, which Schwab has trademarked as "core and explore." The objective of this approach is to increase the odds of besting the market while reducing the risk of badly underperforming. This method holds appeal in a time of modest expectations for equity returns.

Mutual fund purists, particularly John Bogle, make a sound argument that sector funds are unnecessary and should be avoided entirely, because the risk, cost, and volatility are unwarranted. In Bogle's view, every investor should stick instead with core fund selections, such as index funds. Although this is probably true, human nature leads us to want some excitement in our lives as well as in our portfolios. Sector and specialty mutual funds add some spice. Additionally, it gives us something to brag about at cocktail parties and on the golf course.

Growth stock pioneer Thomas Rowe Price took the long view of investing and anticipated long-term trends. He focused on uncovering profitable opportunities in what he called "the fertile fields of growth." These days, T. Rowe Price, the mutual fund family that grew out of his vision, offers an array of specialty and sector mutual funds that attempt to deliver growth by farming in fields that hold promise. Among their extensive family of offerings are six no-load funds that I believe allow individual investors to explore and I hope score financially: T. Rowe Price Health Services, New Era, New Asia, Eastern Europe, Science and Technology, and Developing Technology. All could be given consideration when filling out a punched-up, growth-oriented portfolio.

Investment master John Templeton made his name and amassed his fortune by pioneering the concept of global investing. As far back as the 1950s, Templeton discovered a gold mine by courageously and presciently making investments in the then-tiny emerging market of Japan.

I agree wholeheartedly with Mark Headley of Matthews International Capital Management when he states, "It's just a fact that American investors don't have much overseas exposure." Most portfolios are too light in foreign equities, concentrated instead in the familiarity of the domestic U.S. market. This is a mistake; for, by not casting the net globally, investors miss out on over half the world's investment opportunities.

Not only will such a narrow focus result in a loss of diversification, but most probably you will be limiting your returns as well. The exciting growth prospects of the early twenty-first century are likely to be found in places such as China, India, Brazil, and Poland rather than the United States, Germany, England, or Japan.

A sensible way to participate in this trend is with an investment in an emerging market stock index fund. Two sound choices are the T. Rowe Price Emerging Markets Stock (PRMSX) and Vanguard Emerging Markets Index (VWO).

Likewise, it may be prudent to look for growth in different pockets than in the success stories of the last 25 years. Health care and biotechnology are good bets to emerge as winners in the decades to come. Demographics (think aging baby boomers) coupled with breakthrough advances such as the mapping of the human genome, all point to explosive profit-making growth opportunities.

The new reality is that the U.S. economy is a health economy. The health care and medical industry is now astonishingly larger than the oil, auto, textiles, steel, and mining industries *combined*. I have heard astute and nationally syndicated columnist George Will point out that the largest employer in Pittsburgh is no longer steel, nor is it manufacturing in Cleveland, nor, surprisingly, energy in Houston. The new era fact is that health care has emerged as the dominant growth industry in each of these cities, with world-renowned medical centers.

Management of General Electric (GE), greatly admired for its business acumen, is now looking to derive growth (i.e., expanding markets and profit-maximizing opportunities) in the health field. It has made a string of acquisitions and concentrated investments to form a new division, GE Healthcare Technologies.

In the nineteen-fifties, sixties, and seventies, GE made its mark and revenue from being an industrial powerhouse (turbines, electric motors, appliances, plastics, chemicals, jet engines). During the eighties and nineties the conglomerate's driver of growth shifted to financial services with GE Capital. So, it is telling that GE is focusing attention on the dynamic health segment and is now the number one provider of technology to digitize medical records and radiology imaging and to capitalize on molecular medicine and the emerging trend of personalized medicine.

We have a client who retired after 35 years as an engineer in the computer drives division of a large IBM plant in Rochester, Minnesota. Talking and visiting with him at his home, I saw very clearly that IBM is on the decline in his community. Meanwhile, the omnipresent Mayo Clinic continues to thrive.

As for the ascendancy of the biotech industry over information technology, count Larry Ellison, Oracle Corporation chief executive and recognized captain of Silicon Valley, as a believer. "The next big thing ain't computers," he says. Instead, "it's biotechnology."

My investment strategy, which I call Twenty-First Century New Era Growth, uses selected diversified sector and specialty funds to assemble the exploratory 20 percent of a portfolio.

The search for growth and excitement centers on two major themes. The first, New Science, includes health science and biotech, and developments in areas such as nanotech, fuel cells, and hydrogen energy. The second, New World, means taking a stand in the emerging markets of China, the Pacific Rim, India, and Eastern Europe, along with gateways Australia and Ireland.

10 EXPLORATORY SPECIALTY GROWTH PLAYS

New Science

1. T. Rowe Price Health Sciences PRSSX Specialty Health (open-end).
2. Hambrecht & Quist Life Sciences HQL Biotech (closed-end) *or* iShares *or* Nasdaq Biotechnology Index IBB Biotech (exchange-traded).
3. T. Rowe Price Science and Technology PRSCX Technology (open-end fund).
4. T. Rowe Price Developing Technology PRDX Specialty Technology (open-end).
5. T. Rowe Price New Era PRNEX Natural Resources (open-end).

New World

6. T. Rowe Price New Asia PRASX Pacific Rim, excluding Japan (open-end).
7. Vanguard Emerging Markets Index VWO Emerging Markets (exchange-traded) *or* T. Rowe Price Emerging Markets Stock PRMSX Emerging Markets (open-end).
8. iShares MSCI Australia Index EWA Australia (exchange-traded) *or* Aberdeen Australia Equity Fund IAF Australia (closed-end).
9. T. Rowe Price Emerging Europe TRMX Eastern Europe (open-end).
10. New Ireland Fund IRL Ireland (closed-end).

First, let me state loud and clear that the investment selections I list on the preceding page constitute aggressive growth, and only those investors with the patience and discipline to hold on to these funds for 10 years or longer should fish in these waters.

Always consider the appropriateness of any investment for your own goals and financial situation before investing.

Recognizing the volatility (risk) carried by these specialty funds, limits need to be set and controls put in place to manage the risk and benefit from the return potential. Following my strategy, 80 percent of one's portfolio would consist of the core or plain-vanilla funds. Examples include the traditional mutual funds and Treasury securities that I profile in earlier chapters. By this majority weighting in the middle of the road, the investor will not be taking on an inordinate or imprudent amount of risk.

A strong reason for holding these new-age funds for the long term is that as sector funds they are highly volatile, with extreme ups and downs. For example, T. Rowe Price New Asia (PRASX) soared in 1999, doubling its share price. It had risen an impressive 79 percent in 1993, yet suffered downside losses of 37 percent in 1997. It followed a dramatic rise in 1999 with a 31 percent drop the next year.

Let there be no doubt that a biotech fund, such as Hambrecht & Quist Life Sciences (HQL), is an aggressive investment with soaring peaks and deep valleys. To use a golf analogy, this sector fund is equally capable of scoring an eagle, such as the ace performance (hole-in-one) turned in for fiscal year 2000 of 155 percent, as it is going to the opposite extreme of triple bogeying in the succeeding two years, giving back 29 percent and 26 percent, respectively. Duffer investors looking to shoot predictable pars should not play on this course.

Recognizing the downside, the logical question becomes, why invest in biotech at all. The quick answer is that long-term investors willing to assume substantial risk with a portion of their money cannot afford *not* to have a place at this table.

A legitimate knock on sector funds is that their concentration in a single industry or region spells a lack of diversification. This is true to some extent of my Twenty-First Century New Era Growth portfolio, as we focus on biotech, health care, new technology, Pacific Rim, China, Australia, Ireland, and Eastern Europe.

I would counter that this investment plan does aim to diversify, by using only funds, be they of the traditional open-end, closed-end or exchange-traded (ETF) variety. From financially painful personal experience, I have sworn off dabbling in individual stocks, realizing that I am no stock picker.

For example, I thought it would be smart to buy the names profiled in a *Bloomberg Personal Finance* magazine article extolling the virtues of profitable, growing companies that benefited by being downstream of the Internet boom. Accepted wisdom at that time, circa 1998–2000, was that every growth investor needed an Internet investment strategy, and this play made sense to me. Unfortunately, my stock purchases in consultant Whitman Hart (bankrupt), e-payment software Moebius (big loser) and industry communications firm Gartner Group (barely surviving) taught me a memorable behavioral finance lesson.

Many astute investors believe that biotech's time has come. After decades of fits and starts, biotechnology research has made exciting breakthroughs that should amply reward investors. Biotech is the new frontier, and the mapping of the human genome features the convergence of biology, high-speed computing and engineering, mathematics and physics to produce truly breathtaking results. After years of painstaking research, the big payoff is close at hand, with hundreds of drugs and vaccines in late-stage clinical development.

According to Michael Murphy, editor of *Biotech Investing*, today offers a once-in-a-lifetime investment opportunity, driven by watershed events in scientific discovery. The revolution taking place will play out on a global stage and be pushed by the end consumer.

I discovered Hambrecht & Quist Life Sciences and subsequently purchased this life sciences fund in my own account, recommending it as well to a handful of suitable clients of our firm. Found in the portfolio of this actively managed fund are stock and convertible securities from the fertile fields of biopharmaceuticals, including emerging companies, drug discovery and delivery technologies, health care services, and medical devices and diagnostics. I was reassured to hear Murphy proclaim this particular fund as the best way to invest in biotech. His primary rationale was that diversity is an absolute necessity in biotech investing, as losers will greatly outnumber the few dozen future superstars.

Another way of investing in a diversified fashion in biotech is with an exchange-traded fund (ETF), such as the iShares Nasdaq Biotechnology Index (IBB). The reason for venturing into the volatile biotech waters is the very real possibility of landing a trophy fish. Widely held among growth investors is the belief that the area of biotech will yield more supersized winners than anywhere else.

In the first book by Peter Lynch, *One Up On Wall Street*, this legendary former mutual fund manager introduces the term "ten baggers" to his readers. A ten bagger is a stock that returns 10 times an original investment, turning $10,000 into $100,000, for a big-time gain of 1,000 percent. Lynch explains how valuable a ten bagger or two can be in turbo-charging an otherwise ordinary portfolio.

Recall Michael Murphy's admonition that in biotech, even more so than in other sectors, losers will greatly outnumber winners, so investors must seek the diversification to be found in a mutual fund. The simple strategy is to resist the temptation of individual stocks and cast wide and deep to catch the big biotech fish.

Wise mutual fund managers increased their returns with some of the success stories in biotech stocks. An example of a monster biotech winner can be found in IDEC Pharmaceuticals. A $10,000 investment made at the end of 1994 and held through mid-1999 was worth an astounding $352,600, for a return of 3,526 percent.

The good news is that after decades of false starts, the biotech sector is finally coming of age, as discoveries move from the lab through the testing stage to approvals—and now to the prospect of billion-dollar breakthroughs for drugs and therapies. The momentum is heating up for a maturing industry, as evidenced by the excitement and soaring returns of another stock, biotech pioneer Genetech.

Genetech was launched with much fanfare in 1976. The stock recently turned from cold to hot, rocketing 60 percent in value in a matter of a few trading days on news that its experimental drug Avastin markedly extended the life of some late-stage colon cancer patients. What is truly exciting is that although Avastin is currently approved only for colon cancer, it has shown real promise in trials to combat lung and breast tumors.

Another firm breaking out of the biotech pack is Gilead Science. Its share price has recently doubled in value. It should be pointed out that both Genetech and Gilead Science are currently found among the portfolio holdings of H&Q Life Sciences and T. Rowe Price Health Sciences (PRSSX).

Biotech not only serves solid profit-maximizing opportunities but also puts investment dollars to work in the business of life. Compare this thinking to the rationale to throw money at the silly Internet frenzy that fizzled after great fanfare. I lost my favorite aunt and godmother to colon cancer in June 2002. The idea of drugs in the pipeline that will help relieve the suffering and extend the life of cancer victims hits home with me.

We have clients living with the challenges posed by Parkinson's, diabetes, Alzheimer's, mental illness, multiple sclerosis, and digestive and heart disease. For these people, our discussions and decisions take into account the reality of their health issues, as well as their finances.

Interestingly, T. Rowe Price Health Sciences sector fund is run by two physicians. They are putting their medical background to work in ferreting out potential stock winners in the arcane field of drug development. Here's a prime example: these physicians are diligently searching and analyzing drug firms that have a prescription for defeating the deadly hepatitis C virus, minus the frequently unbearable side effects.

Kris H. Jenner is the fund manager of T. Rowe Price Health Sciences. According to this former doctor, "The hottest area in drug development right now and for the next couple years is hepatitis C." He goes on to predict: "The winner is going to have an extraordinary increase in value because the market is so significant."

In addition to the hope such discoveries offer, the biotech investment story is exciting because there is much fertile ground to yield growth for many years to come. Good news will be coming regardless of the economy. Peter Lynch notes that ten baggers pop up even in lousy stock markets.

The next big thing is likely to be in the area of genomics, combating disease by tailoring personalized medicines that will prove effective without serious side effects. Remarkably, with genomics you potentially hold the drug to treat you within your own body.

CHININDIA

If your objective is long-term, above-average growth, nearly everyone now believes you have to have an investment strategy that includes China. This dynamic and rapidly developing economy is simply too big a story to ignore. The mega-trend is becoming more evident. As Great Britain was the economic powerhouse of the nineteenth century and America was clearly on top in the twentieth, the twenty-first century could well belong to Asia, specifically to China and to a lesser extent India. Industry observers have taken to referring to this dynamic duo of China and India as Chinindia.

The flip side, and there's always a flip side, is that plenty of potholes line the road that could derail unwary investors. China's negatives are many and daunting. As a developing economy it might no longer be an infant, but its growth spurt still leaves the country as a young adolescent, susceptible to wrenching growing pains. China's huge population, which translates to an equally huge market, presents as many tough challenges as promising opportunities. The success of this emerging giant could take longer than expected and should not be thought of as a sure bet. Continued growth and development will require expansion of sound economic, social, and human rights policies, the adoption of more democracy, sound environmental policies, and education of the masses.

One way to participate in the Asian boom is by making an investment in Australia. With its proximity to Asia, its sound financial and banking system, and its educated English-speaking workforce and democratic institutions, Australia offers a smart back-door play on China's upside potential.

Australia has quietly posted a long run of growth, with an economy recognized as the most resilient in the world. Australia boasts of having the most multilingual workforce in the Asia Pacific region. In the financial capital city of Sydney, Chinese is now the second most-spoken language. Importantly, Australia is recognized as a country having among the lowest risk of political instability in the world.

Australia has had over a decade of strong, sustained economic growth, and its future as the shining light in the Asia Pacific region looks bright. As Australian Prime Minister John Howard put it: "We are a strong, sophisticated, medium-sized economy, which is punching well above its weight."

Australia is abundant in natural resources, including the minerals copper, nickel, and iron ore, and other raw materials, and it is benefiting from satisfying the voracious appetite of a hungry industrial China. One example is a long-term, $25 billion deal to supply liquefied natural gas to the burgeoning Guangdong province of China. Australia also is one of the world's largest coal exporters.

Count United Kingdom billionaire Richard Branson among those who are betting on the Australian stock market and economy. This shrewd businessman and investor has faith in the future of Australia, referring to it as a fantastic country.

There are two ways I recommend to invest in Australia as a gateway to Asia. One is an exchange-traded basket of Aussie stocks, the MSCI Australia Index (EWA). An alternative is an actively managed closed-end fund, the Aberdeen Australia Equity Fund (IAF). Both offer a diversified investment mix, with major holdings in banking stocks, natural resources, and consumer firms. The ETF, as expected of an index fund, carries a lower annual expense ratio than the actively managed second option. The discount on the closed-end Aberdeen fund has been running at some 10 percent.

What I find so exciting about investing in Australia is that it covers all of the fertile fields for growth I am counting on to do well for the future. I hope I have made the case that the economic, financial, and trade ties binding Australia with China will continue to propel their stock market. Yet Australia is also a hothouse of innovation, making world-class advances in biotech, renewable energy, and the developing technologies of tomorrow.

T. Rowe Price New Asia (PRSX) is a no-load, open-end mutual fund that invests across the Pacific region. But as its name implies, the fund excludes the fully developed market of Japan. In this fund, T. Rowe Price attempts to employ its vaunted growth discipline and stock-picking ability to tap into the enormous potential of this region. Indirectly, the fund stands to benefit from the dynamic neighboring economy of China.

For many years, the largest country allocation of this fund was in Hong Kong, long considered the best-managed market in Asia, with a heavy concentration in financial services companies. Fund management has now increased its focus on powerhouses India and South Korea. India, the world's most populous democracy, is on a definite roll. A paper published by Goldman Sachs estimates that over the next 25 years, India's economy might well surpass Japan's. Propelling much of India's growth are employment opportunities that translate into many millions of workers stepping up to the middle class and to rapidly rising incomes.

South Korea is the tenth largest economy in the world. Along with Taiwan, it rates among the strongest economies in the region. It has a stable of global brands such as Samsung and Kyocera. Stocks from other Asian Tigers, such as Thailand, Indonesia, Malaysia, the Philippines, and Singapore, so named because of their above-average growth rates, round out this geographically diversified investment fund. Many analysts contend Asian stocks are better values in comparison to those of the United States and other developed countries.

Mutual fund tracker Morningstar rates T. Rowe Price New Asia as "one of the best options for investors who are bold enough to make a pure emerging-Asian play." Bold is an apt description for investors venturing into this region, as it is definitely not for the faint of heart.

The Asian financial crisis of 1997 and 1998 rocked this region. The fund's share price was cut in half over that period. In addition, nuclear threats from North Korea and simmering geopolitical tensions with China over claims to Taiwan and between neighboring nuclear-armed Pakistan and India cast a nervous pall over this region. The SARS epidemic and Southeast Asia's tsunami disaster, as well as a series of terrorist episodes, also have made for volatile markets. In spite of all the challenges, patient investors searching for growth opportunities would be wise to consider a long-term investment in this part of the world.

THE EMERALD ISLAND, A RAGS-TO-RICHES STORY

My absolute all-time favorite movie is *The Quiet Man*, a 1952 classic directed by John Ford starring John Wayne and Maureen O'Hara. Wayne plays the Quiet Man, Shaun Thorton, an American who is starting life over in the simple cottage and pastoral Irish town of his birth. There he falls in love and manages to marry a beautiful redhead named Mary Kate Danaher, played superbly by O'Hara.

In a memorable scene, Mary Kate confides in the local priest, telling of problems in the marriage arising from cultural differences and a dispute with her brother. As a result, the newlyweds are sleeping apart, Shaun in a sleeping bag. The visibly exasperated pastor responds, "Ireland might be a poor country, but here a man sleeps with his wife in a bed and not in a bag."

Indeed, the Ireland of my ancestors was a poor country, but incredibly all that has now changed dramatically. Today, Ireland boasts a per capita income that shockingly is higher than that of Britain, Germany, or France. Ireland has emerged from being an economic backwater to become the shining financial light in all of Europe.

In 1973, the same year Ireland joined the European Union and went down the road of making substantial investments in infrastructure and education, my cousin Dennis and I graduated from college and visited the Old Sod. We were in the first wave of our generation to travel to the land of our roots. Flying into Dublin on that memorable trip, we rented a car in the city's then sleepy airport and drove down the main thoroughfare, O'Connell Street, in light traffic. We found easy parking on the street.

I returned to Ireland in 1997 with Cathy to celebrate our fifteenth wedding anniversary and found a visibly different scene. The capital city today is a vibrant, bustling metropolis. In the ensuing years since my first visit, Ireland has been transformed by smart tax and labor policies that empower a highly educated and productive English-speaking workforce. The result has been rising incomes, plentiful gainful employment, and an environment attracting billions of dollars in direct foreign investment.

Fortuitously, Cathy and I visited my Uncle John during our anniversary trip, two years before he passed away at the age of 92. In calling to arrange our visit, I reminded Uncle John of my first visit in 1973 with Dennis.

"Oh yes, John," he said, "that's when I was good."

My granduncle John Monaghan was the youngest of 10 children. He was born, raised, and resided in a modest thatched roof cottage with a dirt floor and no indoor plumbing. That home is where he had first welcomed me. Uncle John and his brother Pat, who died in 1980 of stomach cancer, never married and stayed on in their beloved village of Clooneen to farm the small family plot. John rode a bicycle, his only mode of transportation, until age 88 when his knees gave out.

During Uncle John's later years, his niece Breda lived nearby in a fashionable district of Galway City. Breda had returned home to

Ireland from England in retirement after being widowed. Breda, my mom's cousin, was an example of an Irish success story. She and her husband had made a nice living in England, first in heavy equipment and later in the London real estate market. She drove a Mercedes-Benz, vacationed in sunny Spain, and regularly visited the States and her sister Winnie in Chicago.

In the final years of Uncle John's long life, with his health declining, Breda offered to take him into her comfortable, modern home. He declined politely, reckoning that since he had spent his entire life in Clooneen, he planned to end it there. Sadly, Breda, my family's closest connection to our Irish roots, lost her own life to cancer (leukemia) in 2002.

Family history aside, many opportunities exist for investing in the Emerald Isle. Sometimes, Ireland is called the Celtic Tiger in reference to its booming economy.

The New Ireland Fund (IRL) is a closed-end mutual fund concentrated in stocks of the Irish stock market. This particular investment has proven the strongest performer to date in my wife's and my personal portfolio. In 2006, it provided us with a not-too-shabby 70 percent return on our investment. In this case, our ethnic affiliation has, at least to date, had a satisfying monetary result.

The top holdings among the approximately two-dozen stocks that make up this portfolio seemingly all benefit from the booming economy. As of 2005, these include financial firm Allied Irish Bank, construction company CRH, hotel and leisure concern Jury's Doyle Hotel Group, airline Ryanair, and the food and beverage Kerry Group.

This actively managed fund elected not to own large-cap stock Irish pharmaceutical giant Elan. This hurt the fund's performance in 2004, when Elan accounted for half the return of the Irish stock market index. Soon after this booming success, however, Elan ran into challenges on a trial for a promising new drug treatment for multiple sclerosis, causing the stock to tumble. IRL's management decision to concentrate on mid-cap growth stocks has had positive results.

I do hope to return to the Emerald Isle with my family in tow.

Our teenaged daughter, Martha, an accomplished Irish dancer, dreams of performing on stage in the land where this art form began. I would love to play golf on its many famed links. Ireland has now become a world-class golf destination, where no less than Tiger Woods tees it up every year in the week before the British Open.

I also long to bicycle the Ring of Kerry in the verdant hills and valleys of Southwest Ireland. This beautiful country offers both tangible and intangible riches to those who seek them.

NEW SCIENCE AND TECHNOLOGY

At the turn of the century in 1899, U.S. Patent Commissioner Charles Duell is purported to have said, "Everything that can be invented has been invented." Obviously, this was an extremely shortsighted, absurd statement, as the next century was transformed and revolutionized by breakthrough advances in science and technology.

In 1900, the manufacturing sector was turning out buggies, barrels, baskets, barbed wire, and bicycles. Over the next hundred years, according to various experts, the five most important engines for growth in the twentieth century included the internal combustion engine, transistor and integrated circuits, lasers, radios, and refrigeration and air conditioning units. Each of this handful of major advances spawned dozens of new industries and new discoveries that dramatically improved the quality of lives.

I have heard investment guru John Templeton recite a litany of inventions he has seen over his long life that affirm his faith and optimism in the even more promising investment opportunities the future holds. T. Rowe Price Developing Technologies Fund (PRDTX) is committed to finding and investing in companies with the potential to unlock these future gains. This small-cap, aggressive-growth stock fund holds some names unfamiliar to us; but, within the universe, a handful hold the potential to be the Microsoft, Intel, Google, or Cisco of tomorrow. Fund management's role is to ferret out the winners. Among the futuristic science poised to break out and develop are nanotechnology, fuel cells, and hydrogen energy.

Circa 1960, automaker General Motors (GM) was the undisputed powerhouse of the era. There was a saying that went, "What's good for GM is good for the country." Its stock was a prominent holding in practically every institutional portfolio. But, oh, how the tide can turn. Decades later, GM faces brutally tough foreign competition, environmental concerns, shrinking employment ranks, declining market share, and a string of losses. This corporate giant is no longer considered a growth engine. To drive home the point of its weakened position, its bond rating has been downgraded from gilt-edged to junk status, and there have even been whispers of a bankruptcy filing.

Tellingly, this old-line manufacturer is pinning its hope for salvation on the developing technology of hydrogen-powered vehicles. In a series of print ads, this maker of Chevrolet, Cadillac, GMC and Buick is touting what its leaders are calling the next generation of GM. GM claims to have over five hundred engineers on three different continents dedicated to making hydrogen cars, where the only emission is water vapor.

Jeremy Rifkin, author of the 2002 book *The Hydrogen Economy*, asserts we are at the "dawn of a new economy powered by hydrogen that will fundamentally change the nature of the market, and political and social institutions, just as steam and coal did at the beginning of the Industrial Age." According to Rifkin, "hydrogen is the most basic ubiquitous element in the universe, that when properly harnessed equals a forever fuel." General Motors' commitment to this technology supports the view that the hydrogen economy is well underway. It is not a pipe dream.

T. Rowe Price New Era (PRNEX) is a natural resource specialty fund that sports a good long-term track record, low turnover, and very reasonable expenses. The portfolio is heavily invested in the energy sector, but management also finds value in forest products, industrial metals, and even water company stocks.

Quite possibly technological breakthroughs will emerge from the substantial research and development expenditures being made by these old-line, highly profitable energy giants. Tomorrow's winning stocks will come from those innovative companies finding economical solutions to meeting the energy needs from greener alternatives to foreign oil.

Another exciting technology is the developing field of nanotechnology. Nanotech involves manipulation at the molecular level. Think of a measure one thousandth of the width of a strand of hair being used to produce new materials with astonishing applications. Listen to Nobel Laureate Horst Stormer: "Nanotechnology has given us the tools to play with the ultimate toy box of nature—atoms and molecules. Everything is made of it…the possibilities to create new things appear limitless."

Writing in *Forbes* magazine, venture capitalist Steve Jurvetson is equally convinced that nanotech is the N.B.T. (next big thing) and revolutionary in its reach. According to him, "It's hard to think of an industry that won't be touched by nanotech."

Another interesting investment choice from T. Rowe Price is its Science and Technology Fund (PRSCX). This sector fund has been around for a while and its performance has run hot and cold. Since the tech wreck of 2000, T. Rowe Price Science and Technology has been cold.

Able investment managers at T. Rowe Price have the freedom and flexibility to go where they find value and see promise. In my mind, someone who is thinking like a contrarian and buying low may consider this fund poised for another leg up.

A glimmer of hope is on the horizon for my client and friend Al, who lives with Parkinson's disease, for my sister, with multiple sclerosis, and for our daughter, with leukodystrophy. Pharmaceutical firms will employ the science of nanotechnology to treat neurological diseases such as these in the future. With our dear Maggie in mind, I read with heightened interest of a revolutionary medical procedure that actually pours a substance directly on the brain to halt the degenerative condition such as faced by our girl. For millions, such advances can't arrive fast enough to combat the progressive nature of certain baffling diseases. Wouldn't it be terrific if the diabetes of my bike-riding friend John could be reversed by nanoshells that protect transplanted pancreatic cells from attack by his own immune cells?

LOOK TO THE EAST

In searching for investment growth in Europe, it may be wise to look beyond slow-moving Western European nations, such as Germany and France, to Eastern Europe. The Czech Republic, Hungary, the Slovak Republic, and Poland, among the most sophisticated markets in the world, became part of the European Union in 2004. In that same year, Romania's stock market was the world's best performer. The Russian economy is awakening and finally embracing a global market economy, while becoming a major player on the energy front.

No less an astute investor than Warren Buffett has made a capital investment in the Russian oil industry. T. Rowe Price's Todd Henry is a fan of Turkey and Russia, based on their reforms and outsized growth potential. He suggests, "Don't be afraid to go into markets on the periphery."

T. Rowe Price Emerging Europe and Mediterranean Fund (TREMX) invests in these periphery countries that, since the fall of the Berlin Wall in 1990, are pro-Western, have adopted pro-growth, tax-wise policies, and are following the path of democracy and capitalism. Steve Forbes, in a *Forbes* magazine column titled "Investors' Paradise," states, "The Slovak Republic is set to become the world's next Hong Kong or Ireland; i.e., a small place that's an economic powerhouse."

Speaking of the burgeoning economies of Eastern Europe, investment manager Frank Holmes sees "positive futures, such as in Poland, with its well-educated engineers and PhDs, where all the populace have access to CNN and the American Dream."

In my personal experience, I have come across impressive young English-speaking students from countries such as Poland, Romania, and Belarus who are working summers in U.S. vacation areas. The

globalization of education and work experience among the college
generation bodes well for the future of investing around the world.

CHASE RECENT LOSERS

A pronounced tendency exists among investors to pile into those
areas of the market that have performed the strongest as of late. This
is often a mistake, especially with sector funds, ignoring a cardinal
rule by buying high. A safer and more profitable strategy over the
long-term is to act as a sensible contrarian and buy low.

For example, in the one-year and three-year periods ending in
2006, the New Ireland Fund, T. Rowe Price New Era, and T. Rowe
Price Emerging Europe exploded. Over the same span, Hambrecht
& Quist Life Sciences and T. Rowe Price Health Sciences turned in
much more tepid returns. Consequently, in making new investment
purchases, laggards such as these might hold the most promise.

ALL THAT GLITTERS IS NOT GOLD

In the fall of each year *Forbes* magazine publishes a special issue
identifying the 400 richest people in America. I admit to a fascination with these super-wealthy, as all of the 2006 *Forbes* 400 possess
a net worth of at least a billion dollars. I am curious how they amassed
their vast fortunes, be it from inheritance, money management, real
estate, technology, energy or entertainment. I read with interest the
capsule profiles on this billionaire set, learning in addition to their
money measure and source of wealth, their age, family status, hometown, and some personal tidbits.

I find a contrast between two members on the *Forbes* 400 of
particular interest from a personal finance and life planning standpoint. Charles Schwab, 68, has $3.8 billion, made his money through
Schwab, the discount stock brokerage he founded, is married with
five children, and makes the Bay Area of San Francisco home. Donald
Trump, 59, has amassed $2.7 billion from real estate deals. Twice
divorced, he calls the "Big Apple" of New York City home, has five
children, and is now remarried to a much younger, beautiful model

and has a new baby. I do not know either of these rich guys person-ally, but disdain the lifestyle of "The Donald" immensely, while feel-ing respect and admiration for Chuck.

For starters, Schwab, despite the challenge of being dyslexic, built Charles Schwab Corporation into one of the nation's largest finan-cial services firms. In doing so, he was truly a maverick and revolu-tionary. He shook up the financial services industry by introducing the concept of discount brokerage, the mutual fund supermarket, and becoming the leading custodian and technology firm serving invest-ment advisors such as ours.

Donald Trump works to give the impression that he cares only about money. In the *Forbes* magazine article he is twice prominently pictured, posing regally in opulent, gilded luxury. Trump craves at-tention, boasting in this piece, "My net worth has tripled." It would be interesting to have this quote juxtaposed on the print advertise-ment appearing in that very same issue of *Forbes* for automaker Daimler Chrysler Jeep, which features the tag line, "Never confuse your net worth with your self-worth."

Trump's hotel and casino resorts business, despite much hyper-bole and ballyhoo, was a financial failure and went bankrupt. Paul Harvey, in his November 22, 2004, national radio program spot en-titled, "All That Glitters is Not Gold," shone a light on Trump's bank-ruptcy filing that listed only $1 million in assets, awash in $1 billion in debt.

In contrast, the publicly traded stock of Charles Schwab Corpo-ration was a phenomenal growth story in the 1990s, with a market value at one time that exceeded financial services giant Merrill Lynch. Profits and the stock price suffered, as they did for all brokerage firms in the tech wreck and bear market of 2000-2002. To change the company's fortunes, Schwab returned in 2003 as chairman of the firm he founded.

Charles and Helen Schwab, through their words and philanthropic deeds, believe in giving something back. They started a foundation, a non-profit agency to provide support and guidance for parents of children with learning difficulties such as dyslexia and AD/HD. Donald Trump gives the impression that non-profit is for chumps. In my opinion, and that of others, his hit TV reality show, *The Apprentice*, presents a sad model for aspiring business people. I refuse to watch it.

Charles Schwab continues to be the public face and pitchman for the financial services firm that bears his name. In a series of TV spots he shared his wisdom and common sense investing. In one, he counsels investors to always seek to mitigate risk. By definition, this means to lessen, moderate, or make less severe exposure to market risk. This is sound advice. Although risk cannot be eliminated completely, it can and should be mitigated to whatever extent possible.

In another ad in the series, Schwab says into the camera, "Investing is about having the appropriate asset allocation so that your investment portfolio has staying power over the ups and downs of the market."

Jon Huntsman of Huntsman Chemical appears on this exclusive *Forbes* 400 list with a net worth of $1.6 billion. The 68-year-old married father of nine children let it be known he made earnest plans to give away the vast bulk of his money in the coming year. Among other causes, he wants his fortune to be used to combat cancer, which has ravaged his family. I found the following quote of John Huntsman compelling: "I want to be remembered for doing something to cure cancer—doing that will really mean something."

Many financially successful people prefer to be discreet and modest concerning their wealth. The late Sam Walton, founder of Wal-Mart, offers a perfect case in point. No one would have guessed this unassuming Arkansas gentleman, attired in off-the-rack clothes from his stores, pumping his own gas, dogs frolicking in back of his seven-year-old pickup truck, was one of the wealthiest men in the country. Happily married to one mate his entire adult life, Sam Walton died in 1998 of pancreatic cancer, a verified multibillionaire.

It's not the same story for the egocentric Donald Trump. In a follow-up to this special *Forbes* 400 issue, he had the audacity to protest he is worth $3.6 billion and not the paltry $2.7 billion they credited him with on the rich list. In fact, he is now suing a published book author who claims The Donald is not a super-wealthy billionaire, but far from it with a measly $250 million.

Trump's source of wealth comes from real estate. It should be noted he dropped off the *Forbes* 400 list in 1990 when his highly leveraged real estate empire hit the wall. As *Forbes* reported at the time in the article "Poor Donald," "as his bankers are learning, to their dismay, his net worth may have actually dropped to zero." One report at the time estimated his net worth at a startling minus $900 million. As concern heightens that the increasingly inflated real estate bubble could deflate with rising interest rates, Trump potentially could again find himself a newsworthy loser.

Donald Trump's marital history is a far cry from my father's. As a devoted family man, my dad honored his marriage vows, faithfully loving my mother until her death. At my father's funeral service I quoted Reverend Theodore Hesburgh, long-time president of the University of Notre Dame. According to the perceptive Hesburgh, "The greatest gift that a man can give his children is to love their mother."

Dad unselfishly worked two jobs without complaint in order to provide for his family of seven children. As a citizen and patriot, he proudly served his country in WWII, earning a Purple Heart after being hit by shrapnel and badly injured. At his funeral service I also spoke of how rock-solid my father was as a friend and neighbor. When I said he would go through a wall for any of those present, I saw them nodding in agreement. One of my previous books carries the dedication: "To my father, Jack McCarthy (1925–1996). May I grow and learn to be half the man he was." His legacy was far richer than money.

GENTLE MOTHER

To balance the talk about the *Forbes* 400's abundant wealth, I find it refreshing to harken to the words of Mother Teresa (1910–

1997), the diminutive Roman Catholic nun and revered humanitarian who worked with the poorest of the poor in places such as Calcutta, India. She gently reminded us by word and deed to "measure wealth in ways beyond money." A reporter once asked her how she could consider herself a success, since the work she did, though laudatory, was a mere drop in the vast ocean of poverty. This towering symbol of the twentieth century rose up and replied, "I'm not on a mission of success. I'm on a mission of mercy." This modern-day saint also told us, "One of the greatest diseases is to be nobody to anybody."

In the fall of 2006, Cathy and I took a memorable tour of St. Ann's Center, a day care facility serving the underserved, located on the south side of Milwaukee. Sister Edna, the director of this warm, inviting, yet bustling place, showed us around personally. St. Ann's, as we came to see and learn, is an intergenerational care facility, serving children, the elderly, and persons with disabilities.

On arriving, we were met in the airy enclosed courtyard by our hostess, who introduced us to a lively 91-year-old woman. To say she was a character would be an understatement. She ignored Cathy and proceeded to flirt with me. I seem to have rapport with elderly women. We soon learned that my admirer regularly played the piano for the other residents.

My first impression of Sister Edna was not at all what I had imagined, as the good-hearted Franciscan nun is quite fashionable. My second surprise was to learn while at lunch that my 91-year-old piano-playing lady friend, Lillian, is none other than sister Edna's own dear mother.

I was profoundly touched by the dynamic I saw taking place at St. Ann's. There was a two-year-old black girl cradled in the loving arms of a matronly woman in a rocking chair. Sister informed us this child started out life as a crack cocaine baby.

Down the hall in another area, I witnessed one of the dozens of wonderful volunteers gently spoon-feeding a severely disabled young man. We learned that it could take the better part of an hour to feed lunch to this man, who was paralyzed from the neck down and strapped in an electric wheelchair. What struck me was how his eyes were fixed on the woman feeding him. I could see the love being transferred as if from a mother to child. It was a beautiful sight. Sister then showed us a specially adapted bathing area, saying that for many residents this was their only opportunity to enjoy a full bath.

We left that day knowing that the faith, hope, and love epitomized by Mother Teresa is taking place at the St. Ann Center for Intergenerational Care. This facility is truly enriching the Milwaukee community with the many acts of mercy performed there.

The following observation was made by psychology professors Ed Diener and Martin E. P. Seligman. "Economic success falls short as a measure of well-being, in part because materialism can negatively influence well-being, and also because it is possible to be happy without living a life of luxury." Mother Teresa's life was living proof of this notion. We can't all be Mother Teresa, but we can put a higher value on family, charity, and living strong than the pursuit of wealth at the expense of these values.

IT IS BETTER TO GIVE THAN TO RECEIVE

The life of James E. Stowers paints an American success story. This soft-spoken, bespeckled Midwesterner was an Air Force fighter pilot during WWII. In 1958 he founded and built Twentieth Century Mutual Funds from scratch.

Recognizing the value of the computer in the investment management business, Mr. Stowers personally designed the computer software programs used by the firm to screen, track, and manage the wide stock universe.

This no-load, no-minimum fund family treated the small investor right and grew over the decades to become a mutual fund goliath. Now named American Century Investors, this premier investment company turned James Stowers into a *Forbes* 400 billionaire.

He and his wife, Virginia, are both fortunate cancer survivors. Having successfully fought and come through this harrowing, life-changing event, they are determined to give back. Looking to make a real difference in the war on this insidious disease, James and Virginia Stowers have given a whopping $1.6 billion of their fortune to create and sustain a world-class research facility in their hometown of Kansas City, Missouri. The Stowers Institute for Medical Research has as its large mission unlocking the mysteries of cancer in order to discover the keys to its cause, treatment, and prevention. Mr. Stower's innovative vision is to parlay his computer success in the investment management field by marrying large-scale science with technology to study and decipher complex genetic systems.

Virginia and James Stowers have four children and five grandchildren. Rather than pass their wealth to their family or have it sorely reduced by estate taxes, they are on record that at their passing, "we're going to give everything we have" to charity for medical research.

I like this thought from the great Winston Churchill: "We make a living by what we get, but we make a life by what we give."

Mega-billionaire Warren Buffett recently made a splash by announcing his decision to give away the bulk of his immense wealth while alive, rather than at his death. As to why he did not pass his wealth along to his children, Mr. Buffett has long said, "I don't believe in dynastic wealth." More colorfully, he refers to the "lucky sperm club." Don't feel the need to pass a hat for his three children, who inherited $10 million each when their mother Susan Buffett died in 2004 from complications of cancer. We know this, by the way, from public records of her last will and testament, on file in the Omaha, Nebraska, county court.

Part of the buzz surrounding Buffett's colossal $31 billion gift is that it was made to the Bill & Melinda Gates Foundation. Bill Gates dreams of applying the same entrepreneurial savvy he employed so magnificently in growing Microsoft to solving the huge challenges in neglected areas of the globe. In addition to having prodigious wealth in common, Bill Gates and Warren Buffett have developed into good friends and are bridge-playing buddies.

Warren Buffett and his right-hand man at Berkshire Hathaway, Charlie Munger, never invest in technology stocks such as Microsoft.

According to Munger, "We have three baskets for investing: yes, no, and too tough to understand." Speaking of his good friend Bill Gates, Buffett says, "He may be the smartest guy I've ever met. But I don't know what those little [computer] things do."

Since its founding in 1994, the Bill & Melinda Gates Foundation has developed an ambitious plan to making a monumental difference in combating the global health challenges of AIDS, tuberculosis, and malaria, as well as transforming the United States' K-12 education system.

It would be a mistake to underestimate Melinda Gate's role and influence as co-founder and director of the Gates Foundation. Melinda is known for the immense energy and passion she brings to this volunteer job. For her considerable efforts, *Forbes* magazine has ranked her among the most powerful women in the world, a few notches ahead of Oprah Winfrey.

I find it of interest to note how these super philanthropists go about deciding which of the multitude of worthy causes to support with their vast treasure. As shrewd investors, they are searching for accountability, measurable results, and the best return on their charitable investment.

In 2004, Danish political scientist Bjorn Lomborg assembled the world's top economists in Copenhagen, where they were presented with the task of evaluating the world's most pressing problems. These scientific thinkers, including four Nobel Laureates, compiled and published a prioritized list of the costs and efficiencies to solve these global scourges.

As a legendary value investor, Warren Buffett is intrigued by findings such as this study turned up: that for every $1 spent on preventing HIV/AIDS, about $40 in social benefits is returned. High on the same lists is the promise of developing a vaccine to eradicate malaria, a major problem in the poorest areas of the Third World.

Former Citigroup CEO and chairman Sanford "Sandy" Weil—like James and Virginia Stowers, Bill and Melinda Gates, and Warren Buffett—has publicly pledged to give away the bulk of his estimated $1.4 billion net worth while alive rather than through his estate. The hard-charging, high-profile financial services executive has already given away some $600 million in the last 10 to 15 years. As part of what Weil has termed a "deal with God," the 73-year-old believes in making the world a better place in real time. Similar to the world's richest men, Weil is opening his personal vault to fighting African diseases. He is helping to set up a Cornell University affiliated medical school in Tanzania.

The late Pope John Paul II felt deeply that the continent of Africa had been forgotten and callously ignored by the modern world. He was known to pray over the fate of Africa. I like to think his prayers are being answered through the actions of these wealthy philanthropic American capitalists.

CHILDHOOD CANCER

During my cancer ordeal I was at Froedtert Hospital every weekday for seven weeks of radiation treatment. Early one morning while I waited in an inner hallway, a young boy around eight years old sat next to me for a couple of minutes. He was slumped in a wheelchair, exhibited the telltale bald head from chemotherapy, and had an IV line inserted in his arm.

I suspect he was brought to the adult hospital from the adjacent Children's Hospital of Wisconsin for a special treatment. Up to that point, I had felt pretty strong, even comfortable, being in the midst of cancer patients, but they were adults. That morning, I was so shaken I could hardly walk. My knees buckled and I prayed to God this unknown child would survive.

In this feeling, I was like Al McGuire. After retiring from coaching, he started Al's Run to benefit Children's Hospital of Wisconsin. McGuire was a tough big-city guy, who didn't back down from anyone. Yet he admitted to having a hard time visiting sick kids. While touring the Intensive Care Unit at the hospital his charity run helped support, he saw many of them. He thought of his own grandkids, and it tore him up inside.

The most moving part of Hamilton Jordan's cancer memoir *No Such Thing As A Bad Day* is the story of Corey Grier. Jordan's wife, Dorothy, is a pediatric oncology nurse, so she must be a special angel. Early in their marriage, Dorothy organized Camp Sunshine in Atlanta for children with cancer. Corey was a favorite camper, described as a 16-year-old African American teenager with a magnetic personality and a light-up-the-room smile.

Unfortunately, in the weeks following one particular summer camp, it became apparent Corey's tumor was taking its deadly toll. Doctors grimly informed the Grier family that Corey had only a few precious months of life, at best. Young Corey had other ideas, determined to live a year so that he could celebrate his seventeenth birthday with his camper friends and counselors at Camp Sunshine the next summer.

Jordan writes, "Camp Sunshine has had a major impact on our lives, especially by giving us the opportunity to witness time and time again dramatic demonstrations of the power of the mind and attitude to alter the course of disease." Corey Grier was one such profile in courage, confounding the medical experts by living to the next summer. He was taken by helicopter into camp on his birthday, a triumphant hero, and enjoyed some of the happiest hours of his too short life. The very next day, Corey died peacefully at the hospital.

During the 2005 telecast of the Tour de France, Nike ran a commercial that has star endorser and cycling phenomenon Lance Armstrong zooming on his bike through a series of changing scenes. At the high point of this memorable spot, Lance looks up from the bike and acknowledges the cheers and support of children on a balcony. They are unmistakably cancer patients, sporting chemo heads and hospital gown attire. There is an obvious connection between these kids fighting for their lives and the world's most famous cancer survivor participating in a sport that leaves no doubt he is living strong. Just thinking of this filmed scene can move me to tears.

I never knew my wife's baby brother, Billy. He didn't get to grow up, as leukemia stopped his life short at age four. At a family reunion to celebrate my mother-in-law's eightieth birthday, I took the time to read the annual Christmas letters written by my late father-in-law. Billy was the youngest of their nine children, healthy, good-looking, and with a great future ahead of him.

Christmas 1969: Billy age 1. "He gets into more things than a mountain goat and has more energy. Exceptionally good set of lungs."

Christmas 1970: Billy age 2. [Diagnosed with cancer, no letter.]

Christmas 1971: Billy age 3. "Some good days—some bad days. Likes to go up north. Knows and accepts the hospital routine for his weekly trips. Wears big boy pants (finally!!!)."

Christmas 1972: [no letter, as Billy died that October.]

Christmas 1973: "We had a good year–certainly a happier year than last."

Our clients Jim and Ruth of Racine lost their youngest son, also named Billy, to childhood leukemia at about the same time, also at Children's Hospital of Wisconsin. I don't want to forget them, or my fraternity brother's son, Emmitt, or our friends Jeff and Wendy's youngest child, Clayton. These youngsters sadly lost out to childhood cancer.

The loss of a child must be indescribably heartbreaking. Not many people know this, but the first President Bush and his wife, Barbara, suffered the loss of a daughter to childhood cancer. Despite all the success they enjoyed and the passage of time, they will tell you that losing a child was the deepest cut of all. It left a permanent scar on their hearts.

The MACC Fund (Midwest Athletes Against Childhood Cancer) was started in 1976, with the major league goal of providing hope through research to children with cancer. Jon McGlocklin retired that year following a sterling NBA career with the Milwaukee Bucks. At the same time, his good friend's two-year-old son, Brett, received a chilling diagnosis of cancer. The ball got rolling, and happily Brett survived, becoming the MACC fund's first success story.

The good news is there is now much more hope for children. Nationwide funding for pediatric cancer research such as that provided by the MACC Fund has resulted in great strides being made. Proof is the rise in the overall cure rate for all forms of childhood cancer from just 10 percent to 75 percent in the past 30 years. Acute lymphoblastic leukemia, the most common form of childhood cancer, is now considered 85 percent curable.

I know one such happy story and statistic personally. Having put his cancer behind him, Matthew is a typical college student, with thoughts of becoming a doctor. Twelve years earlier, battling deadly leukemia, his prospects did not look as rosy.

His dad likes to tell of a funny story that occurred when a nine-year-old Matthew, bald from the effects of toxic chemotherapy, was at the supermarket with his mother. In the checkout line, a young girl about his same age pointed Matthew out, and in a voice loud enough for him to hear. "Look mom, that boy over there has no hair." Matthew relished playing the part, turning to his mother in mock horror, "Mom! Mom! My hair fell out!"

The MACC Fund has as its bold vision all success stories. Their optimistic hope is that through dedicated pediatric cancer research, children will be able to look forward to a 100 percent cure rate.

MY AFRICAN FRIENDS

Along with my family, I had the distinct privilege of welcoming into our home Emmanuel Udo. A native of Nigeria, Emmanuel is a Catholic priest who spent five years ministering and assisting in our parish church, while completing his graduate and doctoral studies at Marquette University in Milwaukee.

The first person who connected with the special warmth of this gentle man was our girl Maggie. At the conclusion of church services, Maggie routinely gave Emmanuel a hug. Through the years, they developed a warm bond. Emmanuel holds a place in his heart and in his prayers for this special child of God.

Maggie is blessed with a complete lack of prejudice. Our family has observed that Maggie has a genuine attraction to people of color, and they for her. Walking past a bus stop, she is likely to greet total strangers with a smile and a "hi friends," which they appreciate and return in kind, smiling. Occasionally, when she comes across a black man, she remarks, "He looks like Emmanuel." Once, I asked Maggie what she meant by this, seeking to determine how much she understood. Her quick and simple reply was, "He is dark, duh."

I am taken by Emmanuel's perception of the abundance of wealth and freedom we Americans take so much for granted. A man of intellect, he has a lot to teach us of the real richness of life. His tribe in Nigeria lives in extreme poverty, and even in this day of modern communications it is very difficult for him to make contact from the United States with his family village. Missionary priests from Ireland educated Emmanuel and nurtured his vocation. This may be why he took so quickly to the McCarthy clan.

A newer African friend of mine is Juvenalis Asantemungu, a native of Tanzania. I have come to know this Catholic priest because like Emmanuel, he resides at St. Jude parish rectory while he works toward an advanced degree at nearby Marquette University.

Father Juvenalis is one of 10 children, three of whom are priests. His homes sits at the base of the majestic Mount Kilimanjaro. He shared with me the fact that his aging parents subsist in a remote Tanzanian village with no road access, no power, or even an adequate water supply. Their health is on the decline, and the rest of his family back home is moving them into town, to be better able to care for them.

A man of impressive intelligence, Juvenalis speaks five languages. He just completed his MBA degree and is now pursuing a doctorate. His bishop in Tanzania recognizes the ability of this gifted priest. They have a grand plan for him to return and use his splendid education and talent to advance the economic and spiritual development of his countrymen.

A highlight of Christmas services for me this year was Father Juvenalis's sharing stories of how this religious holiday is celebrated in his homeland. He said it finally dawned on him why Christmas trees in Tanzania were decorated with cotton. It seems European missionaries did this to replicate December snow from their own northern climates. Until leaving Africa for Milwaukee, Juvenalis had never experienced snow. He said when he goes home he will tell them the significance of the cotton on the trees.

He then gave us a treat by singing a traditional Christmas carol in Swahili, his native tongue. Because he didn't have a drum, he asked parishioners to clap along with him in rhythm. Juvenalis succeeded in capturing the true spirit of the season. I also suspect it managed to bring a touch of home to him.

MARY'S JOURNEY TO CAMEROON

Not only billionaires are working to make a positive difference in Africa. This is the inspiring life mission of Mary, a remarkable woman I have come to know in a client capacity. I first met Mary and her husband, Greg, when they were planning to transition into semi-retirement. Four months later, Greg suffered a fatal heart attack on the seventeenth hole of his golf club. It was a grievous loss that changed Mary's life. In memory of her husband, Mary has directed her energies to the heroic mission of using education to empower young women in Cameroon. I can't do better than share Mary's own heartfelt words with you.

In April of 2001, my life was shattered by the loss of my husband, Greg, a wonderful, compassionate, and generous man. When he first died, I felt nothing but the void in my life. Then, with the help of the mighty and gentle Franciscan Sisters at Milwaukee's Saint Ann Center, I began to see that it wasn't a void, but a doorway. The Sisters invited me to accompany them to Bafut, Cameroon, where they run a medical center and home, and Saint Joseph's Girls Vocational High School. I went . . .and my journey began! In Bafut, I helped the Sisters minister to the sick, handicapped, and the students at Saint Joseph's. I was privileged to share their food and sleeping pallets, their dawns and dusks. My ears still recall the students going about their tasks, singing joyously to face economic adversity and despair.

Cameroon and Bafut represent an agonizing litany of needs. For better education. Better health. Better standards of living for women and children especially. I left full of wonder and questions. Noting how different we are, yet how similar in the many things that pull us daily onward despite hardship. I brought the spirit of Bafut with me when I returned, and made fulfilling the needs of Saint Joseph's my mission. The Saint Ann Center has a not-for-profit organization set up to benefit Cameroon, and the Sisters invited me to collaborate with them. Through this partnership, I've found a way to fill the heart that was so empty after losing Greg.

Wherever you are in your life's journey, please join me on mine. Educating the girls at St. Joseph's is another way to heal the world's voids.

Through Mary, I have met Sister Baki Theodosia, the principal of St. Joseph's Girls Vocational High School. An engaging woman visiting the United States to thank supporters, Sister embodies the value of the mission.

Mary will return to Africa this fall. Her journey involves two seven-hour flights with a seven-hour layover between. The last leg to the village of Bafut takes the better part of a day over bad roads in a vehicle without air conditioning. Mary claims the Cameroon mission has given a renewed purpose to her life. To see a picture of a radiant, white-haired Mary among the schoolgirls of St. Joseph's is verification of this truth.

SKILL, COURAGE, SHARING, JOY

Over the years I have been inspired by being around, watching, and getting to know Special Olympians competing in Special Olympics events. The famed Massachusetts Kennedy clan deserves credit for founding Special Olympics. Like millions of families in America, the Kennedys had a member living with a developmental disability. The late President's sister, Rose, quietly lived out her years at St. Coletta's in Jefferson, Wisconsin. I appreciate that this great organization was named Special Olympics and not Disabled Olympics.

Skill, Courage, Sharing, Joy is the motto of Special Olympics and it appears on all participatory ribbons and medals, which are awarded with much fanfare at athletic events.

I am looking at a picture set showing our 4-foot-10-inch, 85-pound Special Olympic athlete at the State Summer Games. There Maggie competed in track in the 800-meter race walk. At about the three-quarter mark, her coach, Eileen, encouraged Maggie to speed up and pass the competitor in front of her. Maggie responded in a resolute voice with one word that said if that is what you want, "fine." She responded, picking up the pace to a higher gear and took the lead.

Coach Eileen is typical of the many volunteers who make Special Olympics such a resounding success. A veteran nurse and rehab specialist at Children's Hospital of Wisconsin, Eileen is an accomplished athlete in her own right. Her major athletic claim to fame was qualifying for, competing in, and amazingly completing the Ironman Triathlon in Hawaii. This grueling superbowl of triathlons combines a 2.25 mile ocean swim followed by a 115-mile bike road ride. It's topped off by an exhausting full marathon run of 26.2 miles. A highlight of Coach Eileen's Special Olympics career was representing Wisconsin as a coach at the 2003 World Games held in Dublin.

At the medal ceremony following Maggie's race, Eileen and I stood by with teammates and parents and witnessed a pure expression of joy. As her name was announced, Maggie triumphantly raised her fist in the air. Once the medal was placed around her neck, Maggie took a long moment to admire it. Still holding her precious medal, another photo captured Maggie with a smile of unadulterated joy. No athlete at any level, on any Olympic podium, was happier at that moment than our Maggie. As a proud parent, I was so happy for her.

During the latest track season, Maggie trained hard in order to move up and compete in the long-distance, 3,000-meter race walk. Although she did not qualify for the State meet, we all were so proud of our courageous girl, as she competed well, posted a personal best time, and most important, went the full distance.

Nervously watching the 3,000-meter event, I struck up a conversation with a volunteer race official. A retired school administrator and teacher, this nice man said long-distance track is unique among sports, for the loudest cheers are reserved for the final place competitor. Finishing the race is itself a cause for celebration.

Maggie's neurological condition has gradually affected her balance. When she was a middle schooler, we persevered, and with effort taught our determined eldest daughter to ride a two-wheeled bicycle. We moved on to an adult tricycle for her, and now we are riding partners on a tandem bike.

Cathy flew Maggie to the National Institutes of Health (NIH) in Bethesda, Maryland, to have specialists do a work-up on Maggie and assess her very rare genetic disease. Reviewing her records and test results before they saw Maggie, the medical people inquired of Cathy in a phone interview if she was mobile and could walk. Cathy replied Maggie not only can walk but she is also a long-distance race walker, and a winner.

Maggie's brother, Jack, and sister, Martha, are talented and accomplished young students and athletes. Yet in many respects we all feel that Maggie, by overcoming her disabilities to be the best she can be, is truly a champion.

One of the best life experiences I have is marching in the annual Fourth of July parade alongside Special Olympians in our community of Wauwatosa, Wisconsin. It is a grand parade and a slice of Americana. Our 40-member uniformed team steps off some 2.5 miles down the main street of North Avenue, along with rousing high school marching bands, vintage cars carrying local celebrities, horses (watch your step), and dozens of floats.

Thousands of parade watchers line the route and pour out their loudest recognition for the disabled citizen neighbors passing by them. We literally walk through a sea of adulation as they clap, cheer, salute, and even stand up in waves as the Special Olympians march by.

As I said, I have been inspired and enriched by getting to know some very special people. One such person is Tim, who each year leads our group in the parade, revving up the crowd as the American flag bearer. Tim is an exceptional athlete and a natural leader, as well as a productive, long-term McDonald's employee. To me, this red-head with Down Syndrome is the face I put on Special Olympics.

Over the past 25 years, Tim has participated in scores of Special Olympics events and has a boatload of ribbons and medals attesting to his skill. At the State Summer Games, I stood next to his mother, Nancy, as he competed in a hotly contested 400-meter race-walk sprint. Perennial winner Tim was trailing his athletic competitor, and it looked as if he would have to settle for second place. I asked Nancy if her son would be able to live with this disappointment, and she said she hoped so.

In the final turn, Tim took the inside lane, put his head down, tilted to the left in his unorthodox style, and accelerated to the finish line, winning by a step. It was as exciting as anything I have seen in sport. Breathlessly, I ran over to congratulate my hero Tim, telling him I thought it was an amazing race effort. A sweating Tim told me in his halting voice, "John, I was not to be denied." Superstars Brett Favre, Michael Jordan, Tiger Woods, Mia Hamm, and Lance Armstrong don't have bigger competitor hearts than does Tim.

I recently learned some exciting news from Tim's dad, Larry. Tim has the honor of being selected to represent Wisconsin and the USA in the 2007 World Special Olympic Games to be held in Shanghai, China. This is a big deal, and Tim is as excited to go as his parents are happy for him. Coach Eileen and I are thrilled. I have no doubt that Tim, in the finest Olympic tradition, will line up in China and give it his all.

At the State Summer Games, they do things special. For the opening ceremony one year, we thrilled to the sight of an army helicopter landing in an adjacent field and bringing the Olympic flame. The oath recited by Special Olympians is as follows: "Let me win. But if I cannot win, let me be brave in the attempt." A young man with Down Syndrome, representing all the athletes on the podium, took the microphone, and with the verve of Rocky Balboa, told them to "go for it."

PHILOSOPHER COACH

As I say in my opening chapter, the celebrated late Marquette basketball coach Al McGuire had a profound influence on me. It might have had a little to do with the fact that, like me, this fellow Irishman's father was named John, and his mother, Winifred.

McGuire was a streetwise philosopher who believed "there's a rhythm to basketball like there is to life." He also said, "Don't wait to have a drink for a fella once he's dead, better to buy him a drink while he's alive." This quip crossed my mind while I was contemplating the charity-while-alive movement by the super-rich.

At the conclusion of my cancer treatment, I received a good prognosis, but over the course of the summer of 2000 dropped from an athletic 200 pounds to a rail-thin 160. High-intensity radiation treatment to my neck and throat had destroyed my salivary glands, making swallowing difficult. My tongue was burned, taste buds shot, and my jaw did not open fully. Needless to say, eating was challenging, but I was determined to put back 20 pounds, believing it was essential to my recovery. I knew weight loss is a red flag that cancer could be lurking.

Over the next year, I managed to reach my goal.

That fall I took to eating lunch at McGinn's on Bluemound Road, a neighborhood bar and restaurant known for its good food. It was there at McGinn's that I encountered George McMullen. A nice man in his early seventies, he was a retired professor of philosophy at Mount Mary College. A regular patron, he was known affectionately by the bar staff as "Cheeseburger George" for his standard order. The first dollar spent when McGinn's opened was from George, and it is still displayed behind the bar.

George and I became acquainted, as we both preferred eating at the bar in the corner by the window. We also had in common dealing with the ugliness that is cancer. Unlike me, George enjoyed a brandy with his lunch, while I stuck to my iced tea.

Two weeks before George's death, I asked Jeff, the bartender, to let me buy George that drink. A frail George reached over, looked me in the eye, shook my hand, and said in a soft voice, "Thanks, John." It was the best drink I ever bought, and I had Al McGuire to thank.

One of my favorite Al McGuire stories involved his run-in with the legendary Kentucky basketball coach Adolph Rupp. The year was 1968, and McGuire's rising team was set to play perennial college-basketball-powerhouse Kentucky in the quarterfinals of the national championship.

To set the stage, Adolph was at the end of his career and fielded a segregated, all-white team. McGuire's racially integrated team was led by "All American" George "Brute Force" Thompson, recruited from the mean streets of the Bronx, New York.

In the pre-game press conference Rupp kept referring to the young upstart McGuire as "son." Street fighter that he was, Al took this as a talking down and lack of respect toward him and his team. McGuire finally shot back at this perceived slight: "Don't call me son unless you're going to include me in your will."

Always looking to gain an edge, McGuire fired up his underdog team. Marquette went out and played an inspired game, soundly defeating Kentucky and Coach Rupp.

Then there was the game in 1965 when McGuire's Marquette squad was set to tip off against Bradley University in Peoria, Illinois. An arena official was intent on denying the female sports editor of the college newspaper her seat in the courtside press section. Alerted, McGuire came to the defense of this young woman student, threatening, "She doesn't sit in the press row, we don't play this game."

Tom Crean is the most successful basketball coach at Marquette since the Al McGuire era, taking his team to an NCAA Final Four led by the incomparable Dwayne Wade. An astute young man, Crean turned to the wise old owl McGuire as a mentor upon being named head coach.

One piece of life advice the workaholic Coach Crean did not take was McGuire's call for him to back off on some of his demanding work schedule and "smell the roses." "It's time for you to start playing, Coach," said McGuire.

As it was, Crean was a hospice visitor in the final months of McGuire's colorful life. From this experience, Crean learned first-hand that Al always had a plan. Crean observed, "Where I got to watch it was how he said goodbye to everybody and how important that was to him."

Al McGuire's son Allie was a classmate of mine at Marquette, where he played basketball for his father. He appeared on the cover of *Sports Illustrated* as "the man who makes the Warriors go." At his dad's funeral service at Gesu Church on the Marquette campus, Allie spoke movingly of how in the final days, his frail and dying father would struggle to sit up and get up to greet visitors to his bedside. Allie told him, "Dad, you don't have to get up every time. Your friends will understand." Al said yes he did, as they had to see and remember him as being strong. Al McGuire was living strong to the very end.

As my dear mother lay dying from lung cancer, her final words to me were the same as she had told me countless times over my life: "Be good." These two simple words summed up my Mother's paren-tal love and encompassed a wealth of her life guidance.

To my mother, be good meant to aspire to be the best you can be in everything you do. Her frequent admonition was a gentle reminder to be sensitive to others, to make life's path one rich in experience, humor, joy, love, and kindness. Mom was saying also to have the courage to face adversity with grace and a quiet strength, and to live with honor as she had done by her lifelong example.

Mother's call to be good continues to echo in my memory. I think of those words every time I see someone sporting the modest yellow band that has become a global symbol for the life-affirming message to cancer survivors and to all of us to live strong.

My sincere wish for everyone who reads this book is to embrace the journey, to possess the resolve to carry on, and to have the cour-age to always *live strong*.